Unbought and Unbossed

Unbought and Unbossed

Transgressive Black Women, Sexuality, and Representation

TRIMIKO MELANCON

 Temple University Press
PHILADELPHIA

Temple University Press
Philadelphia, Pennsylvania 19122
www.temple.edu/tempress

Copyright © 2014 by Trimiko Melancon

Published 2014

LIBRARY OF CONGRESS CATALOGING-IN-PUBLICATION DATA

Melancon, Trimiko, 1977– author.
  Unbought and unbossed : transgressive black women, sexuality, and representation / Trimiko Melancon.
    pages cm
  Includes bibliographical references and index.
  ISBN 978-1-4399-1145-7 (hardback : alk. paper)
  ISBN 978-1-4399-1146-4 (paper : alk. paper)
  ISBN 978-1-4399-1147-1 (e-book)
    1. American literature—African American authors—History and criticism.
2. American literature—Women authors—History and criticism. 3. Women,
Black—Race identity. 4. Women, Black, in literature. I. Title.
PS153.N5M39 2014
810.9'928708996073—dc23

                                                            2014018279

♾ The paper used in this publication meets the requirements of the
American National Standard for Information Sciences—Permanence
of Paper for Printed Library Materials, ANSI Z39.48–1992

Printed in the United States of America

2 4 6 8 9 7 5 3 1

A book in the American Literatures Initiative (ALI), a
collaborative publishing project of NYU Press, Fordham
University Press, Rutgers University Press, Temple University
Press, and the University of Virginia Press. The Initiative is
supported by The Andrew W. Mellon Foundation. For more
information, please visit www.americanliteratures.org.

For Mama and Daddy

Contents

Acknowledgments

Expressing one's appreciation should never be a meaningless task, but rather a moment filled with heartfelt sincerity. This book has benefited from the cumulative support of so many, to whom I am grateful. For their guidance, generous support, and critical feedback especially during the foundational stages, I extend the profundity of my thanks to James Smethurst, Esther Terry, John Bracey, Andrea Rushing, and Paula Giddings. Words cannot convey how especially grateful I am to Jim Smethurst, whose unwavering support, encouragement, and good humor lifted me at various turns along this journey. No lesser expression of gratitude goes to Paula Giddings, a remarkable source of inspiration and earnest support, as her ever-welcome advice, encouragement, unrelenting faith in me, and generosity of spirit—especially during our invaluably brilliant clarifying "book conversations" stateside and abroad—have enabled *Unbought and Unbossed* to march into fruition. To the W.E.B. Du Bois Department of Afro-American Studies at the University of Massachusetts Amherst, I extend my gratitude for the enormous support—intellectual, financial, and otherwise—that has provided the foundations of my professional and scholarly development, nourished me as a professional and person, and further cultivated my desire for intellectual rigor and social justice.

Others have had a remarkably indelible impact in ways that may never be fully transparent to them. For her pioneering scholarship, as well as intellectual and pedagogical influence on me, Mary Helen Washington—who may never know the depth of her imprint on me while I studied with her as a visiting graduate student at University of Maryland and beyond—deserves my thanks. I am especially grateful to Thadious Davis for her "warmest best wishes," intellectual support, model work, and brilliant advice, which was instrumental in my extended fellowship at Emory. Trudier Harris has been not only a constant source of inspiration, but also a model scholar and professional confidante. I also thank Joanne Gabbin and the Wintergreen Collective for paving a path and welcoming me.

Without the generous financial support of several foundations and institutions, this book may well not have seen the light of day. I express my utmost gratitude to the UNCF–Mellon Mays University Fellows Program, especially Cynthia Neal Spence; Andrew W. Mellon Foundation, especially Lydia English and Armando Bengochea; Woodrow Wilson National Fellowship Foundation, especially Richard Hope, Bill Mitchell, and Caryl McFarland; Social Science Research Council, especially Cally Waite; and Fulbright Commission, especially Reiner Rohr. Additionally, this book was made possible by financial assistance from the Ruth Landes Memorial Research Fund, a program of The Reed Foundation. Loyola University New Orleans awarded me two generous sources of funding: a Marquette and a Bobet fellowship. I also thank the staff members at the Schomburg Center for Research in Black Culture at the New York Public Library; the Manuscript, Archives, and Rare Book Library at Emory University; the Moorland-Spingarn Research Center at Howard University; the Schlesinger Library of Radcliffe Institute for Advanced Study at Harvard University; and the Amistad Research Center at Tulane University, especially Christopher Harter, to whom I express special thanks for an image, Figure 3.1, used in this book.

As I have had the marvelously good fortune of being a visiting scholar and fellow at Emory University's James Weldon Johnson Institute for Advanced Interdisciplinary Studies (JWJI), I am especially indebted to the founding director, the late Rudolph P. Byrd, a trusted advisor, charismatic scholar and human, and model of protocol. A host of individuals at Emory enriched my project and fellowship period: Calinda Lee, Dorcas Ford Jones, Robbie Lieberman, Joshua Price, Tekla Johnson, Mab Segrest, Bill Turner, Evelyn Crawford, Chandra Mountain, Erica Bruckho, and Yolande Tomilson, all in some way affiliated with the JWJI, and Martina Brownley and the Fox Humanities Center. Amy Benson Brown, Randall Burkett, Frances Smith Foster, Brett Gadsden, Bill Gruber, Leslie Harris, Lynne Huffer, Larry Jackson, Mark Sanders, and Kimberly Wallace-Sanders at Emory also deserve my thanks. My most profound and heartfelt gratitude goes especially to Natasha Trethewey, a kindred spirit whose continual encouragement, advice, and unrelenting support have been as welcome and enormously appreciated as her poetics and friendship. I am so incredibly thankful for the crossing of our paths, as she will never fully know that I have traveled and endured this journey far longer, more courageously, and with head and shoulders elevated higher precisely because of her.

At Loyola University New Orleans, I am incredibly fortunate to have not only a vibrant, supportive, and affable cadre of colleagues, but also an intellectual home. To former Provost Ed Kvet; former Dean Jo Ann Cruz; Dean Maria Calzada of the College of Humanities and Natural Sciences; my department chair, John Biguenet; and my colleagues in the Department of English, I extend my deepest thanks. I owe a very special expression of gratitude to Katherine Adams—my former chair and an absolutely marvelous person and colleague—for her steadfast advice, enthusiasm, and good humor; Kate has showered me with much support, which has helped garner fellowships, and I am deeply appreciative. Many thanks go to Barbara Ewell and especially my faculty mentor, John Mosier, a generous and dedicated advisor, for professional support, goodwill, and necessary good laughs over countless good meals, and to Chris Schaberg for his incredibly jovial, intelligent, and ever-willing support and inspiration as I completed this book. I also benefited from colleagues and institutional support at St. Lawrence University, Auburn University, and Freie Universität (Free University) in Berlin, Germany, during my time as a J. William Fulbright Scholar of American Literature and American Studies. For that amazing intellectual and personal experience, I am thankful to my colleagues in the Department of Literature: Ulla Haselstein especially for serving as my mentor, as well as Catrin Gersdorf, Andrew Gross, and MaryAnn Snyder-Körber, who were incredibly welcoming and brilliant—inviting me to present my research at the colloquium, while also providing an international venue in which to engage, research, and teach race and black feminist theories, literary studies, and African American studies. *Sehr vielen dank!*

Words cannot begin to express the profundity of my thanks to Melissa Harris-Perry, who not only served as my mentor for my Woodrow Wilson National Foundation Career Enhancement Fellowship, but also graciously welcomed me as a visiting scholar and fellow at the Anna Julia Cooper Project on Gender, Race, and Politics in the South, of which she is the founding director, at Tulane University. For her constant enthusiastic support, model work, advice, and encouragement, especially as I completed the book revisions and beyond, I am forever grateful. Similarly, special thanks go to Sara Kugler, whose presence and cordial spirit always made work more pleasant. Morgan Franklin, my student researcher at Tulane, and Yolande Tomilson, my graduate research assistant at Emory, deserve my sincere thanks. I also extend enormous heartfelt thanks to the late Rudolph Byrd, Evelyn Crawford, Sandra Duvivier, Melissa Harris-Perry, Cheryl Hicks, Candice Jenkins, Esther Jones, Calinda Lee, and Reanna Ursin for their intellectual generosity and critical feedback on the manuscript. I owe a very special expression of gratitude to Cathy Schlund-Vials, an amazing person and friend, for her always intelligent, deeply appreciated feedback on the manuscript in its entirety, as well as incredible support of this book. I also extend my profound thanks to Robert Reid-Pharr for his brilliant feedback, model scholarship, and enthusiastic support of this project; in each encounter, I have been impressed by his intelligence, approachability, and refreshing humor, which *always* leave me yearning for more academics like him in this world. Last and certainly not least, I was so very fortunate to embark upon this intellectual journey with Catherine Adams, Stephanie Evans, Adam Linker, and Zebulon Miletsky; for intellectual stimulation, camaraderie, and so many incredibly good times, especially when I needed them most, I express my deep gratitude.

Special thanks go to the personal and/or professional friends who have truly made this journey not only endurable but, indeed, pleasant: Tina Alpough, Evelyn Crawford, Durriyyah Johnson, Janaka Bowman Lewis, Carolyn Powell, Cathy Schlund-Vials, Halima Narcisse Smith, Letitia Thompson-Hargrave, Howard Ramsby II, Joy Wilson, and Nazera Wright. Without Kimberly Juanita Brown, Esther Jones, Keisha-Khan Perry, and Reanna Ursin, this "life of the mind" would be far less enjoyable, and so, I thank each of them for inspiring me with her brilliance and enriching my life with their friendships. Also, words (at least none in the English language) cannot even begin to express the profundity of my thanks and respectful affection to Sandra Duvivier, Jamie Gray, and Calandra Tate Moore, my "inner circle" and dearest friends, whom I am eternally grateful the universe saw fit to situate in my life; our nearly half-lifelong friendships are priceless and have provided me with a more balanced, pleasurable, and humor-filled existence beyond the academy.

I reserve my utmost heartfelt gratitude for my family, whose deep, unyielding love and indomitable support have sustained me throughout this endeavor. My parents, Sterling and Ramona, have never lost faith in my abilities to succeed triumphantly and have been unceasing in their encouragement, optimism, generosity of spirit, and selfless support. I am everything I am, entirely and indubitably, because of them, and words could never begin to express or encompass my profound love for and gratitude to them. My sisters Drs. Trina and Trichelle, by earning professional degrees in fields in which African American women are underrepresented, have defied odds, invalidated stereotypes, and served as both personal and professional models for me. I owe my success, in large part, to their exceptional examples. My younger sister, Trichlyn, has forever impressed me with her vibrance, resilience, intelligence, and professional drive; her fortitude, easy laughter, and professional success continue to inspire me. Furthermore, my existence and this project have been enriched tremendously by the likes and lives, fierce determination, and always welcome presence and good humor of Sepehr Saeedi and Alan Wise. Last, my nephews, Shuwn, Sterling Ramon, Aaron, Ian, Aidan, Caleb, Brody, and Owen have always provided warm, pleasant, loving, and welcome distractions from the tediousness and rigidity of writing; I love and thank them dearly, as well as await all that their promising futures hold. Last and certainly not least, my grandparents—living in this world and "up yonder"—never ever cease to inspire me; their love and impression on me are undeniable, and I hope I have to some extent, if even fractionally, made them proud.

For healing conversations and restoring my mind, heart, and spirit, I offer my thanks to Kalpana Murthy, and especially Violet Bryan, Michele Levy, and Eloise Dixon, who have enlightened, supported, advised, and sustained me, as well as have served as exemplar professionals, humans, and now friends. Cecelia Cancellaro has not only provided impeccable feedback but unexpected and welcome support, and this book is better, in part, because of her. My deepest gratitude goes to Janet Francendese for her exceptional enthusiasm, editorial brilliance, constant support, and model editorship; to Sara Cohen for her expert work and always eager support; to Tim Roberts and Gary Kramer for unwavering dedication to this book; and to the three anonymous readers for Temple University Press, for their insightful feedback and intellectual generosity. An earlier version of the second chapter, "Toward an Aesthetic of Transgression: Ann Allen Shockley's *Loving Her* and the Politics of Same-Gender Loving," appeared in *African American Review* 42, nos. 2–3 (Fall/Winter 2008); thanks go to *AAR*, especially to then editor Joycelyn Moody and managing editor Aileen Keenan, for publishing and providing an intellectual venue for my work. And, very many thanks go to D. M. Grant for his generosity in allowing me to use *The Night*, which celebrates black women's sexuality, encapsulating the very spirit and gorgeous cover of this book; and, certainly no lesser expression of gratitude goes to Karine Percheron-Daniels for her extremely timely support and generosity in allowing me use of her provocative artwork *First Lady*.

I am blessed and highly favored. If there is Glory, as there most undoubtedly is, I know precisely to whom it belongs.

Unbought and Unbossed

Introduction: Disrupting Dissemblance

Unbought and Unbossed: Transgressive Black Women, Sexuality, and Representation explores what exercises of sexual citizenship look like, particularly their manifestations through the trope of transgressive behavior, in post-1960s black women's texts. The book's title is taken from Shirley Chisholm's 1968 congressional campaign slogan, "Unbought and Unbossed," and her eponymous 1970 autobiography. As the first black congresswoman and first black to campaign for United States president, Chisholm—in her position in the political arena and her progressive stance on abortion and the rights to the freedoms of citizenship—embodies a particular transgressive subjectivity. One grounded not solely in her political disposition but also in her very presence physically and ideologically within an almost exclusively white and male-dominated political terrain. At the time she wrote her autobiography, the House of Representatives had 435 members: 417 white men, 10 women, 9 blacks; and so, Chisholm herself, as black and a woman in Congress, "ma[d]e it add up right."[1]

While inspired by Chisholm's political motto, this book is *not* about politics—not, that is, in the electoral or legislative sense.

Nor is it about Chisholm, who, willing to go against the proverbial grain and challenge the status quo, is a remarkably dynamic
figure that certainly merits scholarly attention. This book gravi-
tates off of her notion of "unbought and unbossed" as it encapsulates the spirit and essence of *transgression* (an inherent refusal
to be encumbered, unapologetic resistance to "containment,"
and repudiation of racial/masculinist domination or hegemony)
that characterizes post–civil rights black women's literary and
cultural production. *Unbought and Unbossed* critically examines the ways black women writers of the post–civil rights era
deploy black women characters that transgress racial/gender/
sexual boundaries, particularly those relating to black heteronormative gender and/or sexuality, and challenge paradigms of
black womanhood and female sexuality. Writers such as Toni
Morrison, Ann Allen Shockley, Alice Walker, Gayl Jones, and
Gloria Naylor negotiate black women's historical positionality
as racial/communal symbols of Victorian propriety and their
expressions of individuality in a postmodern society precisely,
I argue, through the trope of *transgressive* black women whose
various enactments of recalcitrance and purported misconduct
defy communal sanctions and problematize notions of a unitary black community. To this end, these characters illustrate
the inefficacy of a strategic politics of silence surrounding black
female sexuality, or "dissemblance," as a viable conduit for black
sociopolitical advancement in a postmodern society.[2]

By "transgressive," I mean those unmediated performances,
enactments, or instantiations of (mis)behavior characterized
by a deliberate "violation" of certain racial, gender, and sexual
sociocommunal boundaries whereby the enactor transcends, if
not destabilizes, established normative and acceptable behavior.
Neither transhistorical nor static, transgressive behavior signifies and might best be understood as conduct marked by a defiance, inversion, or traversal of prescribed norms or conventions.
At the center of this work, then, are black women who partici-
pate in various transgressive acts at the very crux of which is
sexuality: adultery, promiscuity, interracial sexual intimacy,

circumvention of marital sex, sexual violence, same-gender loving, and/or other politics of the intimate. In their deliberate (mis)conduct, they are radical agents who depart unapologetically from proscriptive social and sociocommunal definitions of black womanhood and interlocking circumscriptions governing black female sexuality.

Unbought and Unbossed analyzes representative texts in the sociocultural and historical moments of their productions— informed by and in direct response to the political struggles of the 1950s, 1960s, and 1970s—elucidating the ways they disrupt the myopic representations of black women and the silence about their sexuality in the American literary and cultural imagination. Through the trope of sexuality, this study examines characterizations of black women who not only diverge from stereotypical images imposed by ideologies of "whiteness," but also rebel *unapologetically* against constructions of female identity imposed by black nationalism that constitute what I call the "classical black female script": that is, black women's expected racial loyalty and solidarity, sexual fidelity to black men, self-abnegation, and idealization of marriage and motherhood. The "script," discussed at greater length in chapter 1, is (in)formed simultaneously at the interface of two overarching ideologies: the "cult of true womanhood" with its principles of piety, sexual purity, submissiveness, and domesticity; and, second, culturally specific tenets of uplift and obligatory service propounded by black nationalism and nationalist discourse generally.[3] Constituted in response to persistent stigmatization, the classical black female script, as well as black women's adherence to it, was also part of an effort to "normalize" black womanhood and, in turn, black identity in the face of pervasive stereotypes. It is precisely because post-1960s characters "violate" these socially and communally mandated codes of conduct governing black womanhood and racialized sexuality that their purported misbehavior is perceived as threatening to community mores, aspirations, and advancement.

Drawing upon black feminist, critical race, and performance theories, literary theory and criticism, and theoretical discourses on gender and sexuality, *Unbought and Unbossed* analyzes these characters' transgressive behavior, particularly in regard to their sexuality, as a means to create a (post)modern black (female) identity. I argue that these deliberate enactments of recalcitrance, "illicit" sexuality, and intimate "misconduct" undermine nationalist exigencies of creating communal boundaries through black women, if even for uplift purposes, by circumscribing their sexuality. Not only do these subversive acts destabilize and render obsolete black politics contingent upon essentialist or unitary constructions of community, racial representations, and black womanhood, but they also significantly mark a postmodern moment. This book elucidates that the sexual longing, desire, and intimacy enacted in these texts function metonymically for another aspirational desire: a progressive black identity with racialized gender and sexual politics reflective of the sociopolitical temporal moment. Put another way, sexuality in its various instantiations in these post–civil rights texts operates not simply as a trope but rather as a signifier of postmodern blackness that encompasses a desire for, and efforts toward, a more complex black identity ungoverned by outmoded, rigid politics that are overdetermined by race or attendant conventions concerning gender and sexuality.

In the post–civil rights era, "racial politics [could] no longer be premised on models of unmediated representation or of monolithic racial community," as literary scholar Madhu Dubey asserts; what differentiates "postmodern from modern black intellectual and cultural production is its quest for a politics of difference that eschews essentialist constructions of community."[4] What these post–civil rights texts and their transgressive characters reveal is not a wariness or denouncement of "blackness" or community. On the contrary, these authors and texts embrace black culture and racial/communal consciousness even to the extent that they illustrate that nationalist and feminist politics may well, and sometimes do, intersect and conjoin in meaningful rather than tensional ways. They do, however, contest and excoriate narrow constructions of community that, in their privileging of race and rigid deployments of "black-ness," largely preclude more complex, modern practices and discourses on racialized sexual politics and gender that could enrich and empower the community. The narrow constructions and outmoded dictates governing gender and sexuality succeed, paradoxically, in doing the precise opposite of their strategic design: they endanger and compromise rather than protect or advance various individuals—especially women—and the very community itself.

It is no mere coincidence, then, that this phenomenon, this very endangerment, is embodied and inscribed textually in these post–civil rights novels as devastation and racial, physical, and sexual violation. Sexualized violence against black women's (and, to a far lesser extent, men's) bodies and the accompanying communal upheaval, destruction, and/or tragedy punctuate the texts under examination. Whether Renay's college date rape in Shockley's *Loving Her*; Meridian's molestation at a local funeral home in the eponymous novel by Walker; Eva's sexual viola-tion with a "dirty popsicle stick" and subsequent rape in Jones's *Eva's Man*; or the vicious gang rape of Lorraine of "The Two" in Naylor's *The Women of Brewster Place*, these black women characters confront a sexual conundrum riddled with sexual entanglements along a vexed and thorny continuum. Even as they engage in transgressive behavior marked by sexual agency and autonomy, the central focus of this book, these narratives are saturated with female sexual vulnerability (emblematic of a larger *communal* vulnerability, sexual dehumanization and/in a *racial* historical past) so that, even in their adherence to com-munal dictates governing sexuality, these women encounter nonetheless a sexual quandary. Not only does this speak to the inefficacy of a "politics of silence," but it also makes transparent a detrimental corollary: palpable and entrenched danger, as well as what is at stake in the absence of a progressive black sexual politics with which to meet contemporaneous exigencies.

In calling attention to sexualized violence, in no way do I attempt to overshadow or undermine the *transgressive* behavior, sexual agency, or empowerment of these characters or, moreover, to suggest that transgressive behavior operates alternatively or as an intrinsic reactionary stance to sexual(ized) aggression or violence. Nor do I postulate that sexual vulnerability is a prerequisite or, for that matter, conduit for liberatory black female sexuality. Since transgressive behavior, sexual empowerment, and sexual vulnerability are not entirely discrete categories, I am interested in how they imbricate in a Hegelian sense. For, if "sexual violation" constitutes part of a "legacy of racialization," as literary and queer studies scholar Darieck Scott posits, how does (racialized) sexualized violence interface with transgressive behavior—or, in what ways, if any, does transgression in these post–civil rights literary productions operate?[5] To what extent does black women's transgressive behavior, whether expressed as recalcitrance, sexual excess, or subversion of established norms, serve as a medium by which to broach and transgress a complex, albeit at times fractured, past and to navigate—as autonomous subjects—the temporal moment? And, read collectively, how do Morrison, Shockley, Walker, Jones, and Naylor, as literary and sociocultural activists, shift paradigms of black womanhood and female sexuality; and, how do they attend to the concrete issues governing black women of the post–civil rights era and beyond without essentializing the totality of black women's experiences?

Unbought and Unbossed begins its analysis with post–civil rights novels of the twentieth century (while offering critical comparative analysis of other literary, sociocultural, and historical moments) to establish a nexus in which literary texts, movement ideologies, and the politics of identity and representation intersect to provide a broad interdisciplinary discursive framework for analyzing these complex dynamics. At its very core, this book is grounded in critical race studies, black feminist theory, and representations of black womanhood. As such, it is in dialogue with a multidisciplinary cadre of pioneering black feminist scholars, particularly Darlene Clark Hine, Patricia Hill Collins, Paula Giddings, bell hooks, Deborah McDowell, and

Mary Helen Washington, who have produced landmark work in these intellectual arenas. In its conceptual orientation and grounding in interdisciplinary literary and cultural studies, this book is in concert with scholars who have advanced scholarship on constructions of black womanhood, race, and their intersectional affinities with political desire and/or nationalism: most notably, Hazel Carby, Claudia Tate, Ann duCille, and Madhu Dubey—and, more recently, Candice Jenkins and Lisa Thompson.[6]

While this book follows in this literary scholarly tradition, *Unbought and Unbossed* begins its analysis with post–civil rights novels of the mid- to (early) late twentieth century, explicating the ways the political movements mark a postmodern moment and, in turn, affect characterizations of black womanhood and account for themes of "the transgressive" in black women's literature. In fact, the authors deploy postmodernist techniques, in conjunction with a racialized gender politics governing sexuality, that create an ideological and aesthetic tapestry—a black postmodern paradigm—that offers a less monolithic set of representations of black womanhood, sexuality, and black sexual politics generally. Put another way, it is precisely the ideologies, discourses, and aesthetics of postmodernism that these writers infuse with a racialized gender politics concerning sexuality to interrogate notions of subjectivity, identity, politics of differences, power differentials, and freedom/liberation (with continuity and community). They do so to address and broach their particular conditions as black women, since movements such as feminism and black nationalism did not fully encompass or speak to their intersectional identities, experiences, or exigencies.

The heart of the book, which makes notable intellectual interventions, examines a conglomeration of texts of the 1970s and early 1980s that take on different *registers* embedded in the larger notion of transgression. In its focus on texts of this radically and politically charged moment, it seeks to redress a paucity of scholarship in African American and black feminist literary and cultural studies, which have given little critical attention to the interesting *interregnum* period between black nationalism and multiculturalism. As these texts are situated in the post–civil rights, (post) nationalist age of burgeoning multiculturalism, radical discourses on race, systematic oppression, and racist marginality—symptomatic of and deeply rooted in the black nationalist/black aesthetic tradition—represent an ideological and paradigmatic shift. The rising institution(alization) of multiculturalism—as a largely conservative canonizing discourse that recognizes race, particularities of racial/ethnic culture (articulated within a rhetoric of "diversity"), and pluralism— subsumes, if not consolidates, in ways that produce a particular narrative. At the very crux of such narrative is a racial integrationist discourse, an overarching "feel-good" melting-pot mystique that leaves little room (or, for that matter, *tolerance*) for radically critical or critically radical modalities of race and its intersections with other attendant (identity) politics.[7]

Second, *theorizing* black women's transgressive behavior, while simultaneously examining various manifestations of transgression—or what I often refer to as *racialized gender transgression*—this book challenges "mainstream" discourses and theories of transgression, whereby the nexus of race and transgression, especially where black (female) subjects are concerned, typically falls into an abyss of critical inattention.[8] This book analyzes and elucidates black female transgressive behavior and sexuality—while paying particular attention to periodization, politics, and aesthetics of the (late) mid-twentieth century—to expand understandings of the nexus of gender, sexuality, race, and transgression. In its analysis of postmodern characterizations of black womanhood, black female sexuality, and the ways that both feminism and nationalism imposed constructions of black womanhood that inform post–civil rights authors' characterizations of them as transgressive, this book diverges from previous scholarship in this regard and in its utilization of sexuality as a trope and axis of interrogation of hegemonic power, politics of passion, and female (subversive) erotic pleasure.

I deploy the term "transgressive" (and by extension "transgressive behavior" and "transgression") to indicate the ways these black women characters operate out of a particular and strategic politics, agency, and deliberateness that challenge or, at the very least, call into question what constitutes "normativity," while simultaneously destabilizing conventional paradigms governing race, gender, and sexuality. In this regard, political scientist Cathy Cohen's notion of "deviance" resonates as particularly salient. In her landmark essay "Deviance as Resistance: A New Research Agenda for the Study of Black Politics," Cohen argues for an analysis and paradigmatic shift that, building upon discourses and frameworks in African American studies and queer theory, centers those vulnerable and marginalized subjects who—in their deliberate refusal to conform to established "normativity"—embody a deviance that resists socially and sociocommunally prescribed "heterogendered" and "'normalized' understandings and behaviors."[9] Such individuals embody this subjectivity, complicating power relations, regulation/regulatory processes, and "normativity"; and, their deliberate agency in opting out of conformity to the "fundamental concepts/behaviors" governing "desire, pleasure, and sex" provides the basis for transformative politics and the very paradigmatic shift Cohen proposes. Like Cohen's, my work on transgressive behavior and representations foregrounds those (black women) subjects who unapologetically subvert the established sociosexual "norms." While I recognize that multiple valences of representations of black womanhood and blackness operate as transgressive—with blackness signifying, within the literary and sociocultural imagination, anomaly, debasement, resistance, or excess—I do not present black women's transgressive behavior and racialized (gender) transgression as indicative of or coterminous with aberrance, abjection, deviance, or perversion. Nor do I situate them as pathological in ways that fortify or reaffirm heteronormativity, black debasement, or the purported norm. Rather, I read the manifestations of transgressive behavior as grounded in black (female) subjectivity that not only challenges putative normative modalities governing race, gender, and sexuality, but, as stated previously, as also emblematic of desire for and gestures toward a black postmodern moment.

In its problematization and analysis, then, of the ways race and sexuality intersect in constitutive and formative ways, *Unbought and Unbossed* is also in conversation with interlocutors, such as Cathy Cohen, in black sexuality and queer studies: particularly Roderick Ferguson, Sharon Holland, Robert Reid-Pharr, Darieck Scott, Siobhan Somerville, Kathryn Bond Stockton, and, most recently, Aliyyah Abdur-Rahman. These scholars theorize the complexities and intersections of blackness, sexuality, gender, and "transgression," whether notions of transgression manifest as or are articulated within the rhetoric/realm of a politics of deviance, aberration, erotic disarticulation, shame, abjection, or choice in their foundational work.[10]

Roderick Ferguson's work on African American racialized sexual positionality and aberration has particular purchase, especially his explication of the ways in which sociological schools of thought constructed blackness, vis-à-vis the discursive, canonical, and aesthetic, as "corporeal difference" and outside the norms of both heteronormativity and patriarchy.[11] Not only does he argue that heteronormativity, universalized with whiteness, "is not simply articulated through intergender relations," but also "through the racialized body" with African Americans embodying "gendered and eroticized properties" and nonheteronormativity.[12] With blackness imputed as such, Ferguson theorizes the complexities of black representation and positionality:

> I theorize African American nonheteronormative difference as a way of thinking [about] discourse and contradiction in tandem. [. . .] Hence, in saying that African American culture is a site of contradiction, I do not mean to suggest that sociology is not contradictory. I simply mean to suggest that *African American culture's own particular contradiction of being racialized as nonheteronormative produces nonheteronormativity as a site of rupture.*[13]

Problematizing black nonheteronormativity as contradictory and essentially as rupture, Ferguson's assessment is consequential and resonates with my own readings of black women's transgressive behavior, and black transgression generally, as not emblematic of black "anormativity" or with "the black body" at a tangible or "atmospheric level," as literary and black queer studies scholar Sharon Holland avers, that "produce[s] a narrative of degradation to which that body is perpetually mired."[14] In this book, I repudiate notions of inherent black social/sociosexual pathology or perversity and, rather, read transgressive behavior and transgression as vehicles of disruption, a destabilization of sorts, that turns the putative "normative"/"heteronormative" on its proverbial head. *Unbought and Unbossed* thus situates transgressive behavior and transgression as a destabilizing (and, thereby, *differentiating*) agent, site of analysis, and locus of desire that is dialogic: encapsulating a dynamic at once transcendent, in that it emblemizes subversion and troubles what constitutes the "norm," and also transformative in that subjects *traverse* circumscriptions, *disrupt* established tradition, and *circumvent* conditions that seek to compromise them—as black women—in sexual, racial, and gender domains.

Unbought and Unbossed concerns itself with racialized sexuality, particularly as it relates to black women, and how the very stigmatization of "blackness" informs representations of black women through the trope of sexuality along a continuum rather than bifurcated trajectories. I base my critical analyses methodologically and conceptually on representative novels, cultural texts, and theories read within/alongside a larger sociohistorical, cultural, and political context to explicate the degree to which stereotypes and constructions of black women's sexuality are inscribed in black women's literary and cultural production. At times, I utilize contemporary popular culture (as is the case in the next section on transgression) to elucidate the extent to which these dynamics are not isolated in particular (con)texts or confined in a temporal vacuum that comes to a halt in the 1980s.

Unbought and Unbossed is, then, not so much invested in situating transgression hierarchically or in quantifying transgressive behavior—as in what makes one behavior or instantiation of transgression more transgressive than the next. This book, more fruitfully, explicates the nexus of race, sexuality, and transgression by interjecting discourses on transgression with race and gender, and theories of race, gender, and sexuality with black female transgressive subjectivity. As such, it explicates the extent to which transgressive behavior and the methodical deployment of transgressive characters and sexuality operate as a mechanism to contest absolute constructions of "blackness" that, whether inadvertently or deliberately, seek to approximate the gender-sexual politics of larger society. What these texts and a sustained analysis of them illumine is the confluence of race, transgression, and sexuality; or, the degree to which sexuality, and by extension (racialized) sexual transgression, functions, I contend, as a *strategy* of power, *site* of contestation, and *locus* of erotic agency, pleasure, and subversive politics. And, too, they make visible the dynamic interplay of differences, subject positions, and identity politics that constitute black identity and should, concomitantly, inform black racial politics and community in a postmodern moment, as well as critical approaches to analyses of these. For, it is imperative "to think critically about African Americans and African American culture without simply essentializing the category of blackness" or "fixing, reifying, or separating race, gender, and sexuality in the name of their political serviceability to racial blackness," as literary and black queer studies scholar Dwight McBride insightfully avers.[15]

While this book marks a significant departure from the existing scholarship on representations, it is, in part, rooted in and reflective of the larger sociocultural and political milieu/changes occurring at this particular historical juncture (civil rights, black nationalism, women's liberation, gay and lesbian rights, and the sexual revolution especially) that have informed these authors. This is of particular significance since the novels of this era function not simply as literature or fiction but rather as bodies of knowledge that speak to, and have inscribed in them, larger sociocultural, historical, and political phenomena. As such, they are not merely texts but sites of interdisciplinarity, as well as foundational precursors for much of the subsequent theoretical discourses on black feminism, race, gender, and sexuality.

As "some of black women's most dangerous issues were first aired in the 'safe' space of the arts," these post-1960s authors offer textual interventions, broaching some of the most vexed, if not sensitive, racial/communal/sociopolitical dynamics of the era.[16] This gives credence to the degree to which black women's literature should not be disregarded or reduced merely to the imaginative and fictive. For it, as literature in black racialized contexts especially during particular historical moments, speaks powerfully to the social, political, and experiential climate in which it was written. And, too, black women's literature of this era sets a precedent for much of the historical and theoretical discourse that follows. Post-1960s black women's literary production thus constitutes a rich, deliberate site—a *repository*—that expands our ways of considering interdisciplinarity and, importantly, the intersectionality of race, gender, sexuality, and nation, as well as elucidates the ways that literary texts, history, and sociopolitical movements and theories conjoin meaningfully.

Black women's literature, these novels, and the transgressive black women characters in them transgress boundaries precisely because of the various dynamics that complicate the texts and should also govern our readings of them. Not only does this illustrate the complexity of the novels—which may be deconstructed using race theory and cultural studies approaches, feminist epistemologies, and theoretical discourses on gender and sexuality, among other points of analyses—but it also situates these literary narratives within a larger continuum and sociohistorical, political, and cultural context. The novels, while drawing heavily on African American history, culture, and traditions, assume *extraliterary* meanings and significance, thereby serving as complex sites that offer insight not only into black women, the subjects of the literature, but that also expand our very epistemologies of race, gender, sexuality, and the politics of identity in a postmodern temporal landscape.

In its reframing or reconceptualization of this cadre of post–civil rights texts, *Unbought and Unbossed* elucidates the nexus of racialized gender and sexual transgression, and the very ways the writers featured employ erotic characterizations, "theatricalities" of desire, and sexual(ized) black women's bodies to reconstitute black women's positionalities, identity politics, and (sexual) subjectivity, while attending to their exigencies in the post-1960s era and beyond. What becomes transparent, and this book makes evident, are the ways in which these post–civil rights writers destabilize outmoded paradigms governing sexual politics, animating formulations—vis-à-vis representations, theoretical discourse, and transgressive embodiment—of a post-1960s black politics on liberatory sexuality, or what we might consider a distinctly *postmodern black feminist sexual revolution*—discursive, transformative, and emblematic of the post–civil rights temporal/ideological/cultural landscape.

Unbought and Unbossed thus presents other manifestations that illumine the ways that race, gender, and transgression imbricate in relation to black (women's) bodies to demonstrate the *transhistorical* dimensionality of these dynamics, their reach and temporal ubiquity, and how race and sexuality—coupled with gender—collide in historical and contemporary moments that necessitate critical examination. Enlisting movement ideologies, literary and cultural texts, and politics of identity, this book aims to invigorate intellectual thought, pose possibilities, and reverberate what is at stake—and the (counter) stances—if stereotypes dictate comportment, representations, and intimate performances; mediate or govern politics of passion in private and public (racialized) spheres; or reduce any, every, or *all* black sexual expression to perversity rather than situate it along a continuum: one that is not only afforded black women's white counterparts but that is also constitutive of the nature and range of the existential human (sexual) condition.

"Black Is, Black Ain't": Race, Representation, and Transgression

[A]ny black American, simply by virtue of his blackness, is weird, a nonconformist in this society. —AMIRI BARAKA

Black people have, one might argue, always been "transgressive," depending, that is, on how we conceptualize transgression. Manumitting one's self in light of enslavement, disenfranchisement, and legal disownership of self is in many ways transgressive, as is refusing marginalization in a society wherein blackness is deemed inferior. While black people, specifically African Americans, have historically had a complex and precarious relationship to "the transgressive," discourses on black racialized identity and transgression are few and far between. To critically explore the nexus of blackness, which has invariably been marked as unconventional and outside the "normative," and transgression is at once a complicated and consequential endeavor. Such an undertaking necessitates an explication of "transgression" and how it and racialized blackness—and, by extension, black womanhood—converge. And, too, it warrants an elucidation of the ways that black identity, as well as constructions of black womanhood, and "the transgressive" have intersected at various moments in somewhat vexed and constitutive ways.

Significant critical attention has been given in recent scholarship to transgression, which might be characterized generally as "symbolic inversion": any conduct or "act of expressive behaviour which inverts, contradicts, abrogates, or [. . .] presents an alternative to commonly held cultural codes, values and norms."[17] Others problematize transgression as "not merely breaking a code" or "rebelling against normative social or cultural constraints" but, rather, as the "very pulse that constitutes our identities" and sense of subjectivity in the face of "a constant, if discontinuous negotiation with the transgressive otherness by which we are formed and informed."[18] While such conceptualizations are valuable and provocative, they are neither universal nor representative, especially when considered in racialized contexts. What happens when such theoretical notions are applied to black people who, by virtue of their blackness, have functioned historically as the very quintessence of difference: as the embodiment of that "transgressive otherness" by which identities and boundaries have been formed and informed?

Transgression within a racialized context functions, then, dialectically: as that which, located and operating outside the "norm," also simultaneously affirms, defines, or completes it. This is especially so for black people. For, in order for "whiteness" to signify racial/sexual purity, enlightenment, and acceptability, constructions of "blackness" within the American and larger Western imagination came to embody both denotatively and connotatively an entirely different set of meanings and semiotics: as intrinsically licentious, impure, ignorant, and abject.[19] Or, put another way, blackness, at various historical moments, became the entity by which conceptualizations of civilization, national identity, (non)universality, and progress were constituted precisely vis-à-vis racialization—or, with the strategic association of African Americans with "non-normative gender and sexual practices and identities (as the woeful signs of social lag and dysfunction)" in a culture wherein "heteronormativity" and "universalized heteropatriarchy" functioned as signs of order, national identity, and progress.[20]

If transgression is, as Michel Foucault asserts, "an affirmation of division [. . .] insofar as division is not understood to mean [. . .] the establishment of a separation" but rather "retaining that in it which may designate the existence of difference," black identity—whether through mythologies, stereotypes, or social constructions of race—has operated as that very "existence of difference" and antithesis of "normativity" precisely in order to affirm, uphold, and/or preserve it.[21] Herein lies the irony, peculiarity, and complexity undergirding black identity and transgression. Because black people have been characterized historically as "outside" the realm of normalcy—as abject and outside the law (and heterosexual/patriarchal "normativity")—they have served as "the transgressive" background against which established normality has been constituted. Yet, black people's very attempts at social advancement, as well as their efforts to enter into the American body politic and attain first-class citizenship, have paradoxically also been instances marked by transgression. Blacks, in their efforts to gain freedom, enfranchisement, and equality, as well as to "normalize" blackness, were in essence transgressing their relegation to a marginalized status. When mainstream theorizations and discussions of transgression fail to address its racialized contours or complexities, especially where black identity is concerned, they are not merely elisions. Rather, they call attention, I argue, to the ways blackness has been conflated with transgression and, furthermore, marked indelibly as always already transgressive to the extent that it appears "fixed" like a naturalized trope. Moreover, in not addressing the nexus of blackness and transgression, particularly in relation to the "normative," such accounts neglect the history and conditions—inherent in the construction of an "enlightened West," and especially the building of an American democratic republic or nation—that required the fundamental debasement, relegation, and stigmatization of black people. Thus, black people serve as the "indispensable sacrificial lamb vital to [. . . the] sustenance" of American democracy; and, "black subordination constitutes the necessary condition for the flourishing of American democracy, the tragic prerequisite for America itself."[22]

Ruth Landes helps to further elucidate and problematize black women's relationship to established convention. In *The City of Women* (1947), Landes theorizes, explicitly and implicitly, race, gender, and sexuality as intersecting, and, perhaps even more consequential, she elucidates the extent to which these are punctuated by *culture* and, in turn, mediated by the particulars of *positionality*. Even as this text engages Brazilian and not an exclusively American culture, Landes, as an American anthropologist, provocatively examines race relations and black women's subjectivity and sexual freedom; and she problematizes what, in essence, constitutes "conventionality," especially in terms of gender and sexual "norms." In so doing, she elucidates the degree to which convention is static: that is, never entirely fixed, culturally absolute, or "globally 'normativized,'" which also offers insight into conceptualizations of convention and transgression and particularly how black women's bodies and sexualities are situated within the practices and discourses of the West and beyond.

And so, while black people occupy a complex and precarious position in relation to transgression, this relationship is far more vexed and complicated when compounded by gender. In her gendered analysis, Katharine Kittredge observes that transgression is accompanied by terror and danger, and "[w]omen, especially, understand that once they have moved outside of society's behavioral/sexual boundaries, there will be no return and no alternative place of safety."[23] Furthermore, "the alienation that follows transgression gains power because it cannot be clearly seen: the boundaries of acceptable behavior shift over time, place, and circumstance; and the dangers that lie 'beyond' are un-spoken."[24] Her analysis, while important, necessitates far greater problematization and begs a racialized gendered analysis. While neither acceptable behavior nor transgression is transhistorical, black women have long experienced having no place of safety, let alone "alternative" spaces; moreover, the association of black womanhood with hypersexuality, excess, and as being outside behavioral, moral and sexual convention has certainly transcended shifts in time, place, and circumstance, accounting, in part, for the exclusion of black women from constructions of femininity and "true" womanhood. Rather, black women have been cast as embodying the polarized opposite of an idealized white womanhood in order to sustain such a construction as a model, if even illusory and contrived, of "normative" womanhood. Black women, as "other" and outside the parameters of acceptability and protection, became associated with "illicit" and "overt" sexuality, which in turn subjected them to discursive and corporeal sexualized violence, abuse, and attacks on, as well as defamation of, their bodies and character.[25]

Such circumstances surrounding black womanhood, particularly the correlation between and conflation of black women's bodies as sexually degenerate and pathological, are not, however, limited to particular historical moments, nor are they restricted to particular (con)texts. Instead, this phenomenon is a transhistorical occurrence, as a number of relatively contemporary events illumine. In his highly criticized (and later repudiated) remarks, radio personality Don Imus referred to the almost exclusively black Rutgers women's basketball team during their 2007 NCAA championship game against Tennessee as "some rough girls" and "nappy-headed hos"; whereas "the girls from Tennessee," a more visibly white female team, in Imus's estimation, "all look cute." Imus's invectives evoked vicious stereotypes at the heart of which were racialized and sexualized conceptualizations of black women's bodies, as well as their character, that render them always already transgressive and, even within a twenty-first-century context, vulnerable. His comments expose the systematic defamation of black women as both licentious and invariably linked with "illicit" sexuality, regardless of their status, as well as the persistent attack on black women and their bodies contemporaneously. Moreover, his references to them as "rough," in juxtaposition to the designation "cute" he used to describe the Tennessee players, represent deeply racist/sexist conceptualizations of black women ideologically and aesthetically as largely outside the beauty status quo and realm of femininity as less-than-female—as practically "female masculine" bordering masculinity—and, thereby, ineligible for protection.

Similarly, during the 2004 Super Bowl XXXVIII halftime show featuring Janet Jackson and Justin Timberlake, a "wardrobe malfunction" accounted for the exposure of Jackson's breast at the precise moment Timberlake sang, "I'm gonna have you naked by the end of this song." Responses to the singers' performance, whether incidental or a calculated choreographed gesture, inevitably diverged. While there are various factors to consider, such as the performers' obvious age difference, most transparent were their racial and gender differences: Jackson, an African American female pop icon (and sister of the global pop sensation—the "King of Pop"—Michael Jackson), and Justin Timberlake, a former "boy band" group member and breakout white male performance artist. The singers' performance and the public's response to it revealed a particular vulnerability of both an intimate and public nature. Jackson experienced castigation and a lack of sympathy not at all commensurate with her sexualized exposure. Conversely, Timberlake was considered, by and large, a relatively innocent "bystander" who was simply unaware or duped. As such, he, though having actively pulled on Jackson's clothing, did not encounter the same degree of criticism or suffer ramifications to the extent that Jackson did.[26]

These instances are not, however, limited to the interracial realm but also occur in intraracial contexts, as the controversy surrounding Nelly, rapper and music entertainer, reveals. In his highly contentious and controversial video *Tip Drill*, black women appear partially nude, especially in comparison to the fully clothed male rappers donning athletic jerseys. Nelly's swiping of a credit card in between the "posterior" (a.k.a. buttocks) of a woman caused an uproar of enormous magnitude, as did his obtuse and degrading misogynist lyrics. Not only did students at Spelman College plan a boycott of his charity performance, but he was scathingly excoriated by the National Association for the Advancement of Colored People (NAACP). In some ways, Nelly's career still suffers from this incident. What his video and its subsequent public condemnation expose is the extent to which perceptions and stereotypes of black women, womanhood, and blackness generally are entrenched in various segments, including the black community, and perpetuated in troublesome ways. Disseminated are constructions of black masculinity and manhood as regulatory—dictating the terms of their sexuality and desires through women, whose bodies and sexualities are governed by and accessible to (multiple) men. Some rappers, in turn, become representative of or conflated with an "authentically" black (male) subject whose masculinity is constituted, if not governed, by his sexuality—virility, sexual domination, and prowess—in relation to the female body, exploitation, and capital, as evidenced by the title ("*Tip*" *Drill*) and Nelly's dashing money toward women for sexual exchanges and accommodations.

Nelly's video perpetuates problematic constructions of black masculinity and reifies what sociologist Robert Staples observes as black men being "in conflict with the normative definition of masculinity," which, "as defined in this culture, has always implied a certain autonomy over and mastery of one's environment."[27] Part of that "environment," whether in broad or euphemistic terms, is women—and the male authority customarily, and even at times legally, associated with traditional manhood. And so, black men, in the absence of one type of larger social power and outside "normative" constructions of masculinity, might wield masculine authority and subjectivity in relation to women in compensatory and systematic ways through sexual voyeurism of black women's bodies and the commodification of black (female) sexuality. Masculinity becomes conflated "with those traits that imply authority and mastery, femininity with those traits that suggest passivity and subordination"; moreover, "[m]asculinity is tied intimately to sexuality" in that "gender informs sexuality, sexuality confirms gender."[28] Black masculinities enacted in Nelly's video are contingent, then, upon the reproduction of stereotypical and myopic conceptualizations of black womanhood and both racialized and sexualized constructions of masculinity/femininity. This is representative of a masculinist discourse and iconography symptomatic, as well as reminiscent of the black macho hypersexualized image and self-posturing of the Black Power (nationalist) era.[29] Still, the masculinist self-posturing and misogyny of Nelly's video, and arguably of millennial rap generally, is distinct and cannot be conflated congruously with the black macho paradigm that, despite its shortcomings and ultimate outcome, was advanced putatively, in part, in the spirit of black (male) liberation.

What each of these "vignettes"—at the crux of which are the vexed ways in which race, gender, and sexuality intersect with regard to black women in contemporary cultural events—illuminates is that black women, regardless of status, professionalism, background, athletic or artistic achievement, are reduced to stereotypes or "controlling images," to invoke Patricia Hill Collins's terminology. Such representations not only deny black women's subjectivity through objectification, but relegate them to a state of sexual pathology, vulnerability, and accessibility seldom consensual; moreover, they are an indication that the very paradigms, discourses, and modalities regarding race, gender, and sexuality do not and will not suffice. Otherwise, black women will remain unprotected from these racialized gender/sociosexual conditions, stereotypes, and violations that stem from a larger matrix of racial/sexual and racist/sexist oppression, representations, and domination.

This attack on black women, their bodies, and character has long-standing historical underpinnings; and it has long been an issue with varying consequences for and responses from black women. To assert their subjectivity and contest pathologized sexual infamy, African American women of the early black women's club movement, in the late nineteenth and early twentieth centuries, embraced dissemblance and propriety with regard to sexuality. In response to having been marked as morally/sexually depraved and outside the realm of womanhood—and the protection and attendant characteristics this designation provided—black women, mostly from the middle class, adopted respectability, propriety, and a politics of silence surrounding sexuality as a means to challenge their stigmatization as the quintessence of deviance.

This cult of secrecy became deeply entrenched within various segments of the black community, manifesting especially, and assuming its most institutionalized form, in the black women's club movement.[30] The efforts of these clubs, which joined together to form the National Association of Colored Women (NACW), were concomitantly subversive and recuperative. They not only actively challenged racism and sexism, but also sought to rescue black women and the larger black community from sexual and moral infamy by creating "positive" images and adopting conventional bourgeois propriety in regards to sexuality, morality, and domesticity. To this end, late-nineteenth- and early-twentieth-century African American women writers, some of whom belonged to the National Association of Colored Women or other professional organizations and literary societies, were invested in portraying black people, specifically African American women, in accordance with a politics of respectability and the attendant strictures of the racial uplift paradigm.

Frances Harper and Nella Larsen, for instance, created characters in compliance with respectability and the norms of their times, as examinations of Iola Leroy in Harper's *Iola Leroy* (1892) and Helga Crane in Larsen's *Quicksand* (1928) clearly demonstrate. Harper avoids representing Iola as a woman with sexual desire or longings. Moral and respectable, Iola glorifies motherhood and domesticity, all the while exuding "saintliness" and sexual repression. Helga, though appearing in literature nearly thirty-six years after Iola, is not much more progressive in terms of sexual empowerment, expression, or desire. Running from her sexuality and never confronting it or her sexual repression, Helga marries a fundamentalist preacher spontaneously and "prematurely"—with marriage being an institution in which sex is sanctioned and legitimated—not only confining herself to domesticity and motherhood, but becoming even more repressed and despondent.

Emphasizing the ambition, middle-class values, domesticity, and Christian morality of their characters, Harper and Larsen, like several of their black female contemporary writers, restrict black women characters to prescribed ideals to challenge stereotypes surrounding black womanhood. Literary scholars and critics Hazel Carby, Claudia Tate, and Ann duCille have argued convincingly that these early characters serve, as their authors intend, as innovative "rhetorical device[s]" and as "highly political narrative strateg[ies]."[31] Yet, however conscious and deliberate these authors' political and literary strategizing, their black literary "heroines," very rarely constructed outside of the contexts of propriety and uplift traditions with which they were in tandem, are characterized by, and behave in accordance with, the politics of bourgeois propriety and the "norms" of their time. And so, "despite the early writers' efforts to revise homogenized literary images" and challenge stereotypes, as literary scholar Deborah McDowell contends, "they succeeded merely, and inevitably, in offering alternative homogenization; they traded myth for countermyth."[32]

By the late 1930s and well into the 1950s, the role of black literature, as well as its thematic, ideological, and political landscape, evolved. Characterized by the rise of social realism and protest fiction, and appearing in the sociohistorical context of the Great Depression and Jim Crow politics, canonized African American literature witnessed a dramatic shift and took on different meanings. Writers of this period critiqued interlocking systems of oppression in their diatribes against American racism and the white power structure. With few exceptions—Ann Petry's *The Street* (1946), Dorothy West's *The Living Is Easy* (1948), and Gwendolyn Brooks's *Maud Martha* (1953), most notably—published African American fiction during this era was largely dominated by the male protest writers Richard Wright, Ralph Ellison, James Baldwin, and, to a lesser extent, Chester Himes. Their fiction, an indictment of American white racism and its ideological, hegemonic, and violent oppression of African Americans, focused prominently on young male protagonists' struggles against alienation, subordination, and racialized violence. Most black women in the fiction of these male protest writers are peripheral types lacking dimension.[33] Characterized as long-suffering eternal victims and/or seductresses, the black women depicted by these writers exist, by and large, either at men's disposal or as the impetus for black men's demise or tragic death, as is the case in Wright's *Uncle Tom's Children* (1938) and *Native Son* (1940). Wright's characterizations coincide with the particular type of cultural nationalism he deploys to redefine black manhood against its construction as outside traditional masculinity and heteropatriarchy. "Wright's nationalism" necessitates "a specifically masculine revolutionary agency" that not only excoriates "feminization" but that also "prove[s] aggressively heteropatriarchal."[34] In other words, Wright utilizes a version of cultural nationalism vis-à-vis African American literature to overturn, if even by problematic means, paradigms of black manhood as outside the heteropatriarchal and heteronormative domains.

African American women writers at the time, including Petry, West, and Brooks, as well as Alice Childress and later Lorraine Hansberry, challenged "white supremacist capitalist patriarchy," to invoke bell hooks's terminology, yet did so quite differently from their black male counterparts. While they participated in the protest paradigm, they did so in innovative ways that offered a critical reassessment and epistemological recalibration of the very nature of "protest" itself. These women engage, deploy, and *engender* protest that is not grounded in male hegemony or aggression. Put another way, black women's protest literature operates thematically, *not* off an axis of masculine angst, isolation, or prowess, but rather through an intersectional interrogation that provides a more nuanced discursive and ideological excoriation of systematic racist, sexist, and classist oppression and their cumulative effect. Importantly, these ideas are exposed vis-à-vis the prism of *interiority*: an insularity or inner-dimensionality, personal and specific to them as black women, as well as communally and racially collective at large.[35] Petry's delineation of the plight of blacks exposes the consequences of interlocking systems of oppression confronting them, including the sexual vulnerability of black women and their struggle against multiple oppressions (as evidenced by the extent to which protagonist Lutie Johnson goes to protect herself from violence and sexual violation in *The Street*). Hansberry's *A Raisin in the Sun* (1959) offers a dramatic explication of the insidiousness of white American racism, as well as the tensions between Jim Crow politics and the mistreatment of blacks, alongside the black struggle toward upward mobility and against "a dream deferred" (Beneatha's desire to be a doctor, Ruth's contemplated abortion, Walter Lee's attempted business entrepreneurship, Lena's homeownership). Still, there is Brooks's novelistic rendering of the politics of race, segregation, and the experiences of blacks in *Maud Martha* wherein lies a yearning for the ordinary, the "common": purchasing a home, establishing traditions, cultivating one's family and quality of life. As Brooks illustrates, these very "common" things that Maud longs for are not so ordinary *or* (easily) attainable for black people in light of racial apartheid, segregationist politics, and incessant oppression. By virtue of their "blackness," and how race and systematic oppression operate, blacks are not only largely refused fundamental human, civic, and social rights, but they confront institutionalized obstacles that compromise their experiences of the "ordinary" and other so-called common privileges. Her emphasis on public manifestations of racism, alongside intimate renderings of childbirth, establishment of tradition, and family life, serves as an amalgamation of public and private: political protest and indignant insularity.

What black women's literature from the 1930s through 1950s illustrates is the changing ideological, political, and literary/ sociocultural milieu—the very shifting landscape of the politics and paradigms—governing "the politics of silence." While this era is distinct with its own stylistics, literary conventions, and thematic preoccupations, its engagement with and refusal to be silenced in the face of racial injustice, coupled with its acknowledgment of the gender/sexual terrain, allow it to serve as a consequential bridge—a space with larger epistemological and ontological impact—to post-1960s black women's literature. The black women writers of this era gesture toward racial, gender, and sexual liberation and contest the interlocking systematic oppression of black women and the community. They anticipate, then, the post-1960s and second-wave feminist doctrine that "the personal is political." Additionally, these writers make clear that the political (*who* is enfranchised, has access to fundamental rights and full civic, economic, and social subjectivity) is also deeply personal and inextricably bound to one's race, gender, class, ethnicity and/or nation(ality).

What, then, created space for African American women writers to explore the complexities of their intersectionality and diverse experiences as black women with range, depth, and substance? What enabled them to contest limited representations and the matrix of domination, both contributing to and perpetuating black women's oppression, marginalization, and exclusion? And what allowed them to challenge and redefine the politics governing their multiple identities in strikingly new, daring, and consequential ways? Indubitably, it was the political movements ensuing and developing out of the civil rights struggles of the 1950s and 1960s. The civil rights movement, with its focus on renegotiating the marginalized and segregated social space to which African Americans had been consigned, centered itself around ending social segregation, as well as the political and economic disfranchisement of blacks. Challenging the American social disorder that produced and rested on oppositional constructions, the civil rights movement demanded equal rights for all people, specifically African Americans, who had long been relegated to second-class citizenship. Galvanizing individuals around sociopolitical activism and nonviolent action, it raised the racial, class, and political consciousness of Americans. This new awareness made a space for African American women to move forward in their quest for equality and liberation from American social injustice.

In "The Civil Rights Movement: What Good Was It?" Alice Walker asserts that prior to the movement, she had "never seen [her]self and existed as a statistic exists, or as a phantom. In the white world [she] walked, less real to them than a shadow [. . .], wait[ing] to be called to life. And, by a miracle, [she] was called."[36] Much like Walker, the struggle for civil rights "called" many black women into being, not only providing them with heightened ideological and sociopolitical consciousness, as well as political skills, but also empowering them with knowledge.

Awareness of one's condition, and the metaphysical systems perpetuating that condition, is, in itself, life-giving and transformative. In part because of this new awareness, and in part because the term "sex" was included as another dimension in the Civil Rights Act of 1964, African American women began interrogating their position within the movement and society.[37] Having worked exceedingly hard in the black rights struggles, including both the older civil rights and subsequent Black Power movements, black women remained largely overshadowed. With extensive focus on the recovery of black manhood, a major component of black cultural nationalism, it became increasingly difficult for black women to address issues affecting them within the movement, and they strongly desired to contest the simultaneity of oppressions—racism, patriarchy, sexism, heterosexism, and classism—confronting them as blacks and women.

While the Black Nationalist movement, in which black women participated, refuted notions of black political and cultural inferiority, celebrating "blackness" publicly in radical form, its often unitary constructions of black identity privileged black manhood (and heterosexuality) in ways that relegated black women to the periphery. According to black nationalist tenets, and in tandem with nationalisms generally, black women's functions did not extend beyond biological and cultural nurturing. As problematically constructed within these discourses, "all Black women should be heterosexual" with "the primary utility of black women's sexuality" being that of "inspiring her Black man in the privacy of their home. Her own pleasure is rarely mentioned."[38] Many black women contested these unitary, patriarchal, and heterosexist constructions of black female identity in their refusal to have their sexuality regulated through black men, marry, or "make babies for the revolution" and the black nation. Risking possible alienation from the community, these women asserted their agency in revolutionary ways, providing a space and transgressive models for black women who diverge from the nationalist script.

Marginalized in the black rights struggle, some black women looked to the burgeoning women's liberation movement as a way of challenging patriarchy and addressing issues pertaining to them as black women. Yet, the women's movement and related sexual revolution neglected to speak to the nexus of racialized gendered sexual liberation, thereby alienating black women because of racial and class demarcations but even more so because of the varying ways in which white and black women—and blacks generally—have been characterized sexually. The "Sex and Psychology" section of the October 1971 issue of *Ebony* magazine featured an article entitled "Blacks and the Sexual Revolution" that ruminated on the nexus of American sexual liberation and black sexual politics. Because of the historical stigmatization of black sexuality, as well as black people's active participation in the forefront of varied sociopolitical movements, much of "mainstream" America linked the sexual revolution with a "moral degeneracy" that they also associated with blackness, leading them to question if blacks were responsible for it: "Predictably, some whites have gone so far as to associate the sexual revolution with the black drive for freedom and liberation. [. . .] Are they [blacks] unknowingly leading the so called sexual revolution in America, too?"[39]

As black sexuality was entrenched in the white literary, cultural, and social imagination as the quintessence of licentiousness, deviance, and hypersexuality, a significant portion of white America attributed the revolution to blacks, as evidenced by nationwide surveys conducted in 1967 wherein half of the respondents expressed the opinion that blacks had "looser morals" than white Americans.[40] What these sensibilities and statistics reveal is the overarching extent to which "blackness" was viewed in sociosexual ways—or, what Sharon Holland considers "the erotic life of racism." The ways that "racist practice *does* limit human desire by attempting to circumscribe its possible attachments"; for "there is no 'raceless' course of desire" but, rather, "the practiced nature of quotidian racism" and, more specifically, how these very "practices shape what we know of as 'desire.'"[41] As such, the statistics governing blackness and sociosexual dynamics illuminate not only the precise ways race, racism, and desire collide, but also illustrate, concomitantly, that what was constitutive of liberation, sexual and otherwise, varied across racial (and by extension, I would add, gender and class) lines and was not identical or homogeneous among blacks and their counterparts.

Gender further complicates this. Because larger American discourse had categorized white women as emblems of purity and lacking in sexuality (putative justification for the constructions of black women's and men's sexuality, as well as their respective sexual dehumanization and sexualized crimes against their bodies), the largely white second-wave feminists asserted sexuality in more public ways. Black women, castigated and stigmatized as always already sexually transgressive and the antithesis of purity, shied away from public displays of sexuality. Most white women associated with the women's movement were, unlike African American women, (upper) middle-class and benefited from the privileges of whiteness. Yet, unlike their white male counterparts, white women, in exchange for "protection" and white privilege, had been largely consigned to subordinate positions and narrowly defined roles within the male-dominated American social order. Invested in redefining themselves beyond the traditional roles of wives and mothers and outside the realm of sexuality, these second-wave feminists galvanized around renegotiating the dynamics of gender, identity, and sexuality within American society, which black women had long encountered and experienced. As Toni Morrison avers in her 1971 polemic "What the Black Woman Thinks about Women's Lib," black women had "known something of the freedom white women are now beginning to crave. But oddly freedom is only sweet when it is won. When it is forced, it is called responsibility."[42]

Black women were marginalized in the black and women's rights movements, but they were concomitantly influenced by their own efforts toward racial and gender egalitarianism. African American women themselves, forming their own feminist agenda, asserted radically subversive racialized gendered sexual idcntities and politics. The Combahee River Collective, an organization of black lesbians instrumental in black feminism, refuted notions of black women's sexuality regulated through, and as the sole property of, (black) men. They were "actively committed to struggling against racial, sexual, heterosexual, and class oppression" and viewed "[b]lack feminism as the logical political movement to combat the manifold and simultaneous oppressions" confronting black women.[43] The black feminist movement also questioned the regulation of black female sexuality, arguing for a centering of black women's issues and the inclusion of black women who transgress communal circumscriptions—predicated on heteronormative gender and sexuality—for women in favor of more liberatory approaches to sexuality in and of itself.

Politics of Sexuality, Race, and Representation—Or, "Has the Sexual Revolution Bypassed Black People?"

As *Unbought and Unbossed* is invested in elucidating the nexus of race and sexuality as these intersect with representation and transgression, it is important to investigate how these dynamics consolidate and, in turn, manifest in the discourses governing racialized blackness, representations, and the sexual revolution during the 1960s and 1970s? For if, as Siobhan Somerville posits, a fundamental conceptualization of "sexuality through a reliance on, and deployment of, racial ideologies" exists and is predicated on "cultural assumptions and systems of representation about race,"[44] in what ways do sexualized racial ideologies inform our epistemologies and experiences, as reflected in literary and cultural texts that foreground these racial/sexual dynamics? June Jordan's elucidation of the politics of sexuality as "subsuming the different ways in which some of us seek to dictate to others" with regard to "what we should do, what we should desire" and "how we should behave ourselves, generally" is also especially illuminating and applicable to the dynamics governing sexuality—as well as the premise behind the politics of sexual liberation in the post–civil rights, sexual revolution era (and beyond).[45]

Discourses on black racialized sexuality often veer toward certain proclivities, namely to illuminate the extent to which it has been pathologized, regulated, systematically violated and utilized as a form of oppression, and/or linked inextricably to heterosexuality in ways that perpetuate an inauthentic black heteronormativity. Far less attention has been given to black racialized sexuality within the context of a/the sexual revolution or, to borrow from June Jordan, a "new politics of sexuality." Given the assaults against black people and their sexuality historically, and their need to protect and rescue themselves rather than reify stereotypes, it is not difficult to understand why a paucity of literature and scholarship exists with regard to black sexual liberation of the 1960s and 1970s.

As is usually the case with cultural and political movements, the sexual revolution was characterized by a plethora of complex elements that resist simplicity. The designation "sexual revolution" itself was coined in the 1920s. The term does not refer to a particular social phenomenon, and it evolved with each passing decade. During the 1960s and 1970s, the sexual revolution was marked by varied politics, involving an eschewal of Victorian propriety and mores regarding sexuality, a rebellion against and redefinition of what had traditionally constituted sexual "norms," and the liberation of libidinal forces from restrictions that situated them exclusively within the confines of heterosexual marriages. The sexual revolution challenged taboos that traditionally accompanied sexual expressions: namely, premarital sex, masturbation, homosexuality, same-sex loving, polygamy, group sex, open marriages, orgies, extramarital sex, and interracial sexual intimacy, among other sociosexual dynamics. These decades saw changes not only in ideologies and sociosexual practices, but also in the social, cultural, and legal landscape as evidenced by the development of the birth control pill, sex education beyond pedagogies of abstinence, screening and distribution of pornography and hard-core sex cinema in public theaters and for private collections, a repeal of sodomy laws and the removal of homosexuality from the approved list of mental disorder categories, the decriminalization of abortion, and the enactment of no-fault divorce laws, as well as contestations of interracial marriages (as violations of state miscegenation laws) as invariably unconstitutional.[46]

As historian David Allyn notes in *Make Love, Not War*, the various manifestations of the sexual revolution, as well as the ter minology itself, were characterized by ambiguity that lent itself to various interpretations. The sexual revolution emblematized a subversion of the (sociosexual) status quo and an "unexpected period of social transformation," resulting from a calculated effort to overturn "the legal and political pillars of the existing moral regime," and thus revealed the deep inherent "contra- dictions of American life" in the 1960s and 1970s.[47] While his elucidation of the ways in which the sexual revolution worked to undermine the prevailing moral and social codes is useful, his characterization of the sexual revolution as a profoundly and intrinsically "American" revolution, emblematic of the "contra- dictions" of American life, is especially provocative and revela- tory. Some of those contradictions were inextricably linked to sexuality in the white private sphere, which was not nearly as Victorian or puritanical as previously thought. In other words, much of the publicly professed sexual morality did not coincide with the reality of sexual practices and conduct in private, espe- cially within the dominant racialized sociosexual system.

As scientist-turned-sexologist Alfred Kinsey exposed over a decade earlier in his infamous *Sexual Behavior in the Human Male* (1948) and *Sexual Behavior in the Human Female* (1953), widely known as *The Kinsey Report*, what Americans expressed in public about their sexuality did not always reflect their pri- vate sexual conduct. Surveying various subjects regarding their sexual experiences and desires, Kinsey found that a significant percentage of the population, specifically white American males and females, had participated in various sexual activities—pre- marital sex, extramarital sexual encounters, and same-sex desire and intimacy, among other commonly held sexual "taboos"—which illuminated the extent to which individuals' personal sexual experiences and histories did not accord with established public "norms" governing sexuality. The degree to which individuals desired and engaged in particular sexual behaviors, such as same-sex intimacy, prompted Kinsey to create new topographies to more aptly, so he conjectured, categorize sexualities and sexual identities. Whereas three categories—heterosexual, homosexual, and bisexual—had previously existed, Kinsey's data findings prompted him to create four additional gradations reflective of a larger sexual continuum.

While Kinsey's report was indubitably controversial because it exposed publicly an otherwise undisclosed dimension of America's sexual character, particularly as it revolves around constructions of white sexuality, it also provoked charges that it was inherently and methodologically biased. This was due, in part, to the fact that a significant portion of his subjects had formerly been incarcerated, were or had been prostitutes, and/or were self-selected and unashamed of challenging society's sexual codes. As such, his studies were critiqued as not being reflective of the general American population because of the limited demographics racially and otherwise, subject positions, and circumstances of his subject pool. While the Kinsey Institute did, at some point, conduct research on African Americans, finding disparities in the sexual conduct of the working class and the black middle class, the topics of black sexuality, the status of blacks, and the sexual revolution were receiving their own attention in the black community. Black writers, sociocultural and political activists, and black scholars and intellectuals initiated dialogues and studies on sexual diversity, same-sex desire, lesbianism, and black male homosexuality, as well as produced narratives to address these topics and rape, incest, molestation, interracial sex, and other sociosexual dynamics. In his 1970 "A Letter from Huey to the Revolutionary Brothers and Sisters about the Women's Liberation and Gay Liberation Movements," Huey Newton, while supreme commander of the Black Panther Party, not only offers support of the women's and gay liberation movements, which he recognizes as potential political allies; but, perhaps far more consequential, he articulates a politics of shared oppression from the established "norm"—humanizing the women's and gay liberation movements—while instructing his constituents to remain vigilant in not associating revolution with homophobic, heterosexist, or sexist postures. In speaking of gay liberation specifically, he posits, "We haven't said much about the homosexual at all and we must relate to the homosexual movement because it is a real movement"; and, "whatever the case is, we know that homosexuality is a fact that exists and we must understand it in its purest form; that is, a person should have the freedom to use his body whatever way he wants to."[48] Moreover, he avers that, as the Black Panthers were in the process of developing a "revolutionary value system," they should eliminate from their vocabularies any offensive, pejorative language regarding gays and nongays alike. While its support of gay liberation is progressive within the context of its time, this philosophy did not engage a conspicuously racialized element regarding black sexual diversity within the Black Panther Party, nationalist movement, and society at large.

During the 1970s, black general-interest periodicals like *Ebony* magazine featured articles on the topic of blacks and the sexual revolution. *Essence* magazine, for black women especially, produced a monthly column entitled "Your Sexual Health" to address questions on such topics as female orgasms, oral sex, sexual wellness, sexually transmitted diseases, libido, abortions, same-sex desire, and the questioning of sexual identity. On the academic front, the *Black Scholar*, one of the leading academic journals, published a special issue in 1978 entitled "Blacks and the Sexual Revolution." And, a 1971 issue of *Ebony* featured the comedian Dick Gregory and his large family on the cover with his story, "My Answer to Genocide," in the "Race" section. Apparently his answer was, in part, race augmentation vis-à-vis the reproductive capacities of (black) sexuality.

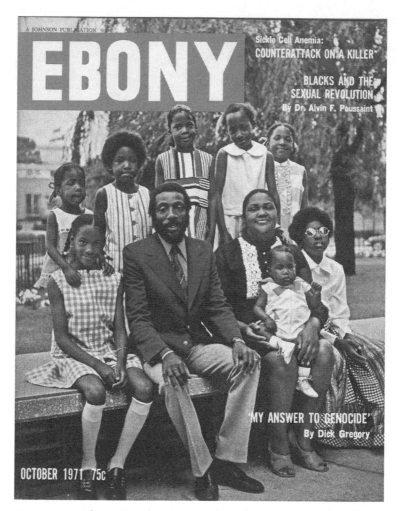

FIGURE I.1 *Ebony*, October 1971, with Dick Gregory and headliner "Blacks and the Sexual Revolution." (Courtesy of Johnson Publishing Company, LLC. All rights reserved.)

Of equal or greater import, Gregory's story was paired interestingly with a feature article in a provocative special "Sex and Psychology" section, wherein Alvin Poussaint disseminated his findings on blacks and the sexual revolution. Foregrounding blacks, the sexual revolution, and liberation, Poussaint dispelled mythologies regarding black sexuality, while calling on black people to remain vigilant and "on guard against the mass media's outpouring of crude and degrading sexual stereotypes." Collapsing dichotomous constructions of black sexuality among class lines, he refuted the notion that the black middle class and bourgeoisie embraced more puritanical sexual views than their counterparts of a lower socioeconomic class. Reportedly, less-educated black women had fewer instances of sexual relations before *and* during marriage than black middle-class women. "Let us keep in mind," he asserts, "our unique social heritage and be thankful that many blacks have retained a relaxed attitude toward sex," he asserts, while concomitantly expressing hope that the sexual revolution would liberate racialized sexual tension so that black people would cease to be the "scapegoats" upon which white sexual repression would be displaced.[49] Poussaint's assertion might, at first, seem curious—as a directive eliciting gratitude and praise instantiated on the basis of "a unique" cultural practice and heritage. His emphasis on this racial/cultural sensibility, coupled with his notion of "relaxed" sociosexual dispositions among blacks, takes on greater magnitude—and indeed significance—when contextualized within the framework of the American cultural proclivity to pathologize black sexuality.

Just six years prior, in 1965, sociologist (and later senator) Daniel Patrick Moynihan, in his now infamous *Moynihan Report*, illustrated the "erotic life of racism."[50] In his report, Moynihan posited that the crux of the degeneration of the black family and black community was the black "matriarchal" family structure, which, in turn, implicates not only (a false sense of) black dysfunction and pathology, but also contrived notions of black female promiscuity and hypersexuality. The illegitimacy rate among blacks, comparatively higher than that of whites, putatively functioned as material evidence, though was skewed and illusory, as the disproportionately higher abortion rate among whites was conspicuously neglected from the discourse of his report. Thus, it reinscribed and reified racist/

racialized stereotypes of an always already aberrant, "anormative" black sexuality, resulting in a castigation of blacks—rather
than systematic American racism, racist oppression, and a long
history of U.S. state and legally sanctioned sexual crimes against
black bodies—for cumulative black familial and communal
"dysfunction."

As literary and sexuality studies scholar Aliyyah Abdur-Rahman cogently notes, historical "sexual aberrance incorporated a
logic of racial and corporeal identity by which to make it visible"
with "transgressive sexuality" being constituted by conventions
predicated on aesthetics and phenotypes, notably "appearance"
in the "arena of race, by which to make it known."[51] What this
brings into stark transparency are the contradictions of American life, deeply paradoxical, of the indeed racially sexualized
constructions of American sociosexual character. For, as the
individual and aggregate findings of Kinsey and Poussaint had
shown, while black people's sexual lives were varied, they were
neither as exaggerated nor pathologically anomalous as the
stereotypes or *The Moynihan Report* otherwise suggested. Contrastingly, white sexuality lacked the puritanical character that
had historically been attributed to it, as the studies exposed that
whites engaged more frequently in clandestine taboo sexual acts
and a sexual culture that belied their presumably "normative"
sexual character.

Three years later, in a 1974 issue of *Ebony* with a cover featuring the then sex symbol Billy Dee Williams, sociologist Robert
Staples, in "Has the Sexual Revolution Bypassed Blacks?," argued
that although blacks, unlike their white counterparts, were far
less involved in certain sexual behavior, such as pornography,
"swinging," and open marriages, college-age blacks were more
likely to engage in premarital sex than their white counterparts
during the sexual revolution.

Such statistics, however, necessitated calibration around the
issue of frequency given that, while engaging in premarital sex at
higher rates, black college students were less engaged than whites
in one-night stands, but rather were in longer-term committed

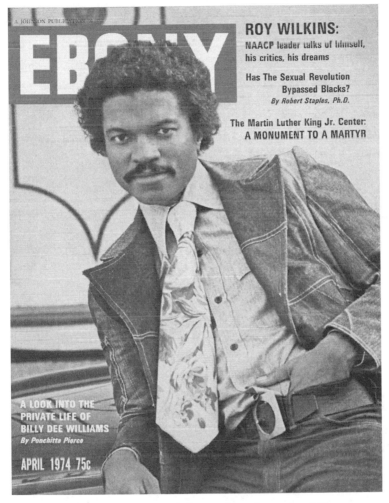

ROY WILKINS:
NAACP leader talks of himself,
his critics, his dreams

**Has The Sexual Revolution
Bypassed Blacks?**
By Robert Staples, Ph.D.

**The Martin Luther King Jr. Center:
A MONUMENT TO A MARTYR**

A LOOK INTO THE
PRIVATE LIFE OF
BILLY DEE WILLIAMS
By Ponchitta Pierce

APRIL 1974 75¢

FIGURE I.2 Billy Dee Williams featured on the cover of *Ebony*,
April 1974, with a headliner on the Sexual Revolution. (Courtesy of
Johnson Publishing Company, LLC. All rights reserved.)

relationships wherein sex was more frequently involved. All
in all, Staples's research indicated that black sexuality was
neither outside the realm of "normalcy" nor hyperpuritani-
cal. In response to his initial query, "Has the sexual revolution
bypassed blacks?," the answer was relative and contingent on

"which feature of the Sexual Revolution we mean and which segment of the black community we are talking about. The most reasonable answer" appears "to be that some blacks have been passed by, others are catching up and a significant number are today just as sexually together as they have always been."[52] Within the black community, sexual expression was not monolithic, practiced and experienced unilaterally, but instead black people negotiated their sexuality and its politics in ways that were not quintessentially aberrant or racially/communally disintegrating, although sexual stereotypes, *The Moynihan Report*, or skewed general public opinions would suggest otherwise. To further complicate this point, Staples discusses black male homosexuality; and, even though his treatment of it is, at times, problematic—in his depiction of it as a circumstantial response to black female-headed households, black male incarceration, or the general castration of black men in society as a whole—he nonetheless acknowledges its presence in black communities and the United States in ways that do not deracialize (or characterize as "nonblack") homosexuality and same-sex desire.

The sexual revolution also had positive and liberatory ramifications for women: freeing them from patriarchal limitations and "the restraints of a male-dominated value system that defined sexual pleasure as an exclusively male prerogative," a point that black feminist scholar-activist Toni Cade (Bambara) elaborates.[53] In her 1969 manifesto "The Pill: Genocide or Liberation?"—reflective of her ineffable, mutually inclusive commitment to black nationalist and women's liberation struggles—Cade illuminates the intersections of the two movements, as well as the extent to which they should not be deemed isolated or mutually exclusive within the black community. While she recognizes the "rearing of warriors for the revolution" as a "noble thing," she dismisses the notion that doing so entails "dumping the [birth control] pill":

> The pill gives the woman, as well as the man, some control. [. . .] And after all, it's through the fashioning of new

relationships that we will obliterate the corrosive system
of dominance, manipulation, exploitation. [. . .] On the
other hand, I would never agree that the pill really liberates
women. It only helps. It may liberate her sexually (assuming that we don't mean mutually exploitative when we yell
"sexual equality"), but what good is that if in other respects
her social role remains the same?[54]

What the pill thus provides, she posits, is choice: the fundamental
agency and ownership of her body—or "at least some of the major
events in her life"—and it also gives women the space, in terms of
opportunity and temporality, to fight against systematic oppression and for liberation in these and other areas.[55] Cade argues
that a right to choice is a powerful conduit toward liberation and
racial/gender/sexual empowerment for not only black women but
the community as well. The very ideologies that W.E.B. Du Bois
articulated nearly a half century earlier in his (then) radically progressive polemic "The Damnation of Women," in which he avers
that racial advancement and liberation should be predicated *not*
on "our idiotic conventions" but on women's right to education
and motherhood, sexual and reproductive agency, at their own
discretion, reverberate in Cade's assessment.[56]

Du Bois's polemic resonates, too, in Shirley Chisholm's 1969
reflection on "the abortion question," women's reproductive
rights, access to safe contraceptive devices, and the necessity
for the end of compulsory pregnancy—which, as she notes, is
an issue affecting not only women but America at large. At the
crux of these discourses are reproductive rights as they relate to
larger issues of racialized gender, freedom, and (sexual) liberation, and also the fact that equality itself necessitates equity in
the social and sexual terrain simultaneously—or, it necessitates
one's sexual citizenship: the fundamental right to orchestrate,
dictate, and define the terms of one's (adult) sexual life in accordance with one's desires and with respect to one's privacy.[57]

What becomes transparent in terms of black sexual politics and sociosexual dynamics within the black community of

the era is that black sexuality, intimacy, and desire constituted something with far greater complexity and liberalism, to evoke the word in its broadest sense, than how society and history alike have written it. Instead of black sexuality as steeped in a conservatism at the crux of which was an inauthentic heterosexism and homophobia (based on a religious or fundamentalist tradition), the black sexual revolution embodied a complexity that spans a continuum, not only in terms of the varied sexual expressions, loving, or sex purely for sex's sake; but also in its multifaceted effort to narrate and iterate the varieties of black sexual expressions and experiences. In this regard, this articulation of racial/sexual sensibilities and identities typifies the extent to which, when we engage or speak of race, in this particular case "blackness," we also "always already" speak "about gender, sexuality, and class" in an "intricately negotiated amalgam" of these intersecting dynamics.[58]

Unbought and Unbossed: Transgressive Black Women, Sexuality, and Representation, while interested in instances of transgressive behavior and sexual citizenship in post–civil rights texts, does not insinuate that these literary characters epitomize black women's lives. Nor does it suggest that they should be read within a sociological framework as transparent transcriptions of a particular experiential reality of behaviors, as doing so would be problematically misguided. Some of the scenes and behaviors operate out of extremities and conventions customary in literary contexts, and rely on sexual spectacle and the spectacular (as is the case with *Eva's Man* and its fictionalization of the grotesque ramification of the cumulative effects of sexual dehumanization and madness). This book seeks, then, *not* to perpetuate sexualized stereotypes or reify racist constructions of black sexuality as pathologized; nor does it aim to achieve the diametrical opposite: to uphold what literary scholar Mary Helen Washington refers to as "sacred cow" images of black women. Its goal, rather, is to engage and analyze these textual moments to produce a literary/cultural tapestry that troubles as well as reimagines the politics and *possibilities* of representation; the potentialities of empowering subversive erotics; the "pedagogies" of these black feminist postures toward liberatory sexual politics; and the intersectionality of black womanhood, racialized sexuality, and transgression.

Organized conceptually, *Unbought and Unbossed* delineates and explores the aesthetics of transgression in five representative chapters and a conclusion. In chapter 1, I flesh out some of the foundational conceptualizations and arguments posited in the introduction, particularly as they relate to paradigms of black womanhood and the classical black female script, which is historicized and contextualized in relation to overarching ideologies of race and womanhood. Through a close reading of Toni Morrison's *Sula* (1973), I explore the ways in which the script, at once racialized and gendered, is inscribed and manifests itself in post-1960s literature, specifically *Sula*—wherein the eponymous character, emblematizing transgressive behavior, not only subverts the script but also reconstitutes paradigms of black womanhood and sexuality.

Foregrounding politics of sexuality, chapter 2 examines "transgressions" against essentialist binaries regarding "blackness," same-sex desire, and homosexuality. As rigid discourses on sexuality do not provide apt paradigms to capture or illuminate the complex terrain of black women's sexuality, in this chapter I use "same-gender loving" as a theoretical and discursive framework to challenge limited discourses on sexuality. Illustrating the utility and applicability of "same-gender loving," I analyze it and the ways that politics of sexuality are entrenched in Ann Allen Shockley's *Loving Her* (1974), which characterizes same-gender loving within an interracial context that challenges heteronormativity and the regulation of female sexuality through men. I suggest that Shockley both castigates the ideological conflation of homosexuality and same-sex desire with nonblackness, and subverts nationalist and societal constructions of womanhood, manhood, family, and the black nation.

Chapter 3 begins with scholarship and discourses on "community" and the individual to elucidate the dialectics of transgression and sociocommunal belonging. Whereas most characters examined in previous chapters are shunned or isolated because of their transgressive and unconventional behaviors, Meridian Hill, the protagonist in Alice Walker's *Meridian*, diverges from this paradigm. I argue that in her characterization of Meridian—who confronts and negotiates sociocommunal politics governing race, gender, sexuality and community or "nation"—Walker complicates myopic, if not oppositional, constructions of female identity vis-à-vis community. This chapter examines the ways in which Meridian, transgressing strictures for women while fulfilling a vital communal role, expands unilateral conceptualizations of womanhood and community, thereby demonstrating that individuality and community are not mutually exclusive.

In chapter 4, sexuality and violence, as they intersect with "madness" and entrapment, are explored in Gayl Jones's *Eva's Man* (1976). In part, I suggest that, in this novel, transgression manifests in a physicality that is marked by a perversity of desire that almost always erupts into sexual violence, all the while mediated through the "madness" of the protagonist, Eva Medina Canada. Her madness, as it relates to sexuality and violence, engages mythologies regarding black sexuality, but also demonstrates the degree to which "madness" or insanity is, in itself, transgressive and potentially radical. Analyzing the presentation of the psychology of Eva, then, this chapter elucidates the extent to which madness is, at times, conscious, calculated, and performed, as well as unconscious and unintentional—ultimately speaking to the precarious ramifications of particular silences and politics governing race, gender, and sexuality.

Chapter 5 analyzes the ways that transgressive behavior and sexuality intersect with solidarity and healing, serving as a vehicle of transcendence—or at least potential transformation—for black women and the community in Gloria Naylor's *The Women of Brewster Place*. While myriad representations and experiences of black women pervade Naylor's novel, within each vignette, sexuality is interwoven both overtly and in nuanced ways into the tapestry of the larger narrative toward individual

and, ultimately, communal/collective healing and empowerment. This chapter examines Naylor's utilization of a range or
sexual continuum—from asexuality to hyper-(hetero)sexuality,
lesbianism and same-sex desire to conventional and compulsory
heterosexuality—among other instantiations of sexual expressions and desire. Not only does it provide a larger commentary
on black female sexuality and community, but it also makes
larger claims and commentaries regarding black sexual politics,
community, transgression, and the sexual revolution in black
racialized and communal contexts. Finally, emphasizing the
importance of examining the junctures and disjunctures surrounding racial identity, black women's sexuality, and the politics of representation, the conclusion analyzes representations
in the age of First Lady Michelle Obama to expand discourses
on black women, as well as provide new ways to further examine and deconstruct black womanhood in/and the "nation" in
potentially revolutionary and progressive frameworks.

1 / "New World Black and New World Woman": Or, Beyond the Classical Black Female Script

Not all women are intended as mothers. Some of us have not the temperament for family life. Clubs will make women think seriously of their future lives, and not make girls think their only alternative is to marry.

—*WOMAN'S ERA*

A relationship between black people, representation, and political subjectivity has always existed and, at times, has been contingent upon representations of black womanhood. Still, this relationship has been more pronounced during particular historical moments. During the nineteenth and early twentieth centuries, African Americans, having been negatively stereotyped as uncivilized, ignorant, and licentious within a racially hegemonic society, were relegated to an inferior status and deemed ineligible for full civic and political rights. In an effort to counter ubiquitous negative images and secure sociopolitical equality, some African Americans, largely under the influence of black intellectuals and activists, subscribed to certain codes of conduct—namely, respectability and propriety—to uplift and empower the race through acts of self-definition and determination. Bourgeois behavior and mores, including the espousal of Victorian sexual conduct, served for blacks, then, as a means of racial and sociopolitical advancement.[1]

While such strategies affected the black community collectively, they had their most pronounced effects on black women, who were seen as symbols of their race. Having been characterized as licentious and immoral, as the very antithesis of "ideal" (white) womanhood, black women were perceived as responsible for so-called black deviancy and pathology. In light of this and their sexual violation by white men especially during slavery, Reconstruction, and Jim Crow—with their putative lasciviousness serving as justification for such crimes—black women embraced respectability as both protection and counter-myth. Deploying propriety and a rhetoric of moral superiority in various aspects of life and culture, they challenged prevailing images of black women particularly and African Americans generally. Their comportment and public display of "respectable" behavior served as forms of counterrepresentation, as well as racial uplift and advancement. These very female behavioral codes surrounding black womanhood can be seen not only in black women's literature and the black women's club movement, but also in newspapers, journals, and periodicals of the late nineteenth and early twentieth centuries, as this chapter's opening epigraph illustrates.

Published in an 1894 issue of *Woman's Era*, a Boston-based African American women's journal, the article from which the epigraph was taken speaks to the nexus of womanhood (proscriptions for women), motherhood, and club life in ways that are remarkably progressive. Most black women's clubs, temperance societies and churches, among other organizations, advocated domesticity and its attendants, marriage and motherhood, for black women. Propagating such discourses and "mandates" regarding black womanhood, these organizations and the black middle-class individuals or intellectuals who were prominent in them, largely encouraged women to embrace domestic values, as well as respectability, Victorian sexual propriety, and Christian moral virtue. Such expectations were not merely arbitrary or deliberately dictatorial. Through domesticity—marriage, motherhood, and the creation of black nuclear families—and conformity to conventional behavioral codes of conduct, black women, as race bearers, would, so the logic went, advance the movement toward racial uplift and equality. They would use this personal and cultural politics of respectability to renegotiate their status and positionalities, as well as dispute discourses replete with racist ideologies at the crux of which was a rhetoric of racial differences, white superiority, and black inferiority.

This chapter begins with an articulation and elucidation of some of the sociocultural, historical, and political ideologies governing black womanhood of the late nineteenth and early twentieth centuries, particularly as they intersect with racial uplift for a variety of reasons: first, to elucidate the calculated efforts black women made to combat mainstream racist discourses and practices; second, to illustrate how particular racialized ideologies and politics regarding women and gender conventions intertwined, impacting constructions of black womanhood as well as black women's lived experiences; and finally, to demonstrate the ways that blacks mediated, vis-à-vis discursive and performative gestures, the racist/racialized and systematic oppression confronting them. This turn-of-the-century and early twentieth-century politics exposes the ways in which representations of black women and racial advancement interface, interestingly, for both black and white people. Just as constructions of black identity hinged upon particular paradigms of black womanhood, ideologies and constructions of "whiteness" militated against and were contingent, dialectically, upon the stereotypes and negative imagery associated with blacks. Constructions of black womanhood, and the dissemination of "positive" images of them, intersected in vexed and provocative ways with racial uplift and black nation-building enterprises. Conversely, "negative" representations and mythologies of black women and blacks collectively fortified constructions of "whiteness" as dominant, mainstream, and acceptable—or, in other words, as "normative" and, thereby, deserving of full citizenship, as well as the accompanying rights and privileges.[2]

A consequential correlation between these dynamics existed, so much so that they compounded, resulting in the creation of certain prescriptions for black women. These circumscriptions, necessitated by the desire to redefine black racialized (and sexualized) identity, as well as "normalize" it in the face of persistent attacks and vilification, consolidate to embody *the classical black female script*. By that, I mean a particular set of ascribed roles governing what constituted "good," acceptable, and appropriate black womanhood in relation to racial advancement and nation building. The script—constituted by black women's expected racial loyalty and solidarity, sexual fidelity to black men, self-abnegation, and idealization of marriage and motherhood—demonstrates the ways in which race, gender, sexuality, and nation imbricate. Embodied in these tenets and prescribed roles is a particular "race" work for black women: one contingent upon gender, sexuality, dissemblance, and convention that approximated black women's allegiance to the race. To a certain extent, inscribed in the classical black female script is a particular deference to and prioritization of racial loyalty, characterized by gender and sexual prescriptions, as well as outright sanctions governing black womanhood that—if followed by women— would not "jeopardize" or compromise the already tenuous racial/gender codes, injunctions, or status quo.

Conformity to these principles signified women's loyalty and solidarity, as well as commitment to racial uplift and the black nation; whereas nonconformity to them situated black women outside race work or, essentially, as betrayers of the race. Not only does this call particular attention to black women's positionalities and how they intersect with and predicate upon conformity to particular racialized/gendered dictates largely punctuated by sexuality, but it also interestingly underscores racialized efforts toward self-redefinition and determination, as well as the construction of ideologies of white supremacy and racialized practices that further define and demarcate "whiteness." At the crux of such formulations of whiteness, and its differentiation as privileged and putatively superior, were, in part, constructions of womanhood and white feminine character that are often associated with the "cult of true womanhood."[3] "[W]hite America's perceptions of racial difference were founded on the different way they constructed black and white women," notes historian Deborah Gray White, whereby the latter "endured their own race-determined sexism."[4] Constituted by four fundamental tenets—piety, purity, submissiveness, and domesticity—the cult of true womanhood excluded black women, yet relied on negative stereotypes and mythologies regarding black womanhood and its "illicit" sexuality and character. The cult of true womanhood and larger interlocking discourses on "whiteness," as well as black racialized iterations of racial uplift and nation building, all played a role in the formation of the classical black female script. Put another way, black women's exclusion from "true womanhood," even when they possessed the principal elements constituting it, led overwhelmingly to their public display of the classical black female script, a variation of which constituted the racial and/or communal obligatory roles expected in uplift/nationalist discourse. The tenets of the script, and the very phenomenon of the script itself, emblematize the particular exigencies of the black race, especially as they relate to black women's roles, comportment, and positionalities during this particular historical moment.

Given the calculated efforts toward black racial uplift, and the ideological and sociopolitical contexts undergirding them, sentiments such as those expressed in the 1894 issue of *Woman's Era* are emblematic, to say the least, of a progressive and radical approach to the role of black women, as well as a competing discourse on black women's positionalities. Diverging from constructions of black womanhood monolithically or exclusively within the realm of the domestic, the quotation used as this chapter's epigraph challenges narrow conceptualizations that relegate black women to a domestic position, if even for uplift purposes. Rather, it advocates "alternatives" for black women: options and choices beyond, not myopically or exclusively constituted by, marriage, motherhood, and traditional familial trajectories. Anna Julia Cooper, widely known for her advocacy of and commitment to racial uplift, recognized women's positionality in racial progress as integral. "Only the Black Woman," as she eloquently asserted, "can say when and where I enter, in the quiet, undisputed dignity of my womanhood, without violence and without suing or special patronage, then and there the whole Negro race enters with me."[5] What Cooper's position on the role of women illuminates, whether in specific or broader terms, is the nexus of black womanhood—unencumbered by marginalization, restrictive dictates, disenfranchisement, violence, and gender conventions within the confines of the domestic sphere—and black racial and sociopolitical progress. Racial progress, that is, was contingent upon, rather than inhibited by, women and their access to education, protection, enfranchisement, and progressive politics neither punctuated by marginalization and female gender deference nor characterized by rigid, limited, or patriarchal perspectives.

As *Unbought and Unbossed* is invested in the historical, ideological, and sociopolitical dynamics governing black womanhood and the representational, this inaugural chapter provides a lens, historic and contextual, by which to explore the shifting paradigms of black womanhood and prescriptions for women in the early era: emblematized by the classical black female script and "alternatives" (as "new world black and new world woman," as explicated in the discussion that follows), as these evolve and operate in post-1960s (con)texts. I am particularly vested in the nexus of the script and postmodern modalities of black womanhood; second, in those instances wherein women's roles and positionalities are not contingent upon particular racialized dictates; and, third, those "alternatives"—to allude to the opening epigraph—to prescribed conventionality and how these are treated, broached, and/or subverted in post–civil rights black women's literary and cultural production. I turn, to this end, to the post 1960s novels of black women to examine how black women writers like Toni Morrison, whose work is the central focus of this chapter, revisit, subvert, or defamiliarize prescriptive tenets and positionalities for women predicated on (outmoded) Victorian and racialized constructs. Or, framed yet another way, I examine how Morrison deploys such postmodern techniques as disruption, (de)fragmentation, and (re)inscriptions with regard to black women's bodies and sexuality to gesture toward a postmodern "new world" (female) blackness.

If transgression, denotatively speaking, emblematizes a defiance of the "norm" and traversal of the social order and status quo vis-à-vis participation in the ostensibly illicit, Morrison's 1973 novel *Sula* (and the eponymous character) achieves just that. Whereas the classical black female script functions as the medium through which conformity to female circumscriptions manifests, transgression (and in turn transgressive behavior), as it unfolds in *Sula*, is marked by recalcitrance, rebellion, subversion, or a destabilization of the script. The novel's chapter titles, comprised of years rather than words, span "1919" to "1965," in ways that dialogize—or put into dialogue—the historical eras and competing sensibilities, yet another reason why, though the novel was published in 1973, I do not restrict analysis of it to a strictly post–civil rights temporal moment. In fact, the novel's historical range, bridging the early 1900s and post-1960s moments, offers a critical ideological, sociopolitical, and cultural space for a postmodern (re)consideration of the particular dynamics and vestiges of the early "racialized Victorian" era. In the same fashion that some black writers routinely revisit and renegotiate dynamics governing slavery, race, and freedom—corporeal, psychic, and existential—via the modern neo-slave novel/neo-emancipatory genre, women writers such as Morrison (and the others examined in this volume) have, in a similar spirit, I contend, revisited the fundamental ideologies and dynamics surrounding black womanhood in the post-1960s black feminist moment and beyond.

What this chapter suggests is that post-1960s authors challenge black women's positionality as racial/communal symbols of Victorian propriety and advancement through a rearticulation of black womanhood not predicated on (restrictive) modalities or outmoded and inefficacious tenets for racial progress. No longer divorcing black women and their bodies from sexuality, shrouded in a politics of silence, these writers illustrate the complexities of black womanhood, defining it in ways that do not "revise beliefs about black hypersexualization by erasing sexual matters," as literary scholar Lisa Thompson insightfully avers, but rather "challenge concepts of acceptable sexual behavior."[6] As such, they reclaim and redefine black womanhood and community from racist discourses that pathologize black female sexuality and, concomitantly, "rescue" it from racial/nationalist efforts that, in the name of advancement, regulate black womanhood through black men in racialized/communal contexts.

In "Unspeakable Things Unspoken," Toni Morrison describes the eponymous character of her novel *Sula* (1973) in poignant terms that expand, if not reconstitute, blackness and femaleness within a post–civil rights era. "I always thought of Sula as quintessentially black, metaphorically black," Morrison notes, "which is not melanin and certainly not unquestioning fidelity to the tribe. She is *new world black and new world woman* extracting choice from choicelessness, responding inventively to found things. Improvisational. Daring, disruptive, imaginative, modern, out-of-the-house, outlawed, unpolicing, uncontained and uncontainable. And dangerously female."[7]

Morrison's assessment of Sula, as well as her rationale and inspiration for creating such a daring and dangerously black and female character who, until then, was unimaginable, is provocative, as it is indicative of a particular articulation, and indeed anticipation, of a more complex configuration of black *and* female identity: one not impeded by monolithic or obsolete definitions of race and interlocking conventions regarding gender and sexuality. Morrison's characterizing Sula as embodying "new world" blackness, as it intersects with and informs her "new world" female identity, is calculated and illuminates the often "contradictory, resistive, subversive, and celebratory effects" and manifestations of blackness (and black womanhood).[8] The designation "new world," whether pertaining to or qualifying "black" or "woman"—as it applies in the context of this work—transcends a certain provincialism or absolutism that would restrict blackness or black identity to the limited or territorial. As it pertains to female identity, in the sense of "new world woman" (and not divorced of race), it signifies a particular womanhood uninhibited by traditional strictures and categorizations, taking it into liberatory or, at the very least, unfathomable trajectories.

In his monograph *Appropriating Blackness*, performance artist and black queer studies scholar E. Patrick Johnson theorizes about the various constructions and appropriations of blackness, arguing that blackness is not fixed but is, rather, a slippery and multifaceted dynamic. The "mutual constructing/deconstructing, avowing/disavowing, and expanding/delimiting dynamic that occurs [. . .] in the production of blackness is the very thing that constitutes 'black culture.' What happens," then, "when 'blackness' is embodied? What are the cultural, social, and political consequences of that embodiment in a racist society?"[9] This important question about the embodiment of "blackness," as it pertains to and, I would add, is compounded by gender and sexuality (be it intimacy, desire, or behavioral and sexual identity), undergirds *Sula*. In Morrison's characterization of the eponymous character as the embodiment of blackness not only metaphorically and phenotypically but also "quintessentially," she appears to essentialize black identity, situating "blackness" as fixed and homogeneous. Yet, she achieves the opposite, revealing its multidimensionality, which exceeds the unitary or unilateral and is, in turn, emblematic of a postmodern gesture: one that defamiliarizes the absolute in a destabilization or disruption of what literary, race, and sexuality studies scholar Robert Reid-Pharr brilliantly identifies as the very "seamlessness of black ontology."[10] That is, Morrison's assertion problematizes conventional assumptions and ways of considering the existence, manifestations, and functions of blackness or black identity. Blackness, in this regard, is not rendered monolithic; nor is its heterogeneity compromised for an elusive (if not singular type of) racial solidarity. Rather, the "limited boundaries" are "redraw[n]," as literary scholar Deborah McDowell insightfully notes, "to move the discourses on blackness to terrains beyond those whose topographies keep us locked in opposition and antagonism."[11] To this end, Sula functions as the embodiment of disruption—that corporeal manifestation of transgression, contestation of the status quo and convention, and traversal of the established "norm"—within the context of her community, the Bottom, even while she has a symbiotic relationship to it; for, she is a result of her community and its sanctions. Symbolic of the "modern(ized)"—a *new world black and new world woman*—Sula signifies this destabilization in her community.

The novel begins in the post–World War I moment ("1919") and ends in the civil rights era ("1965"), while alluding through flashback to the antebellum and post–civil rights era.[12] In the book's opening scene, the omniscient narrator, or narratorial consciousness, characterizes, in an elegiac voice, the status of the Bottom and the valley town of Medallion, Ohio—marking the Bottom's current constitution postgentrification and industrialization juxtaposed with its previous historical composition: its cultural insularity and genesis rooted in "[a] joke. A nigger joke." The Bottom's founding is based on a racialism, a racist history, and narrowly defined constructions of race (its name deriving from a joke played on an enslaved black man by "a good white farmer"), yet the Bottom transcends this irony in its progress. Conversely, however, it is practically defeated by its inability to continually evolve, and by a relatively stymied organic growth, and is eventually crippled by and victim to gentrification and industrialization: a reverse enactment, a reenactment of sorts, of the initial joke. Whereas the Bottom's genealogy is rooted, paradoxically, in the race-specific joke accounting for its existence, the community's partial, if not eventual demise, is at the hands of both the nondescript "they"—euphemistic white referents—and the black residents themselves (as evidenced in the tragic National Suicide Day march and mass deaths).

Sula, as a product of this environment, is both informed by as well as cultivated within this communal context, yet is neither defined nor entirely restricted by it. She flouts the community's history and communal sanctions governing race, gender, and sexuality unapologetically with her deliberate transgressive behavior and subversion (and cultivation of an existence outside the strictures) of the classical black female script. Whereas most of the novel's other characters, in their affinity to racial/communal sanctions, embrace conformity and gender-specific regulations, Sula does not. Not only does she explore the "choices [. . .] available to women outside their own society's approval," but she experiences "the risks of individualism in a determinedly individualistic, yet racially uniform and socially static, community."[13] In her deliberate nonconformity to bourgeois conventionality and sociocommunal circumscriptions for women, Sula subverts the script, while simultaneously destabilizing a fixed categorical blackness predicated on particular deployments of racialized and gendered (black female) respectability and performance. In her "alterity," she embodies other paradigms of black womanhood and black identity generally.[14]

"Something Else to Be": *Sula* and Transgressive Behavior

In part 1 of *Sula*, she and her best friend, Nel Wright, are cognizant at young ages of the limited roles ascribed to black women. Having "discovered years before that they were neither white nor male, and that all freedom and triumph was forbidden to them, they set about creating something else to be."[15] In their search for "something else," they create identities that extend beyond that of their female progenitors and challenge oppressive forces that infringe on their agency and threaten to relegate them to an inferior status. Sula grows up in a household marked by seeming "dysfunction" and chaos, the structural material embodiment of unconventionality. She is the granddaughter of Eva Peace, a one-legged woman who dominates the lives of her children, friends, strays, and boarders (30), inculcating in her offspring "manlove": "simply [loving] maleness, for its own sake." Her questionable and ambivalent behavior as a mother eventually leads her daughter Hannah Peace, Sula's own mother, to inquire, "Mamma, did you ever love us?" (66). And yet, it is with a similar intergenerational "distant eye" and insatiable love of men, coupled with maternal ambivalence, that Hannah raises

Sula. After the death of her husband, Hannah, who "rippled with sex" and refused to live without the "attentions of a man," immersed herself in "free love" and required some "touching" every day (42, 44). She exercises utmost discretion, however, when it comes to the location wherein she has sex: her bedroom is her least favorite place. This is not "because Sula slept in the room with her but because her love mate's tendency was always to fall asleep afterward and Hannah was fastidious about whom she slept with. She would [have sex with] practically anything, but sleeping with someone implied for her a measure of trust and a definite commitment" (43–44).

Hannah's differentiation between casual sex and committed sexual intimacy challenges not only heteropatriarchy and heteronormativity—which emblematizes a "modern regulatory apparatus" that marks "sexuality as the object of rationalization and control" customarily in the private domain within a "heteropatriarchal household"—but also the classical black female script; and, Hannah's sexual life (as her daughter Sula will later replicate) falls clearly outside its strictures.[16] Her rationalization for or hesitation about abstaining from (frequent) sexual activity in her bedroom stems not so much from how the "impropriety" might impact her young, impressionable daughter but, rather, from her own discomfort with and repudiation of the emotional responsibilities society attaches to sexual intercourse. It comes as absolutely no surprise, then, that of the two "lessons" Hannah indirectly teaches Sula, one explicitly concerns sex: "that sex was pleasant and frequent, but otherwise unremarkable" (44). This sensibility accords with the ideological discourses and politics of the sexual revolution—contemporaneous with the novel's moment of publication—with its overarching reclamation of sexuality and libidinal forces from a Victorianism or moral compass that would glorify sex as precious or necessitate reserve and sexual abstention. This "unremarkability," however, also interestingly deexceptionalizes sex in a way that resists the particularities and the very nature of racialized (black) sexuality within a larger sociohistorical and political context. That is, for (aspiring middle-class) black people, in this case black women especially, who, by virtue of their lack of governance (legally and otherwise) over their bodies during the sexual atrocities of slavery (and with little protection or recourse throughout the Jim Crow era), sex had otherwise operated as a function: nothing special, grandiose, or "remarkable." Hannah's sexual experiences serve as a counterparadigm in that sex for her is constituted not by a racialized legacy of sexual trauma, violence, or shame. As such, it lends itself provocatively to a degree of sexual agency and liberation, as well as, importantly, to a politics of choice, desire, and freedom: a "freedom of choice" that animates the notion that "the individual's ability to choose—or not choose—family, intimacy, parenthood, and so forth as a basic human right" indicative of the ever-changing nature of the "common sense of sexual and erotic choice."[17] That Hannah's sexual experiences are unencumbered by sexualized violence also speaks to a black feminist politics of pleasure governing black women's sexual intimacies.[18]

Hannah's notion of the unremarkable nature of sex with a "nothing-worth-talking-about" essence might also account for her not talking about sex or instructing Sula through a practical, meaningful discourse on sexuality. This choice, then, is not merely negligence of her maternal role. Rather, it also reflects the extent to which silence surrounding black women's sexuality is deeply ensconced in the community. In an environment or culture wherein the script circumscribes women's behavior, with its particular dictates governing sexuality, even Hannah, who engages in sexual intercourse frequently, does not entirely overstep its boundaries. She engages sexuality in its physicality, never exceeding the domain of corporeality that would, otherwise, manifest in the discursive, vocalized, or the spoken. Thus, in silent disposition regarding sexuality, she, in essence, does not "articulate any conception of [. . .] sexuality," to evoke black feminist scholar Evelynn Hammonds, or "the possible varieties of expression of sexual desire."[19] Instead, sex is performed and enacted but, "quiet as it's kept," it is never vocalized, spoken about, or taught through a discursive pedagogy of instruction or intergenerational transmission of experiential knowledge.

Hannah, in addition to this "lesson" on sex—which Sula learns incidentally after witnessing her mother having sex in the pantry—also imparts a second lesson to Sula: "there was no other that you could count on" (118–19). Sula learns this upon overhearing her mother admit that, while she loves Sula, she "just don't like her" (57). Hannah's differentiation between lov ing and (not) liking her daughter—which alludes interestingly to Hannah's inquiry to Eva of "did you ever love us?"—exists, much like her ideologies regarding sexuality, in direct opposition to the script, which demands women's idealization and exaltation of motherhood. Hannah demystifies the gradations, obligatory dimensions (or lack thereof), and contingencies of "love" in a demarcation between duty/obligation (love) and agency/choice (like).[20] Hannah not only destabilizes fallacious or generalized assumptions regarding the "quality of love," particularly where mothers are concerned, but also illustrates that "love" and "like" are not coterminous notions—nor do these entities fall along the same emotional-committal continuum. For, fundamental to Hannah's notion of love is what feminist sexuality studies scholar Jennifer Nash recognizes as a "black feminist love-politics" in which love engenders a "resistant ethic of self-care"; or, put another way, "love is a politics of claiming, embracing, and restoring the [. . .] black female self."[21] Thus, none of the inadvertent "lessons" Hannah instills in her daughter, namely about sex, love, and nondependency, offers Sula any substantial or pragmatic instructions on girlhood/womanhood or, more specifically, codes of conduct for female behavior. Hannah's not instructing Sula in these areas, however, provides Sula space in which to create a self unaligned with conventionality— "a resistant ethic of self-care." And, too, it functions, in part, as an impetus and foundation for Sula's later transgressive behavior and interrelated prioritization of her "self."

Unlike Hannah, Nel's mother, Helene Wright—the apotheosis of motherhood as it is defined by the classical black female script—"rose grandly to the occasion of motherhood" (18); and, in counterdistinction to Hannah, she raises her daughter in strict accordance with bourgeois propriety and respectability. In fact, "under Helene's hand [Nel] became obedient and polite. Any enthusiasm that little Nel showed was calmed by the mother until she drove her daughter's imagination underground" (18). Yet, while Nel is raised in accordance with the script—which is, in her case, severely "maternally imposed" and socially mandated—she eventually comes to question her own identity in relation to her maternal female progenitors. Nel's sojourn begins in 1920 while she rides a segregated train to New Orleans with Helene, who is objectified and sexualized by the patriarchal gazes of male passengers. After having witnessed her mother's victimization and silent composure, ten-year-old Nel vows that no man will ever look at her that way. For, she would never let "midnight eyes and marble flesh [. . .] accost her and turn her into jelly" (22). Nel's experience on the train is far from innocuous, exposing her to the extent to which black womanhood is subjected to (hyper)sexualization (as evidenced in the sexualized metaphor "jelly") that renders black women—even those like her mother who are the quintessence of respectability and decorum—vulnerable to sexual dehumanization, objectification, or violence. While in this instance the sexual violation is not physical, its psychological aspect is no less acute or deleterious. Unprotected as such, Nel, as a black female, cannot necessarily elude and transcend the inevitability of racialized sexual vulnerability, yet what she can and does do, is divest herself of associations with her intergenerational female progenitors who have already encountered varied instantiations of these sexual entanglements. Thus, upon their return to the Bottom, while looking in the mirror, Nel proclaims, "I'm me. Not their daughter. I'm not Nel. I'm me. Me" (28).

Nel's experience on the train and her newfound "me-ness" foster her creation of a self, like Sula, outside the confines of girlhood/womanhood, and exclusive of the repressive middle-class Victorian values of her mother and licentious behavior of her grandmother Rochelle Sabat, "a Creole whore" (16). Not only does Nel dissociate herself from the sexual disarray, marked by both agency and vulnerability, but she undergoes, concomitantly, a journey toward her newfound identity: a "me-ness" rooted not in an already fixed state of being but, rather, gained through an existential process marked by catharsis in which her identity (politics) is not only transformed but actualized. Nel's cathartic experiences reverberate with what Deborah McDowell recognizes precisely as the "notion of character as static *essence*" reinstated "with the idea of character as *process*. Whereas the former is based on the assumption that the SELF is knowable, centered, and unified," as she further avers, "the latter is based on the assumption that the SELF is multiple, fluid, relational, and in a perpetual state of becoming."[22] And so, Nel establishes a "self" incongruous with the diametrically opposing identities of Helene and Rochelle, the apotheosis of propriety and promiscuity, respectively. She enacts her/this incongruity through her cultivation of a friendship with Sula, the embodiment of nonconformity.

Sula's and Nel's inventing themselves outside the script and its strictures materializes in "1922" in two consequential correlating events: their masturbatory and homoerotic "grass play" scene and, second, the interlocking tragic interactions with Chicken Little. Both events evidence their disengagement with expectations governing black female behavior through their empowering homosocial relationship, as well as illumine their gestures toward liberation, if even metaphorically, from patriarchy and the regulation of female sexuality. Transpiring near the riverbank, the grass play scene involves Sula and Nel, "without ever meeting each other's eyes," stroking blades of grass "up and down, up and down." Upon taking possession of a "thick twig," Nel removes its bark with her nail, stripping it down to "a smooth, creamy innocence." Sula replicates Nel's move with a twig of her own, before the two begin uprooting grass to make a bare spot, on which to trace "intricate patterns" with their twigs, after which they "poked" them "rhythmically and intensely into the earth, making a small neat hole that grew deeper and wider with the least manipulation of [the] twig" (58). After "more strenuous digging and [. . .] rising," the holes grew deeper and larger, and "[t]ogether they worked until the two holes were one and the same."

Sula and Nel engage in performative gestures deeply rooted literally and symbolically in the erotic, homosocial, and sexual. The passage not only emphasizes a fluidity of gender and sexuality, but also embodies intimacy and sexuality in its physicality without an utterance or vocalized discourse. Moreover, it also reflects the notion that sexuality and intimacy are, in and of themselves, their own language—aural, sonic, orgasmic—that exceeds syntax yet has its own verbosity. While there is no spoken word, but rather a politics of silence that is palpable, the passage itself utilizes another language, a language and iconography of intimacy, that manifests in a lexicon rife with metaphoric references to sexuality, the sexualized body, and erotic acts: "twigs" and "holes," symbolic genitalia, alongside the "bare spot" and textured "intricate patterns" that, after deep and "strenuous digging," culminate with the "two holes" together becoming one. Much could be extrapolated from the passage that would bear claim to myriad interpretations regarding the specificity of Sula and Nel's sexualized acts, especially regarding where they are situated along a continuum of sexualities. I am less concerned about categorizing the sexualized experience of these girls—twelve years old, "wishbone thin and easy-assed," as the narrative voice describes—within a limited topography, and more interested in illuminating the ways in which they perform an external manifestation of their sexualities or sexual desires vis-à-vis acts that neither gender/sexualize the body nor regulate their intimacy through men.[23] Their intimate exchange defies conventionality, transgressing restrictions of female sexuality, particularly those expressed in the script (and racialized/nationalist discourses undergirding it), thus the necessity for its privatization. To this end, the interlocking event with Chicken Little—who, upon infringing on their "illicit" sexual grass play, is eradicated—is consequential and, as I will illustrate, latently *sexual*.

While "an unspeakable restlessness and agitation," at once titillating and perhaps orgasmic, engulf Sula and Nel after their grass play scene, their homoerotic moment ends abruptly as Chicken, "a little boy in too big knickers," approaches from the lower side of the riverbank. Chicken's presence is, in a (sexual) sense, not consensual: it is an unwelcome, uninvited intrusion. The language of the passage is rife with references to the sexual, though far more nuanced (especially in juxtaposition to the grass play scene), but nonetheless engages the erotic. Chicken's entry from the "lower banks" of the river, emblematic in both physiological and anatomical terms, of the body's lower regions where the genitalia, the sex organs reside, reinforces the sexual and his unwelcome infringement upon Sula and Nel. His immediate death, then, marked by an ambiguity of calculation versus inadvertence with regard to Sula and Nel's intentions, resembles the playful and accidental, yet borders on the ambiguously deliberate and punitive: with Sula picking Chicken Little up by his hands, swinging him "outward then around and around" as his "knickers ballooned" before he "slipped from her hands." As he sailed "over the water they could still hear his bubbly laughter" before the "water darkened and closed quickly over the place where [he] sank" (60–61). In this scene, vis-à-vis actions, gestures, language, and imagery, the sexual is provocatively encoded in, first, the embrace: the picking up and "foreplay"—the stimulating pleasure from touch and movement, the outward gyration that proceeds "around and around" in the swinging motion—resulting in the ballooning of Chicken's pants. The response is titillation: the ballooning knickers, symbolic male corporeal gratification, the excited body with emphasis on the pants (the regions of erectile stimulation and pleasure)—with (orgasmic-like) "shrieks of frightened joy"— that culminates with a penetration, a submergence wherein he reaches a cumulative peak of stimulated pleasure, in a painfully tragic (sadomasochist) climax: *death*.

Sequentially, Chicken's death follows Sula and Nel's homo-erotic intimacy; and, just as Sula and Nel methodically concealed their symbolic sexualized gestures, filling the holes with debris for concealment, so, too, is Chicken Little eliminated—his body drowned and engulfed by water—to keep their homo-erotic scene private. If, as Sharon Holland posits in *Raising the Dead*, readings on "the dead" animate "death" as emblematic of "a figurative silencing or process of erasure, and as an embodied entity or subject capable of transgression," Chicken's unwelcome presence elicits his death; for, he, to evoke Holland, not only embodies the capability of transgression, but also, I would add, marks and, indeed, underscores Sula and Nel's very own capacity for transgression.[24] As a male meddler intruding upon and threatening their female intimacy, his death, regardless of their intent, enables them to maintain their agency through the eradication, physically and metaphorically, of oppressive (and "masculinist") forces that threaten, infringe upon, or restrict female sexuality, the homoerotic, and/or homosocial relationships.[25]

His tragic death, moreover, marks a consequential turning point in the lives of Sula and Nel. While Nel subsequently chooses a life of conformity, Sula becomes all the more radical. Chicken drowns in 1922, yet the reader's next encounter with Nel does not occur until 1927, when she—though "never [. . .] hell-bent to marry" (82–83)—accepts Jude's marriage proposal. Forsaking her childhood "resilience" with Sula, Nel marries, immerses herself in family life, integrates into the community, and leads an ostensibly conventional middle-class existence. Sula, conversely, leaves the Bottom—the night of Nel's marriage, a heterosexist institution intervening on her and Nel's union—for ten years, during which time she attends college in Nashville and travels to Detroit, New Orleans, New York, Philadelphia, Macon, and San Diego (120). Upon her return she sleeps with Nel's husband, Jude—accounting for the demise of their marriage and the "extrication" of Jude, another male presence and infringement (like Chicken Little) on her "one-ness," woman-freedom, and intimate friendship with Nel.

While characterological in nature, one might ask why Sula would leave the Bottom, curiously during the celebration following Nel's wedding, and go off to college? Sula's leaving to attend college and refusal to work or "give back" to her community afterward animates some of the early debates regarding black women's positionality, education, and racial uplift. Women's education and enfranchisement in the early twentieth century were consequential issues engaged among race men and women. Women's education, as some race men and even women conjectured, might, so their logic went, violate gender dynamics and conventions, devastate traditional gender roles and "natural" sexual differences, and compromise the black family, as historian Kevin Gaines posits. Virtually "desexualizing" black women, education and suffrage would ostensibly make them no longer suitable for or desiring of marriage and motherhood, putatively creating racialized gender mayhem wherein women would pose a threat to male leadership, the roles/occupations of black men, and the overall system of male hegemony and patriarchal authority.[26]

Sula, in 1927 and thereafter, practically does just this. In addition to leaving Medallion (instead of settling down and marrying like other Bottom women), she returns from college refusing to use her education in the interest of the community and in the service or uplift of the race. Moreover, she travels intranationally, a luxury unavailable to most black women (save blues singers), demonstrating her uncategorically autonomous lifestyle. Her existence, simply put, is not coterminous with boundaries for women or self-abnegation for anyone or anything: men or race. While Sula's behavior during the 1920s dialogizes larger sociopolitical and racial discourses of that era, she—as a character of a novel produced during a later historical and sociopolitical juncture—also offers provocative commentary on discourses and concerns contemporaneous with the post–civil rights, black feminist era in which Morrison's book was published. In the same year that *Sula* was published, 1973, the National Black Feminist Organization was founded in the spirit of challenging the racism and elitism of the women's movement, as well as politics that privileged masculine authority, patriarchy, and sexism that marginalized black women and their exigencies within the struggle for liberation. As the Combahee River Collective, an organization of black feminists and lesbians founded the year after *Sula* appeared in print, asserts, their politics embrace black and women's liberation, and are defined by a consciousness and feminism they utilized as "political analysis and practice" to struggle against oppression.[27] While predating the collective's "A Black Feminist Statement" (1978), *Sula* personifies the idea, one of its central premises, that black women's liberation is essential, "a necessity not as an adjunct to somebody else's" but, rather, as indicative of their "need as human persons for autonomy."[28] Similarly, as Morrison herself writes in her 1971 manifesto "What the Black Woman Thinks about Women's Lib," in light of the plethora of duties and responsibilities of black womanhood, black women "had nothing to fall back on"— "not maleness, not whiteness, not ladyhood, not anything"—and "out of the profound desolation of her reality," the black woman may "very well have invented herself."[29] Sula embodies these collective philosophies and feminist ideologies in her nonconformity to convention or the status quo that would relegate her, as black and a woman, to a marginal or adjunct status. And, it is with that same sensibility, as the narratorial consciousness asserts, that she—upon recognition that she was neither white nor male—created "something else," an alternative, by which to exist.

"And [. . .] She Became Dangerous": Sula's Subversive and Transgressive (Adult) Behavior

Published in 1973 while Morrison was an editor at Random House in New York City, where she created a list in black literature reflective of the racial consciousness of the black political movements, *Sula* dialogizes not only black nationalist ideologies, but also black feminist sensibilities, including intersectionality, and the sexual liberation prompted by the sexual revolution. In that same year, in the *Roe v. Wade* decision, the

Supreme Court decreed that abortion was legal, a landmark ruling in tandem and contemporaneous with the liberal politics of
the sexual revolution. Sula functions as the material embodiment of black female subjectivity that embraces blackness that
neither compromises nor negates her woman-freedom or liberation, sexually or otherwise. Functioning, then, outside the
parameters of sociocommunal prescriptions and modalities for
women, Sula transgresses convention and concomitantly invests
in her "self" rather than live a life of conformity.[30] Sula is unlike
other Bottom women because she uncharacteristically repudi-
ates conventional life (particularly marriage and motherhood),
as well as transgresses the classical black female script, whose
tenets her various enactments of "misbehavior" resist and subvert. In her obstinate and fierce refusal to marry and "have some
babies" to "settle" her down—as her grandmother Eva suggests
immediately upon Sula's return to Medallion—Sula insists that
rather than "make somebody else," she wants to invent her "self"
(92). Her refusal to acquiesce or conform is transparent, then,
in her transgression against communal expectations for women
regarding reproduction, which also undermines a fundamental
tenet of the (black) nationalist agenda: that black women should
"make babies for the revolution." As reproduction is fundamental to nationalist paradigms and agendas, Sula's refusal to reproduce also calls into question and scrutinizes nationalist visions
of (an imagined) black nation. She challenges a modality centered around reproduction and presents another model—a "new
world blackness," to revert to an earlier argument—that destabilizes and presents a postmodern black notion of "nation." At
the crux of this new world black subjectivity is *not* an intrinsic
expectation that black women reproduce. It is critically important, then, that shortly after Eva encourages Sula to marry, bear
children, and thereby conform to the roles society ascribes to
women, Sula, going against all cultural ethics, commits her to a
nursing home: "At the sight of Eva being carried out [. . .] Sula
[stood] holding some papers against the wall, at the bottom of
which, just above the word 'guardian,' she very carefully wrote

Miss Sula Mae Peace" (94, emphasis mine). Sula committed Eva to a nursing home and took particular delight in that act, illustrating her disregard and contempt for both cultural ethics and (Bottom) communal mores. Her pride in, and determination to preserve, her independence and single-woman status is evidenced by her careful and deliberate inscription of "Miss" on the documents and her unwillingness to allow exterior forces, even her own grandmother, to threaten her agency and infringe upon her lifestyle, autonomy, and woman-freedom.

"With a twist that was all her own imagination," as the narratorial consciousness indicates, "she lived out her days exploring her own thoughts and emotions, giving them full reign, feeling no obligation to please anybody unless their pleasure pleased her" (118). In her quest to please herself, she, upon her return to the Bottom, disrupts social "norms." A wanderer and neither wife nor mother, she exists incongruously with the women of the Bottom and concomitantly "violates" community sanctions: she sleeps with other women's husbands (including Nel's), wears no underwear to church functions, and, far worse by community standards, putatively has sex with white men. It is Sula's sexual "escapades" with white men that diametrically oppose the script, as well as flout the tenets of black nationalism, which explicitly demands black women's sexual fidelity—to black men—as a way of countering dominant society's stigmatization, denigration, and association of black women with sexual deviance and pathology, as well as in allegiance with nationalist ideologies.

In black nationalist accounts, as literary scholar Wahneema Lubiano posits, the survival of the black nation depends upon its being constituted by "strong black families with strong (and responsible) black patriarchs"; thus, within this framework, the black nation and "family is perceived [...] as 'weakened' by black female deviance (sexual and economic) or as 'weakened' by external forces."[31] Sula's ostensible sexual interactions with *white* men elicit unfavorable responses, particularly from black men, namely because her sexual "indiscretions" directly conflict with the community's goals of racial/communal advancement. Sula's sexual "misconduct" contributes to, if not justifies (presumably), the dominant culture's exclusion of black people from the privileges of citizenship, as well as civic and political subjectivity, and opposes black nationalist narratives of the black family and black women's expected role in its construction. Thus, Sula's intentional willingness to "sleep with" white men constitutes a direct threat to the black family, the nation, and (black) manhood/patriarchy, as cultural nationalists imagine these, and is thereby regarded as a deliberate and intolerable betrayal of the race. It also has larger implications regarding the shifting racial, sociosexual culture prompted by issues of interracial sexual intimacy (another aspect of the sexual revolution and litigation in this era) and miscegenation, as instantiated by the 1967 landmark case of *Loving v. Virginia*. Mildred Jeter, a black woman, and Richard Loving, a white man, married in the District of Columbia, where interracial marriage was legal, in 1958. When they returned to live in their home state of Virginia, they were arrested for violating the state's miscegenation laws. With the assistance of Robert Kennedy, the United States attorney general, they filed suit against Virginia for violating their constitutional rights. They ultimately won their case, and, in so doing, they forever changed the course of history and the racial, sociosexual political landscape where interracial sex, marriage, and law were concerned, as well as demystified the discursive, ideological, and legal strategies deployed to "naturalize the categories of 'black' and 'white'" in matters governing race and sexuality. As Siobhan Somerville avers, the "boundaries between 'black' and 'white' were being policed and enforced in unprecedented ways, particularly through institutionalized racial segregation."[32]

While Sula's (and other black women's) sexual "misconduct" with white men is perceived, then, as threatening and intolerable, black men's sexual interactions with white women are, in a double standard, not judged in this way. As the novel's narratorial voice contends, one might think that "the willingness of black men to lie in the beds of white women [would be] a

consideration that might lead them [black men] towards tolerance" (113). Yet, this is not the case, since in nationalist discourse
and ideology, women—*not* men—"are typically construed,"
as feminist scholar Anne McClintock maintains, "as the symbolic bearers of the nation[, . . .] as biological reproducers of the
members of national collectivities," and, of even greater magnitude, "as reproducers of the boundaries of national groups
(through restrictions on sexual or marital relations)."[33] And,
too, it animates some of the competing sociosexual politics of
particular segments of the nationalist movement—particularly
the more concrete emphasis on black sexualized masculinity,
male authority, and sexual prowess and virility—as displayed
by some Black Panthers, among other segments of the black
nationalist movement. Not only do the politics elucidate the way
racial political ideologies regarding liberation manifest vis-à-vis
black sexual politics; but they also illumine the appropriation by
some black males—the "black machos"—of the very stereotypes
that had historically endangered them, rendering them victims
to lynchings and other (racialized/sexualized) U.S. terrorist hate
crimes.

Sula's story, in several regards, demonstrates Morrison's
conscious and deliberate attempts to not only dialogize but
critique black nationalist ideologies and proclivities that, both
consciously and inadvertently, (re)inscribe and (re)inforce patriarchal and masculinist notions, as well as circumscriptions for
women. Morrison's efforts to destabilize and resist nationalist
tendencies that emphasize black men's oppression over, or at the
expense of, black women is certainly evident in Sula's response
to Jude's "observation that a Negro man had a hard row to hoe in
this world" (103). And so, while Nel—following the protocol of
the classical black female script—placates her husband's "whiney
tale that peaked somewhere between anger and a lapping desire
for comfort," Sula refuses to either commiserate or sympathize
with Jude but asserts that "I don't know what the fuss is about. I
mean, everything in the world loves you. [. . .] It looks to me like
you the envy of the world" (103–4).

Sula's hyperbolic and facetious remarks, deliberately trivial-
izing black men's experiences, destabilizes black nationalist dis-
cursive/ideological sensibilities regarding the reclamation of lost
black masculinity and black men's systematic oppression that
consciously or inadvertently minimize or neglect severely black
women's experiences of marginalization, oppression, and violation. While Morrison does not privilege the plight of black men
at the expense of black women, she does address, even if through
Sula's facetiousness, the historical circumstances accounting for
exterior displays of respectability among blacks and, ultimately,
the script: the pathologized sexual character and infamy of black
people that resulted in the violent sexualized crimes (lynchings
and rapes) against their bodies. Moreover, while these phenomena are historicized and contextualized, Morrison does not
exonerate the ways in which some black nationalists, through
particular ideological elements of nationalism (not nationalism
in and of itself), attempt to situate black men as the apotheosis
of oppressive victimization, whereby black women must heal or
serve as balm for their wounded and/or deflated masculinities.
Sula's refusal to comport herself as such, or recognize the experience of black male victimhood, also "accords with the black
nationalist goal of fashioning a new black identity free of the
oppressive past."[34]

Morrison deftly provides a counterparadigmatic alternative
to nationalist configurations of black masculinity, and how
they could intersect progressively with constructions of black
femininity, in her delineation of Ajax and Sula's nonpatriarchal
romance. Despite the fact that Ajax, a lover whom Sula does not
disregard casually after sex, is nine years Sula's senior—"she was
twenty-nine, he thirty-eight" (124)—their relationship is not
based on hierarchical or hegemonic notions of male authority
and female subordination. Rather, it is marked by more progressive gender politics, if not, to some extent, gender egalitarianism.
Their relationship is not stymied by, but instead precludes, certain mandated patriarchal and social prescriptions for women.
Ajax's attraction to Sula stems precisely from her nonconformity

and "elusiveness and indifference to established behavior" (127). With the exception of Ajax's mother, a conjure woman (and outlier), Sula is "perhaps the only other woman [Ajax] knew whose life was her own, who could deal with life efficiently, and who was not interested in nailing him" (127). And so, it is precisely because Ajax treats Sula both as a woman who owns herself and his equal, rather than an object or extension of himself, that she is attracted to him; and she finds what she had not found in previous relationships with men: pleasure, contentment, fulfillment, and, above all, unconditional acceptance.

Ajax, as a gender-progressive man, accepts and encourages Sula's unconventionality and complexities as "brilliant," autonomous, "tough," and, most importantly, complete. Both Sula and Ajax engage comfortably in their unrestrained relationship. Sula's receptivity to, and behavior with, Ajax does not even remotely resemble any of her previous (inter)actions with men—whom she usually used and then discarded—because these men, unlike Ajax, only objectified, sexualized, and longed to dominate her. It is precisely because of Ajax's fair treatment that Sula is able to consider, if not desire, what she never before had. As Morrison elucidates in an interview:

> [T]he one man who talked to [Sula], and thought she was worthy of conversation, and who let her be. [. . .] [Ajax] was a man who was not intimidated by her; he was interested in her. He treated her as a whole person, [. . .] not as a vessel, not as a symbol of himself. He was secure enough and free enough and bright enough—he wasn't terrorized by her because she was odd. [. . .] When a man is whole himself, when he's touched the borders of his own life, and he's not proving something to somebody else—white men or other men and so on—then the threats of emasculation, the threats of castration, the threats of something taking over disappear.[35]

In her characterization of Ajax and his relationship with Sula as "unconventional," Morrison provides an alternative (re) configuration of black manhood and womanhood, as well as an alternative paradigm governing heterosexual relationships, outside nationalist constructions and the classical black female script. In her assessment of Sula and Ajax's relationship, and especially Ajax's openness to Sula—and the agency, woman-freedom, and unconventionality she engenders—Morrison indicts and critiques those black cultural nationalists who, in their quest to reclaim black manhood, internalized hegemonic ideologies and, thereby, viewed liberated black women as both threatening and emasculatory.

In such a relationship—governed by gender egalitarianism and neither masculinist nor patriarchal constructions of hetero-sexual intimacy—Sula grows even deeper and more intensely, especially in terms of her sexuality. Though Sula had, prior to her relationship with Ajax, gone "to bed with men as frequently as she could" (122), she was filled constantly with "utmost irony and outrage in lying under someone, in a position of surren-der" (123). When involved sexually with Ajax, Sula experiences, instead, passion and uninhibited sexual ecstasy. Whereas prior to Ajax Sula had waited impatiently for other sexual partners—whose names she could not recall during sex—to "disengage," "turn away, and settle into a wet skim of satisfaction," her sexual experiences with Ajax serve as a context and space for her to embrace an intimate, intense, and empowering "postcoital pri-vateness in which she met herself, welcomed herself, and joined herself in matchless harmony" (123). If the erotic, to invoke black feminist poet-scholar Audre Lorde, constitutes "a well of replenishing and provocative force" that, as "a source of power," culminates in empowerment, "an internal sense of satisfaction" and "fullness," then, for Sula, sex with Ajax is no longer merely "sex for sex's sake."[36] Rather, it operates as a conduit by which she enters a deeper, richer, more powerful and intense relation-ship with herself, a communion with her *self*, uninhibited by strictures placed on female sexuality.[37]

With Ajax, Sula discovers—or, better yet, *recovers*—the full-ness, intensity, self-awareness, and empowerment that erotic and sexual experiences can provide, but that her community—and the rigidity and sexual repressiveness of the script—deny her.[38] "In that space of the erotic—the political and the personal—we might be able (if not ready) to revise or even resist," as Sharon Holland insightfully posits, "the object(s) of our critical desire as we come to understand just what it takes to make the erotic such a generative space."[39] Holland's illumination of the complex and generative nature of the erotic, as it intersects with agency, personal politics, and desire, has particular purchase. I draw upon Holland (and Lorde), as what I suggest is not at all that women's sexual and erotic gratification, empowerment, pleasure, and/or identity lie within the parameters of heteronormativity at men's orchestration, or that female sexual liberation is enacted through or predicated on men. Such an assessment would be simplistic, problematic, and counterintuitive to any discourse on female sexuality and especially transgressive behavior. What I suggest is that sex with Ajax is not so much an approximation of sexuality governed by men within a heterosexual, heteropatriarchal, or nationalist-masculinist paradigm but, rather, is the embodiment of the sexual freedom and empowerment, accompanying the erotic, that transcends modalities in which gender conventions and (sexual) power relations are intrinsic.

Sula destabilizes or "queers," to evoke Robert Reid-Pharr, "narratives that are obscured by" an "overprivileging of traditional scripts."[40] Sula and Ajax's sexual exchange is, that is, mutually inclusive with sexual pleasure and reciprocity, overturning the insistence on the suppression of female sexual pleasure for the sake of male sexual gratification. Sula embodies sexual freedom and agency that challenges patriarchy, male (sexual) hegemony, or what literary scholar Erica Edwards identifies as "a gendered hierarchy of [. . .] value that grants uninterrogated power to normative masculinity."[41] This offers a crucial reconfiguration of heterosexual intimacy and the politics of passion in the novel, as well as a reconsideration of heteronormativity and the traditional (post)coital heterosexual paradigm. Moreover, it constitutes "a gender and sexual disruption to heteropatriarchy and inspire[s]" alternative modalities, "practices and formulations" for (sexual) subjectivities to those propounded by nationalism.[42] As such, Sula redefines the politics and possibilities of sexual intimacy—without "normalizing" heteropatriarchal dictates— in ways that privilege ownership of her sexual self, subjectivity, and (black female) sexual citizenship.[43]

Sula and the Politics of Radical Black Subjectivity

In "The Politics of Radical Black Subjectivity," black feminist scholar bell hooks differentiates between opposition and resistance, neither of which is, she asserts, synonymous with subjectivity. The process of becoming subjects emerges as one comes to comprehend the ways in which matrixes of domination work in one's own life, "as one invents new, alternative habits of being, and resists from that marginal space of difference inwardly defined."[44] As a radical agent who transgresses convention and societal definitions of "normative" behavior for women, Sula, even by hooks's definition alone, typifies radical black subjectivity. Not only does Sula well understand, and indeed embody, the simultaneity of oppressions confronting black women, but it is also precisely out of this realization that she rejects her marginalization and exists.

Even as hooks recognizes Sula's unwillingness to accept or capitulate to the social modalities and communal proscriptions ascribed to blacks and women, she asserts that Sula does *not* constitute radical black female subjectivity, insomuch as Sula, while reveling in "self-assertion and [a] celebration of autonomy," is "we also know [. . .] not self-actualized enough to stay alive."[45] "Her awareness of what it means to be a radical subject does not," hooks purports, "cross the boundaries of public and private; hers is a privatized self-discovery."[46] hooks's reader-response critical approach, as well as her characterological assessment of Sula, presents at least two dilemmas. First, whether deliberately or inadvertently, it equates existential or metaphysical notions of living/being with actualization, whereby Sula's dying—or,

"inability" to live—is indicative of Sula's lack of self-actualization. What I suggest is that Sula's death in the narrative should
not be confounded and read as indicative of a lack of self-actualization, consciousness, or subjectivity. Rather, it reflects more
acutely the limited options (especially when *Sula* was written)
for female characters like Sula who challenge racial/sociocom-
munal boundaries and transgress restrictions, especially those
pertaining to female sexuality and marriage, and who ultimately choose a life of "self-discovery" rather than one of racial
uplift and conformity. As literary scholar Mary Helen Washington avers, "The demands of racial uplift and racial loyalty" have
meant that such characters—those "who do not uphold these
ideals"—are invariably characterized with a fate of conformity,
expiation for their perceived transgressive behavior, and far
worse: death.[47]

Yet, it also typifies other attributes that death represents,
to revert back to Sharon Holland, in that the dead—and I
would argue, in this case, also the dying (Sula)—operates "as
an embodied entity or subject capable of transgression."[48] In
Sula's instance, death/dying marks her destiny, and, even in
the process of dying, she does so unconventionally and with an
unbreakable spirit of autonomy, nonconformity, and subjectivity. She herself, upon her deathbed, revels in the knowledge that
she is unlike other black women dying "like a stump" across
the nation. "Me," Sula notes, "I'm going down like one of those
redwoods. I sure did live in this world," a point to which I will
return momentarily (143). Second, and of even greater magnitude, hooks asserts that Sula's "self-discovery" is "privatized"
and thereby fails to extend beyond public and private boundaries. Given that the personal *is* political, as many scholars and
second-wave feminists have argued convincingly, it is precisely
because Sula's personal "indiscretions" and recalcitrant actions
are *not* privatized and are, indeed, exposed and open for public
consumption, that her personal transgressions take on a larger
sociocommunal and *political* significance and educe public/
communal responses.

To return, then, to Sula's quality of life, even on her deathbed, Sula unapologetically and boldly asserts her right to subjectivity. In her final conversation with Nel, which occurs shortly before Sula's death, Sula expresses no regrets about her unconventional and transgressive lifestyle. Despite the fact that she is an anathema in the Bottom, Sula (still) offers no apologies but, rather, takes particular pride in her unconventional status. Whereas other black women who lived lives of conformity in traditional roles "had had the sweetness sucked from their breath" (122) and were dying, Sula, even in her ill-stricken state, differentiates herself not only in how she lived her life but also in how she is dying—*triumphantly*: unencumbered. She transgresses, then, even *in* death and transgresses *as* dying. And, what she has "to show for it," as she asserts to Nel, is her "mind" and "what goes on in it. Which is to say, I got *Me*" (143, emphasis mine). Her possession, as well as evocation, of a "me-ness"—unrestricted, uninhibited, and unregulated by established sociocommunal boundaries—privileges paradigms of black womanhood (in/and community), thereby offering a restructuring, a shifting politics if you will, based on Sula's experiential and existential conditions. What has transpired throughout her life and becomes further concretized at its end, does not advance a reinscription of communal paradigms, at the crux of which are family, reproduction, heteropatriarchal models, or nationalist configurations that "normalize" a regulatory black "nation-state" wherein women perform racialized gender and sexual roles. As such, it becomes emblematic, to revert to my earlier arguments, of "alternatives"—of a postmodern blackness that is at once expansive and inclusive where politics of race, gender, and sexuality are concerned—rather than of communally derived constructions of "blackness" that operate along a unilateral (exclusive/isolated racial) axis.

As Madhu Dubey insightfully avers regarding black literary and cultural postmodernism, the "idea of a cohesive and singular black community" is a "strained" sensibility; and "literary and cultural critics are recalling and refurbishing models of community and of racial representation developed earlier in the century" in the post–civil rights, postmodern era.[49] To further complicate Dubey's claim and take it a step further, I suggest that models of community are not just "recalled" or "refurbished" but reexamined and scrutinized in a way that subverts particular politics that consolidate around race, gender, and sexuality to show the interplay of differences—not, that is, in a fashion that results in a disintegration of racialized community, but rather in one that illuminates its potential and transformative politics. To this end, and as these manifest in *Sula*, the eponymous character serves as the corporeal entity/ reality, the transformative capacity of postmodern blackness, who queers—destabilizes, transgresses, subverts—the "normative." Sula "queers" or "throw[s] shade on" the putative norm and its very "meaning" as it relates to blackness—challenging "heteronormativity and heterosexism"—while concomitantly disrupting "notions of assimilation and absorption" associated with particular constructions of the designation "black."[50] Sula's sentiments regarding having practically nothing—no financial wealth, no husband, no children—and owning, instead, her "self" are revolutionary concepts for women, in which reverberate female subjectivity and postmodern black desire enacted throughout her existence. Not only does she comprehend and refuse to submit to the matrixes of domination confronting her as a black woman, but she invents new alternative states of being, resists marginalization, negotiates uncharted territory, disdains binaries, destabilizes patriarchy and a heteropatriarchal "normativity," as well as traverses the classical black female script and its racialized gender (sexual) confines. In so doing, she, as a "new world black and new world woman," not only transgresses convention but also claims and asserts her right to black female subjectivity.

2 /   Toward an Aesthetic of Transgression: Ann Allen Shockley's *Loving Her* and the Politics of Same-Gender Loving

Through the repetition of deviant practices by multiple individuals, new identities, communities, and politics might emerge where seemingly deviant, unconnected behavior can be transformed into conscious acts of resistance.

—CATHY COHEN

[W]e know more about the elision of sexuality by black women than we do about the possible varieties of expression of sexual desire. Thus what we have is a very narrow view of black women's sexuality.

—EVELYNN HAMMONDS

The differences made by race in self-representation and identity argue for the necessity to examine, question, or contest the usefulness and/or the limitations of current discourses on lesbian and gay sexualities [. . .]; from there, we could then go on to recast or reinvent the terms of our sexualities, to construct another discursive horizon, another way of thinking the sexual.

—TERESA DE LAURETIS

Rigid discourses on sexuality do not provide apt paradigms to either capture or illuminate the complex terrain of black women's sexuality, which has both historically and contemporaneously been hypervisible, yet paradoxically suppressed and shrouded in a politics of silence.[1] If it is difficult to examine the sometimes "nebulous" circumstances surrounding black women's intimate lives, how, given the limitations of discourses on sexuality, do we analyze black women's complicated sexual relationships with women? Existing sexual categorizations and labels, while valuable, do not always encompass the essence of black women's sexualities or own self-established identities.[2] As such, these sexual categories or subject positions further obfuscate, rather than delineate and reflect, the particularities of black women's sexual lives.

Responding to these limitations and the need for a discursive lens to further explore the sexual, in this chapter I provide, under the rubric "same-gender loving," an analytical framework by which to examine the intricacies of certain sexual intimacies between women.[3] By same-gender loving, I mean those sexual engagements between individuals, regardless of their *perceived* sexual orientation, marked by same-sex desire and physical sexual acts accompanied by sexual fidelity, commitment, love (romantic, universalist, political, or broadly construed), and/or a lack thereof.[4] As an analytic, same-gender loving provides a discursive paradigm by which to capture and analyze the nuances and complexities of particular sexual acts between individuals that are, given the rigidity of sexual labels and categories, otherwise overlooked or misinterpreted.[5] I do not at all wish to delegitimize or, far worse, depoliticize sexual categories, labels, or individuals' own self-identified sexualities, as expressed through the language and/or acts by which they define themselves in sexual terms or vis-à-vis intimate expressions. Nor do I argue that sexual categories or sexual self-definitions—and by extension black queer theory or what Roderick Ferguson recognizes as *queer of color critique*—are inadequate, useless, or unnecessary. Quite the contrary, since such a framework and critique, with its epistemological analysis and assessment, crystallizes the precise ways that culture "compels identitifications with and antagonisms to the normative ideals," modalities, and ideologies.[6] For, in the current cultural and temporal milieu, "the imperatives of race and sexuality must give way to messier but more progressive strategems of contestation and survival," as well as discourses and ways of capturing the specificities of the "historical and cultural" particularities that shape our sexualities and expressions of desire.[7] What I suggest,

then, is that sexual labels and categories, in all their specificity and, at times lack thereof, do not always reflect the sexual
intimacies, the very physicality of the sexual, or the corporeal
reality (and continuum) of passion and its politics. Same-gender
loving is useful in such instances, then, as it enables a critical
examination of *sexual intimacies*, the sexual/behavioral/bodily
acts; and it offers insight into the specificity of black women's
sexualities, particularly those sexual expressions that exceed,
and indeed transgress, sexual taxonomies and labels. It expands
existing discourses on sexuality, as well as the ways in which
we conceptualize and theorize about sexual desire, intimacy, the
erotic, and "the transgressive," especially within a black racialized context.

As has been established, *Unbought and Unbossed* examines
different registers of transgression, as it intersects with and is
instantiated by the sexual (regarding shifting representations
of black womanhood)—and its relational aspect to racialized
ideological discourse. While chapter 1 examined racial/gender/
sexual logic, particularly "alternative" constructions and enactments of black female identity, resulting in a subversion of the
script and heteropatriarchal constructions of the intimate, this
second chapter builds upon these ideas, yet takes them into
other sociopolitical, ideological, and sociosexual trajectories.
It examines the aesthetics and politics of transgression, as it
manifests and is embodied in Ann Allen Shockley's 1974 novel
Loving Her, which, published both a year after *Sula* and after
homosexuality ceased to be categorized as a mental disorder,
foregrounds an interracial same-gender loving relationship.[8]
Transgressive behavior, as it unfolds, is thus constituted by a
traversal of regulations of black female sexuality through black
men within a heteropatriarchal construction of family (man/
woman/child), as well as in an eruption of heteronormativity,
as it intersects with and fractures nationalist configurations of
universalized racial politics, sexuality, and community. What
this chapter, in part, examines and elucidates are the ways
Shockley inscribes, complicates, and polemicizes same-gender

loving, which functions as a paradigm and affirmation of transgression. In her characterization of her black female protagonist (who leaves her husband for an interracial same-gender loving relationship), Shockley challenges the ideological conflation of same-sex desire, homoeroticism, and homosexuality with "nonblackness"; subverts nationalist ideologies and social constructions of womanhood, manhood, family, and the black nation; and, problematizes, vis-à-vis the inscription of same-gender loving in a black context, illusive notions of a fixed, unitary black heteronormativity.

What becomes evident, then, is the *heterogeneity* of black experience and, of perhaps even greater ideological and political significance, the counterparadigmatic narrative that emerges: a black postmodern one that disassembles, if not ruptures, notions of racial/gender/sexual universalism, while concomitantly offering a groundbreaking politics of difference around an axis of sexuality. Shockley articulates a politics of pleasure to illuminate and challenge systemic structural inequalities, while presenting, *in 1974*, a postmodern approach to black sexual politics: one situating black women's sexualities (and sexualities more generally) not within a bifurcated trajectory, but along a sexual continuum. This provocative, novelistic articulation thus importantly serves as a *harbinger*—a presage that anticipated subsequent advances in sexuality discourses, particularly black queer studies and theories governing fluid gender and sexualities. Shockley complicates, then, sexual labels, black racialized sexuality, and sexual identities—particularly what constitutes a "lesbian"—in a moment of black nationalist political and cultural resurgence.[9]

"What's in a Name?": Same-Gender Loving—A Context

The Black Power and gay liberation movements of the 1960s and 1970s challenged and redefined identity politics, especially the meanings of "blackness" and "homosexuality" respectively. Neither of these movements, however, did much to create a

space to empower black "sexual minorities" who were marginalized in American society because of both their race and sexual
orientation.[10] Black nationalist discourse, a major ideological
and discursive component of Black Power, largely ascribed heterosexuality as "normative" and, thereby, as a requisite for its
essentialized notion of "blackness"; and the term "gay," within
the rhetoric of gay liberationists, almost always connoted
"whiteness."[11] While heterosexuality typically constituted "normative" sexual behavior in the Black Power movement and black
nationalist thought, within the Black Panther Party lesbians and
gay individuals also served, sometimes openly, in positions of
authority. For, as David Hilliard, Black Panther Party founding
member and chief of staff, posits, "There were gay operatives in
the Black Panther Party working at the highest levels of leadership. [. . .] Still, no one ever asked you to define your sexual orientation. We didn't divide ourselves like that. First and foremost
you were a Black Panther."[12]

Hilliard's remarks complicate the organization's stance surrounding sexuality within the movement: the Party—and, arguably, the larger black nationalist movement—was not exclusively
heterosexual, and its constituents were not required to specify
their sexual orientation. Yet, its prioritization of race and racial
solidarity precluded, if not overlooked, the intersectionality of
race and sexuality: sexual diversity within a racialized collective
context. The Black Panther Party—much like, if not reflective
of the larger Black Power movement—further compartmental-
ized race and sexual orientation into an "either/or" binary. And
so, while the movement succeeded unequivocally in transforming the racial, sociocultural, political, and class consciousness
of black people, it did not fully embrace or acknowledge the
sexual politics within the movement and the black community
at large.[13]

The gay liberation movement, on the other hand, offered
a valuable discourse on sexual politics that challenged heteronormativity, as well as the stigmatization associated with
homosexuality. As a largely white (upper-) middle-class urban

movement whose ideologies were reflective of these demographics, it was largely inattentive to the needs and struggles of its
nonwhite, non–middle-class constituents.[14] It did little to break
away from social stratification predicated on race and class or to
articulate a racialized sexuality. It largely conflated homosexuality and sexual labels such as "gay" and "lesbian" with whiteness. Thus, white middle-class sexual minorities came to define
and represent, if not constitute, "the gay identity." Black sexual
minorities in the gay liberation struggle, similar to those in the
Black Power movement, were trapped, then, within what black
feminist scholar Barbara Smith identifies as the "contradictions"
and "invisibilities" of being black and gay: further silenced,
excluded, and marginalized by the pervasive homophobia and
racism in the black and gay movements, respectively.[15]

Pat Parker, in *Movement in Black* (1978), critiques the com-
partmentalization of identities, namely race and sexual orientation, as well as the exclusive politics in black and homosexual
communities; and she addresses the ways that black sexual
minorities are almost inevitably "othered" and displaced, either
because of their race or sexual orientation, in black and gay
communities:

> If I could take all my parts with me when I go somewhere,
> and not have to say to one of them, "No, you stay home
> tonight, you won't be welcome," because I'm going to an
> all-white party where I can be gay, but not Black. Or I'm
> going to a Black poetry reading, and half the poets are
> antihomosexual, or thousands of situations where some-
> thing of what I am cannot come with me. The day all the
> different parts of me can come along, we would have what I
> would call a revolution.[16]

While Parker critiques structures that demand and perpetuate
the compartmentalizing of black sexual minorities' multiple
consciousnesses or identities, she, perhaps most significantly,
calls critical attention to the revolutionary possibilities of a
simultaneous racial and (homo)sexual identity. It is, in fact,

precisely this revolutionary notion of foregrounding racial and sexual identities concomitantly—rather than negating or situating them within hierarchical or diametrically oppositional categories—that accounts, in part, for the relatively under-considered discourse on same-gender loving.

As a concept, same-gender loving materialized in the early 1990s as a conduit for black sexual minorities—black women who love women (sexually and emotionally) and black men who love men (sexually and emotionally)—to express their sexuality in ways that resonate with the distinctiveness of black culture and life. Coined by activist Cleo Manago as a culturally affirming designation for black and "sexual minorities" of color, same-gender loving, unlike the black and gay liberation movements and discourses, is dialogic: attentive to *both* the intersectionality and inseparability of racial and sexual identities. It does not marginalize individuals or demand the prioritization of either racial or sexual identity but provides a space for black sexual minorities to celebrate the totality of their experiences, struggles, multiple identities, and subject positions.

While same-gender loving does not eradicate the pervasive homophobia, heterosexism, or racism in American society and culture, it challenges these oppressive forces and thereby serves as a pragmatic and ideological site of resistance. Forcing the black community to acknowledge the multiple and diverse ways of loving and sexuality, it allows for a more complex and inclusive self-definition of black sexuality. Moreover, it also challenges the ethnic invisibility, as well as the inscribed "whiteness," that gay and lesbian discourses and queer theory largely produce.[17] The motivation of the same-gender loving movement, then, is to meet particular exigencies:

> [It is in] this spirit of self-naming, an ethnic/sexual pride, [that] the term "same-gender-loving" (SGL) was introduced to fortify the lives and illuminate the voices of [sexual minorities of color]; to provide a powerful identi[t]y not marginalized by "racism" in the gay community or "homophobic" attitudes

in society. [. . .] It is the intention of the [same gender loving] movement to break this cycle.[18]

Black sexual minorities' engagement of same-gender loving has myriad sociocultural and political implications, especially since it acknowledges both sameness *and* difference.[19] Moreover, it resists the essentialism, in terms of race and sexuality, that black nationalist and gay and lesbian discourses, as well as queer theory, largely occlude.

The revolutionary possibilities of same-gender loving lie in its ability to draw critical and necessary attention to racialized same-sex acts and illuminate the realities of black sexuality, rather than problematically, and at times erroneously, reduce some individuals to confining sexual labels and identifiers. Even the term "homosexual" itself emerged, as Michel Foucault avers, as a clinical description for a *type* of individual rather than a sexual activity.[20] Same-gender loving, unlike most sexual categories, resists and avoids the all-too-pervasive tendency to define and/or demarcate individuals on the basis of sexual orientation or reduce black sexual minorities merely and inevitably to a sexuality. Same-gender loving expands the ways we conceptualize black sexual desire, eroticism, and loving; and it resists and destabilizes the politics of silence surrounding sexuality, especially black female sexuality, that has long persisted. Forcing us to engage sexuality and gender discourses seen primarily as disclosures in the black community and society at large, it enables us to discuss with depth and accuracy the particularities of black sexual lives, intimacies, and desires without being stymied by sexual labels, silences, or boundaries.[21]

Though replete with revolutionary possibilities, same-gender loving is not without its ambiguities and implications. One such ambiguity, at least as it relates to this study, is that the "requisites" for same-gender loving are not clearly defined. While created by and for sexual minorities of color, it is not apparent who, in terms of race/ethnicity, can identify with or embrace same-gender loving. As such, it is not clear whether relationships exclusively between sexual minorities of color constitute same-gender loving, or if it also applies to same-sex relationships marked by interracial sexual intimacy between white individuals and people of color. While such uncertainty exists, my study assumes an anti-essentialist understanding of same-gender loving and thereby extends its use and application to interracial intimacies. To this end, it not only further problematizes limited notions of racialized sexualities and interracial same-sex intimacy, but also expands the ways in which we conceive and theorize about the dynamics of race, gender, and sexuality.[22] For, "history has a very limited reach where black/white bodies are concerned" such that it does not recall the historical racialized "events" that punctuate and bear "mark upon our sexual proclivities."[23] Moreover, the "black-white polarity," as Marlon Ross avers, "continues to deny the polymorphous" (and, for that matter, *polyamorous*) "courses of all human desire."[24]

Racially conscious, same-gender loving has an etymology grounded in an Afrocentrist thinking that lends itself to a gendered/male-centeredness.[25] Even in its articulation of and resistance against the essentialism of race and sexuality in the black nationalist and gay liberation movements, its very gender dynamic has not necessarily operated in the service or for the utility of (black) women. In addition to its race-conscious, gendered genesis, it also emblematizes a class-based orientation that resonates among middle- and upper-middle class blacks; and, as such, it does not divorce itself of or escape a "(homo)normative" thrust. Its emphasis on and privileging of the rhetoric "*loving*" emblematizes and might perpetuate a discourse or narrative that tempers, if not dictates, the terms of desire and politics of the intimate within a framework of commitment, romantic love, and/or sexual monogamy. "That might perpetuate" are the operative words, especially since in this context I do not render "love" as synonymous with a romanticism at the heart of which is the "modern concept of love" as "almost exclusively limited to the bourgeois couple and the claustrophobic confines of the nuclear family," to quote Michael Hardt and Antonio Negri, who explicate their frustrations with limiting constructions of love.[26]

In all of its complexities, nuances, and implications, same-gender loving has a particular purchase in relation to Shockley's *Loving Her*, which, on the one hand, transgresses the typical nationalist/racialized paradigm in its engagement of interracial same-sex desire and intimacy, as it eschews a categorization of the protagonist Renay's sexual orientation with "whiteness" in ways that challenge conflations of same-sex desire with non-blackness. Renay, as evidenced in both her intraracial heterosexual marriage and interracial same-sex relationship, for instance, operates off of or performs a "normativity" that reinforces domesticity, family, and bourgeois class positionality. As characterized, Renay (in terms of race/gender performativity) is complex: she embodies the markers of class and a drive toward "normativity" throughout the novel that, in ways, parallel (or are not dissimilar to) that of the same-gender loving movement itself. As such, she operates off of a "normativity" that subverts pathologized notions of blackness as aberrant as she functions in the contexts of her (interracial) relationship, calling into question not only fixed notions of blackness where gender/sexuality or concerned, while she destabilizes simultaneously issues of race/class governing (white) homonormativity. Even as Renay appears to uphold "normativity," then, as a "racially marginalized" subject, she "compel[s] a critique of homonormative formations"; for, such "homonormative formations achieve cultural normativity," as Roderick Ferguson maintains," vis-à-vis "the person of color" who is rendered "the cultural anthitheses of a stable and healthy social order" (a point to which I will return).[27]

Ann Allen Shockley's *Loving Her*—A Brief Overview

In 1974, Ann Allen Shockley—Tennessee librarian, critic, fiction writer, and self-identified "feminist with lesbian sympathies"—published her pioneering novel *Loving Her*, which, as Alycee Lane asserts, is not only "the first African American novel written with an explicitly lesbian theme, but [. . . also] the first to feature a black lesbian as its protagonist."[28] While Shockley does foreground overt lesbian themes instead of addressing them covertly through codification, *Loving Her*, I would argue, does not feature a black lesbian protagonist; rather, it depicts a black woman (Renay Davis) who has been *perceived* historically as a lesbian character.

Renay, after several years in a heterosexual marriage, engages in an interracial same-sex relationship and neither expresses nor specifies her own self-established sexual identity. In fact, upon being called a "lesbian" (by a white lesbian who had never before encountered a black one), Renay—who "knew of no visible changes in herself [. . . and . . .] still talked, looked and acted the same"—asserts that the conclusion had been made "that she was a Lesbian simply because she was with Terry. Wrong judgments had been made that way."[29] What Renay does, then, is transgress and problematize limited constructions of lesbian identity predicated on (mis)conceptions regarding what constitutes a "lesbian"; and she demonstrates, more precisely, that she does not embrace the term "lesbian" because it, with all its rigidity and (un)ambiguousness, neither captures nor reflects the complexity of her sexual life, desires, and experiences.

Despite how Renay has been (mis)categorized historically along the sexual continuum, Shockley creates a protagonist who is a black same-gender loving woman. That alone certainly is radical and groundbreaking, especially given the sociocultural and political contexts out of which she emerged. Shockley foregrounds interracial same-gender loving and homosexuality in her novel during the Black Power/Black Arts movement, when black writers were expected to espouse and inscribe black aesthetics in their works: to qualify for "blackness" meant to promote black consciousness, racial loyalty, and unquestioned solidarity.[30] Moreover, she foregrounds a black same-gender loving protagonist during the gay rights movement and, in so doing, confronts and destabilizes representations—propagated by gay liberationists—that conflate homosexuality and same-sex desire with whiteness and (upper) middle-class status.

Equally consequential, Shockley engages interracial same-gender loving, which also frustrates particular black feminist conceptualizations and paradigms of black women loving other *black* women. And so, as Alice Walker asserts in her laconic 1975 review of the novel, *Loving Her* "has immense value. It enables us to see and understand, perhaps for the first time, the choices certain women have made about how they will live their lives"; and, it "allows us glimpses at physical intimacies between women that have been, in the past, deliberately ridiculed or obscured."[31] This "ridicule" or deliberate "obscurity" was not merely a discursive affront from some black nationalists, white feminists, or gay liberationists, but it also came from black (lesbian) feminists who maintained a critical (dis)position with regard to interracial (same) sex relations—and "uncommon affinities," to evoke Jewelle Gomez—and representations of black lesbians in the literary and cultural imagination.

Walker's remarks, though salient and apt, were written shortly after the novel's publication. With few exceptions, most reviews of *Loving Her*, despite the "immensity" of its value, predate 1980 and are brief, antiquated, relatively inaccessible, and/or hardly scholarly or meritorious.[32] Despite these historical sociocultural/political dynamics, one might ask why this seminal text has been afforded relatively little critical attention. Why has it been largely overlooked by scholars, critics, and academicians? And, more significantly, why, in the 1970s and 1980s—when African American women writers were flourishing and scholars were recuperating black women authors and their texts—were Ann Allen Shockley and *Loving Her* still not recognized and given critical attention?

A multiplicity of factors—poor publicity and inimical reviews, editorial and regional biases, and racism, sexism, heterosexism, and homophobia—account for its neglect and have hindered, for more than a quarter century, critical examinations of *Loving Her*.[33] Moreover, the novel is not without its shortcomings stylistically and otherwise: it is replete with authorial interjections; unsubstantiated generalizations regarding race, gender, and sexuality; and, largely unmediated ideological stereotypes about nationalism, as well as the gay and lesbian movements, that at times reify, rather than challenge, mythologies. Despite these shortcomings and scholars' tendency to largely dismiss the novel, it is, nevertheless, a seminal text: it participates in critical debates on issues affecting black women not simply in the 1960s and 1970s, and it provocatively foregrounds same-gender loving, as well as confronts racism, patriarchy, and heterosexist institutions that threaten black women's agency.[34] Challenging particular identity politics, as well as subverting narrow definitions of "woman" and "normativity" in American society, *Loving Her* further illuminates black women's multifarious experiences, thereby expanding limited constructions of black womanhood—while concomitantly situating sexual expression along a continuum of sexualities.

The novel opens as Renay Davis, a gifted pianist and devoted mother, leaves her abusive, alcoholic husband, Jerome Lee—who embraces black nationalism and articulates masculinist and heterosexist ideologies—for Terry, a white self-identified lesbian. Not at all content, Renay transgresses her victimization and convention by taking their seven-year-old daughter, Denise, and deserting Jerome and their repressive heterosexual marriage. Rather than deny her sexual attraction to Terry, Renay rejects both essentialized blackness, which her husband espouses, and externally defined definitions of womanhood that label same-gender loving, same-sex desire, and homosexuality as deviant. With Terry, then, Renay finds "what she wanted and needed most. She was now aware of herself and the part she had tried to deny" (28).

In fact, Renay had never been attracted to men and had, on countless occasions, repressed and disguised her feelings. When the star football player and "best-looking boy on campus," Jerome Lee, pursued her relentlessly in college, she capitulated, dating him merely to avoid her roommate's increasingly persistent interrogations of her sexuality: "You *do* like *men*, don't you?" (14). Though Renay despised dating Jerome and especially detested him kissing her, she—in a deliberate performance of male attraction and desire—would on those occasions stand "as stone, feeling nothing, knowing nothing, willing nothing"; for, she was, as the novel's narrative voice asserts, "only superficially acting out the woman's role she thought she was expected to play in the context of their relationship" (15). Rather than disclose her lack of desire for men—and, consequently, be labeled, shunned, expelled, or reduced to a sexuality—Renay, through a pattern of constitutive acts, to evoke Judith Butler, performs the gender role socially constructed in strict heterosexual terms for women.[35]

During the course of their relationship, Jerome rapes Renay, which leads to her pregnancy and, in turn, accounts for their decision to marry. Once wedded, Renay, miserable within the confines of her forced marriage, is expected to submit routinely to Jerome's will and to specific gender roles or, otherwise, suffer Jerome's violent beatings. Renay maintains the household, raising their daughter and working to pay the bills with little assistance from Jerome, who drinks heavily and never secures a steady job. Misdirecting and displacing his resentment (which stems from his inability to support his family and his abandoned dreams of finishing college and becoming a professional athlete) onto Renay, Jerome lambastes her as a salve for his bruised manhood: "You know we black men have a hard enough time as it is making it in the white man's world. [. . .] I could have been somebody if it wasn't for you. All you castrating black bitches want to keep a man down. *Ruin* him. [. . .] And *you*. What goddam good are *you* to a man? Not even a good screw!" (29).

The myth of the black matriarchy resonates in Jerome's highly castigatory remarks (which fail, ironically, to acknowledge that his condition is the result of his own doing—of his having raped Renay). Promulgated by sociologist and later senator Daniel Patrick Moynihan and later appropriated by some black nationalists, the myth assumes that black women, in collusion with the white power structure, emasculated black men, thereby preventing them from maintaining their "rightful" position in the black family and society at large.[36] In his evocation of black matriarchy rhetoric, Jerome, as Shockley clearly intends, is equated allegorically with black nationalist discourse, which he epitomizes throughout the novel. Moreover, in his assertion that Renay serves no purpose for men—that she is, as he claims, "not even a good screw"—he not only objectifies her but, like those black nationalists who viewed black women's only position in the movement as "prone," he also reduces her to a marginal sexual role.[37] Compensating for his inadequacy and negligence as a husband, father, and provider, Jerome espouses nationalist ideologies regarding "lost manhood" and asserts himself "by any means necessary"—through both physically and verbally abusive manners—as patriarch of his household.

Shockley, in her rendering of Renay and Jerome's abusive, patriarchal relationship—and especially her characterization of Jerome as nationalist discourse incarnate—conflates black nationalism with unprogressive politics that, instead of liberating black women, at times threaten and violate their agency and autonomy. Yet, readers should not perceive Shockley's characterization of Jerome as indicative of black nationalists' violent stance toward black women. Rather, it is best read metaphorically as a delineation of the ways in which particular sexist and patriarchal ideologies undergirding nationalism "endanger" black women and pose for them a life of submission to black men within fundamentally hierarchical or masculinist constructions of the black family, manhood, and womanhood.[38] Equally consequential, we might read Renay's interracial same-gender loving relationship with Terry in a similar vein in that Renay resituates: leaving one type of domesticity in a (racialized) black nationalist domain for another domestic partnership that also does not, like her relationship with Jerome, divorce itself of a gender patriarchy/hierarchy/hegemony, which Terry, like Jerome, often embodies. Renay thus negotiates two competing "nationalisms," propagated by the Black Power and gay liberation movements, at the crux of which is "citizenship": black and sexual citizenship, respectively.

"A Love So Bold": The Politics of Interracial Same-Gender Loving

Renay meets Terry Bluvard, a wealthy writer, at the supper club where she plays the piano to earn money to pay the bills. When she receives a song request, accompanied by a twenty-dollar tip and an invitation to join Terry at her table, she accepts. Not long afterward, Terry invites her for a drive, during which she expresses a sexual preference for women and desire for Renay: "I'm wealthy. I'm used to getting what I want [. . .]. I'm one of those women who prefers her own sex and I want you" (22). Slightly bemused yet not surprised, Renay reflects on Terry's remarks and, though not responding verbally, thinks that within herself "a desire to be loved and to love existed [. . .]. But could it be met in this form?" (23).

After an episode with Jerome, who threatened to beat her if she did not cook for him and his drinking buddy, Renay acquiesces and then leaves for work, where Terry invites her home for a drink. Accepting Terry's offer, Renay accompanies her to her house, where she shares with Terry her revulsion for Jerome, equating her life with him to a "drowning, a wish unfulfilled, a death." In an act of consolation, Terry puts her arms around Renay, who, "surprised by her [own] boldness," insists that Terry not remove them (26); and, from there, Terry, after first receiving consent and affirmation, kisses Renay, as the narratorial voice describes:

> The mouth meeting [Renay's] was soft like her own and very, very gentle, unlike the hardness she had been accustomed to feeling. Then it increased its pressure and the tongue went into the cavern of her mouth as if it belonged there, joining hers, and the hands brushed over her face

and down to her neck where it stopped. Her eyes were closed, and she felt a warmth consume her—a warmth she had never known before. She didn't want Terry to stop. She wanted the lips and hands to return to her—to where they belonged. (27)

Drawing upon a language of intimacy, a lexicon replete with the sexual and erotic, this passage is provocative and consequential. Disengaging heterosexist sensibilities that ascribe stigma and abnormality to same-sex affection and desire, Shockley inscribes a "natural-ness" and normativity to Renay and Terry's kiss that legitimizes, naturalizing as authentic, their same-sex intimacy. Mainly through the use of a rhetoric of belonging—Terry's tongue belonging in the caverns of Renay's mouth, as well as Renay's wanting Terry's lips and hands to return "where they belonged"—Shockley challenges heteronormativity by demonstrating that intimacy and sexual desire are not restricted solely to heterosexual relationships. The narrator (and thereby Shockley) achieves this by juxtaposing Renay and Terry's affectionate exchange with that of Renay and Jerome—the latter operating as the antithesis of the former.

Whereas Jerome's kissing Renay had been marked invariably by roughness and the absence of desire, the kiss shared between Renay and Terry is gentle and sensation-filled, invoking in Renay newly experienced feelings of undisguised passion, erotic longing, and desire. This longing, this very erotic desire expressed through the sexual and intimate arousal, has far greater implications, serving, as I have argued previously, metonymically for another aspirational racial desire: a racialized blackness that is ungoverned by reductionist or retrograde politics overdetermined by race divorced of racialized gendered sexuality. If black racial politics (of the 1960s and 1970s) rooted in the nationalist agenda construct "racial identity and its centralizing of race as the sole axis of emancipatory politics," Shockley rejects such reductive constructions.[39] Not, that is, for "a racial authenticity that erases the differences within the black experience," but, rather, for one that embraces/expands the heterogeneity of racialized (black) conditions through the sexual (a point to which I will return momentarily).[40]

This is evidenced and enacted in a seminal passage: when Renay's acclimation to physical desire and erotic pleasure expresses itself beyond her and Terry's kiss in their first inter-racial sexually intimate scene imbued with sexual ecstasy and pleasure. Terry, with a double entendre and vocative, "Renay—come," escorts her into the bedroom, after which:

> Renay opened her eyes and stood up shakily to follow Terry to the other room. Eyes clouded with passion, she hardly saw the large bed. [. . .] Then Terry undressed her and left her for a cold instant on the smooth white sheets while she quickly threw off her own clothes.
>
> Immediately Terry was beside her again, and she was no longer alone. She closed her eyes, shuddering at the delicate kisses being showered all over her body like light rain.
>
> "You're so golden brown, so beautiful," Terry murmured in the hollow of her neck. [. . .]
>
> Shyly [Renay] put her arm around Terry, exploring the white body that was new to her—the downy hair like peach fuzz on Terry's back, the strength of her limbs, the small firmness of her breasts which nestled against her own like twins.
>
> When Terry's hand began feeling, exploring and knead-ing, [Renay] shut her eyes once more, losing herself in the gloriously strange wonderment of it, lying back and think-ing nothing until the pressure of the fingers created a little fire of sensuous pain she hadn't known before [. . .].
>
> [. . .] Then Terry was above her, moving, and just as she had known and wanted this all her life, she matched the love movements of body against body—movements which increased to such an intensity that Renay cried out, star-tling even herself.
>
> [. . .]

Cradled later in Terry's arms, [Renay] said: "It was the
first time I've ever had an orgasm." (27–28)

Densely loaded, this passage "legitimates" same-sex intimacy
and destabilizes (heterosexist) hegemonic notions regarding sexuality. It displaces heterosexuality by foregrounding
another paradigm of sexual longing and erotic desire. Emphasizing the "pigmentative" qualities of Renay's and Terry's skin—
Renay's golden brownness and Terry's whiteness—the narrator
reiterates the interracial-ness and (racial) difference between
them (Renay's black body alongside Terry's white body); yet,
it locates their sameness—asserting their breasts were like
"twins," signifying their commonness—especially biologically
and physiologically. The narrator establishes, at once, their
sameness and difference within the context of Renay and Terry's interracial same-sex union. Moreover, its emphasis on the
(sexual) converging of black and white female bodies that have
historically been constructed as diametrically oppositional—
black and white womanhood(s) as constructed dichotomously
and contingent on myths of each other—undermines the history and tensions undergirding the social constructions of
both black and white womanhood. Terry's emphasizing the
beautiful blackness of Renay's body, emphasizing its racialized
aesthetic beauty rather than reifying its historically pathologized status, and Renay's exploration of the whiteness of Terry's body destabilize socially constructed ideologies regarding
black and white femaleness; and, too, reiterate that race—and
in this case gender, as well—neither determines nor precludes
sexual longing and desire. Renay's and Terry's abilities to transcend race in sexual terms/terrain, as well as the (historical)
"semiotics" of black and white female bodies, exemplify the
nexus of memory, meaning, and the body: that is, that once
the body "forgets" (or "un-remembers") in its quest for pleasure, it, like Renay's and Terry's bodies, liberates itself from
historical memory and reductive social constructions—race,
gender, and sexuality that "police" the body. What matters,

as Shockley reveals, is not so much shifting social constructions but, rather, how one('s) (body) feels.[41]

Renay and Terry's sexual intimacy disrupts heterosexist sensibilities surrounding sexuality and the privileging of male desire
and pleasure in heterosexual intercourse. Their sexual intimacy
is marked by a delicateness and sensuality that creates in Renay
intense feelings of passion, erotic desire, and orgasmic ecstasy,
which differ significantly from her experiences with Jerome, as
she and the narrator contend:

> "I didn't know it *could* be like that—" It had never been
> with [Jerome]. The hurried mounting of her, the jabbing
> inside her with the acrid whiskey odor heavy in her nos-
> trils. It had always been over in seconds; then he would
> turn over and go to sleep. (28, original emphasis)

Invested solely in his own gratification, Jerome exerts dominance and power during sex with Renay, as evidenced by his
"mounting" and "jabbing inside" her, which resembles and
alludes to her earlier rape (and accounts, in part, for why in
their nearly seven years of marriage, Renay never experiences
an orgasm with Jerome). Unlike Jerome, Terry is invested in
pleasing Renay, who, during their very first sexual experience,
reaches unprecedented sexual climax. In fact, when Renay
assumes, during their postintercourse dialogue, that Terry had
gotten "nothing out of [sex]," Terry contends instead, "Yes, yes
I did. Pleasing you. In time, as we begin to know each other,
we'll grow together" (28). Terry's remarks reveal not only the
mutually constitutive (sexual) nature of their relationship, but
also the space that exists in their blossoming romantic friendship for reciprocity in terms of sexual pleasure, accompanied
by both sexual/relational growth and longevity. Juxtaposing Renay and Terry's relationship with Renay and Jerome's,
Shockley privileges female desire and sexual subjectivity, while
excoriating the ways in which female sexuality is confined,
regulated, and/or compromised as the object of male longing
and desire. She also transgresses the false notion that women's

bodies are for the exclusive sexual pleasure and gratification of men.

The significance of their interracial intimacy also lies in its transformative potentiality and symbolic import, particularly where race, blackness, and political longing are concerned, wherein the racial integration that occurs consensually within the bedroom operates, to return to my previous premise, as an enactment of larger racial aspirations. In this case, not only for a more complex construction of black identity outside its strategic deployments within the uplift paradigm that relies on respectability and repression, but also as a suppression of racialized (gendered) sexuality. Here, consensual interracial sexual intimacy and the sex act are not marked by nor do they elicit violence (against, as has historically been the case from the antebellum period throughout Jim Crow, black female and male bodies). As such, they are representative of racial progress (or a desire thereof): emblematic of what the extension of full civil rights to blacks (*all* humans), regardless of skin color, race/ethnicity, or phenotype, might produce: harmonious bonding, literary and figuratively, instead of violent or racially hegemonic (and unequal) confrontation. As literary and sexuality studies scholar Aliyyah Abdur-Rahman illustrates in a poignant assessment and cogent analysis of the nexus of interracial sexual intimacy, politics of race, and political longing, "Cross-racial love engages with the civil rights agenda" in that it "grants African Americans the power of choice in sexual matters across the racial boundary"; and literary charactizations of "cross-racial longing often take seriously the transformative power of interpersonal connectivity to foster ethical citizenship"—or, that is, the potential of "transforming felt desire of sexual intrigue into a broader political vision and enactment of social and racial equality."[47]

Such interracial engagements, sexually intimate across color lines, transgress much of the overarching sensibilities, including the legal philosophies, regarding interracial intimacies. In *Loving v. Virginia*, the case mentioned earlier regarding the interracial marriage of Mildred (Jeter) and Richard Loving, a black woman and white man, the trial judge asserts that "Almighty God created the races white, black, yellow, malay and red, and he placed them on separate continents. And but for the interference with this arrangement there would be no cause for such marriages. The fact that he separated the races shows that he did not intend for the races to mix."[43] His statement, based on a purported natural and religious order, implies that the Lovings had violated not only the state's miscegenation laws, but also the laws of nature and God; their interracial union is portrayed as not merely illegal but also unnatural and immoral. Cross-racial longing and sexual intimacy, such as that of the Lovings and that depicted in literary characterizations like that of Renay and Terry, also destabilize the doctrine of "color-blindness" that developed out of civil rights litigation and held that color, in the racial sense, ceased to be a factor or determinant in the law. The doctrine of color-blindness did not produce a postracial environment that delegitimized (white) racial dominance; instead, it resulted in a system wherein race was seemingly not instantiated, mentioned, or articulated but was, nonetheless, always already present, entrenched, and functioning systematically as a principal, and principled, determinant.

As the erotic is, as Audre Lorde contends, a wellspring or source of power, and if black sexuality functions as "a vehicle for" and of "black freedom and power," then Renay's sexual encounters—her very lovemaking—imbues her with liberatory subjectivity and power. With Terry, as the narratorial consciousness notes, Renay feels "alive again, living to love, loving to live" (39); and her experiences with Terry function as both impetus and affirmation for her to leave Jerome: as "[n]ow she knew she could never [be with Jerome] again, for she [had] found what she wanted and needed most. She was now aware of herself and the part she had tried to deny. So much [. . .] had been wasted in the past" (28). Unbeknownst to Jerome, Renay takes their daughter, Denise, and leaves him to live with Terry, her white lesbian lover. Renay's abandoning Jerome, their marriage, and nuclear family structure to live with Terry unequivocally mark her defiance of convention and established social norms through her deliberate participation in two "taboos": one, an interracial relationship; and, two, a same-sex union, both of which have greater social, sociocultural, and political implications. Reading Renay's behavior, especially along the ideological backdrop of black nationalism, illuminates the ways in which she, via her engagement in an interracial same-sex union, disrupts nationalist tenets regarding womanhood, the family, and the "nation."

Within the nationalist paradigm, men and women have diametrically opposing roles. While men generally occupy the domain of power as patriarchs of their household and, thereby, "guardians" of women and children, women are usually ascribed marginalized roles based largely on a reproductive framework, as Tamar Mayer asserts in *Gender Ironies of Nationalism*:

> [W]omen's national importance is based on their reproductive roles, which include biological and ideological reproduction, reproduction of ethnic or national boundaries, transmission of culture and participation in national struggles. Their centrality is also based on women's symbolic status, connected to their reproductive roles, as representatives of purity. Only the pure and modest women can re-produce the pure nation; without purity in biological reproduction the nation clearly cannot survive.[44]

Because Renay engages in a same-sex relationship—that, without exterior intervention, is biologically nonreproductive—she is incapable of producing offspring with Terry. For this reason their relationship, particularly within the nationalist paradigm and society at large, would be considered threatening to the heterosexual family. Since it is an interracial union, Renay does not fulfill her "role" as transmitter of culture and nationalist ideologies to her progeny. In this way, she, in her existing relationship with Terry, overturns essentialist definitions of "woman" and "womanhood" constructed in strict biological, generative, and (re)productive terms. Moreover, because Renay deliberately diverges from the heteronormative paradigm of sexuality and intimacy, she engages in a putatively deviant lifestyle that seemingly excludes her from nationalist conceptualizations of "purity." Yet, her relationship with Terry is, as the narratorial consciousness consistently demonstrates, deeply embedded with elements of purity—though not "purity" as it is conceived in the traditional limited sense.

Of equal if not greater import, Renay challenges nationalist ideologies by fostering a relationship, inclusive of her daughter, Denise, with Terry: by establishing a counterparadigmatic model of family, she ruptures nationalist constructions of both "the family ideal" and "the black family," as they have been imagined. Renay, Terry, and Denise function as a family unit. Renay and Terry are described as "resembl[ing . . .] a married couple," serving as joint caretakers of Denise, who refers endearingly to her mother's partner as "Aunt Terry"; and, Terry "read to [Denise] every night and brought her surprises and took her for drives while Renay cooked dinner" (39). Terry fosters a relationship with Denise, whose father, Jerome, was too seldom at home and usually too inebriated to cultivate a father-daughter relationship with her. Thus, Renay/Terry/Denise's operating collectively as a family unit, as well as their domestic lifestyle, challenges the notion of what constitutes "family" in American society; delegitimizes black or larger nationalist constructions of the family paradigm; and subverts definitions of "family" that characterize it within an exclusively heteropatriarchal framework.

Renay's (re)formation of family (Renay/Terry/Denise), read in dialogue with her former family (Jerome/Renay/Denise), calls attention to the contradictions undergirding nationalist constructions of the black family. For, if within black nationalist discourse, the foundation and survival of "the black nation" is contingent upon the formation of "strong black families with strong (and responsible) black patriarchs," Jerome—who engages nationalism only so far as its tenets regarding female circumscriptions and male-dominance are concerned—utterly fails to perform his designated role within his family unit. He neglects his responsibilities as a husband and father—not supporting his family financially and functioning as more of a *violator* than a "protector" of his wife—and, therefore, does not meet the "requisites" for manhood within the nationalist project. Jerome's negligent behavior, I would argue, threatens the survival of his family and accounts for its eventual demise. Whereas Renay's behavior, her deliberate engagement in an interracial same-gender loving union, is perceived almost automatically as the "real" threat to their family, it is Jerome, ironically, who is responsible for its destruction.

What Shockley does, then, is twofold: first, she exposes the contradictory nature of nationalists who, like Jerome, embrace ideologies regarding womanhood, manhood, family, and the nation that rarely, if ever, translate—at least in any progressive way—into praxis. Second, she reveals the potentially precarious and destructive, rather than generative, nature of black nationalist constructions of gender roles and family particularly and of nationalism generally. Shockley, to this end, lambastes nationalist tendencies to relegate women to unprogressive gender politics that commodify or render them objects to be acquired, possessed, and/or disposed at men's will, while women are expected to exercise no agency. This she does most conspicuously via Jerome's reaction to his discovery that Renay has abandoned him, as the narratorial voice delineates:

> His male vanity had once again risen to the surface. He just *knew* she was coming back. She *had* to come back. It would have been all right if *he* had left *her*, but he could not believe that *she* had left *him*. That she would not be with him anymore and, above all, that she could go the way of the world without him, was inconceivable to him. She was a commodity to him, something he had bought with a wedding license and, like all possessions, was a part of his many belongings. To him, losing her was a loss of property. (42, original emphasis)

Jerome's narrow conceptualization of Renay is symptomatic of a larger masculinist (gender) hierarchy in nationalism that characterizes women as appendages or adjuncts of men who can/should not operate independently of them. As such, women putatively function off a male-derived axis that centralizes men. Moreover, nationalist discourse constructs women as "feminized entities" or objects that "emphatically, historically, and globally—are the property of men."[45] In his failure to view and thereby treat Renay within a politics of equality, as the passage demonstrates, Jerome subscribes to a male proprietor/female commodity binary, as evidenced through his conceptions of Renay within a discourse of possession. Renay's deliberate abandonment of Jerome—and especially her assertion that, "I'm not coming back, Jerome Lee. Ever. I'm getting a divorce"—uncharacteristically marks her progression in that she expresses, for the first time verbally, her refusal to acquiesce to Jerome and serve as a mere extension of him. Of far greater significance, it signifies her disavowal of nationalist and larger societal tendencies that, in the process of nation building, largely objectify and disempower women.

Shockley, thus, indicts black nationalists like Jerome who, in their construction of family and nation, reify dominant patriarchal ideologies that result in the enforcement of male hegemony and an unequal distribution of power between black men and women. The author does this via Renay's stance toward Jerome's request for her to "C'mon home":

> "Why?" she asked. He had said nothing about being sorry. Why did he want her back? To be his scapegoat? To be the blame for his alcoholic weakness? To be an escape mechanism [. . .]? But above all, to be the doormat upon which he could wipe his feet. Wasn't that what most black men wanted their women for? To take their anger at themselves and the world about them, hold their sperm, spew out their babies? This was what made them feel manly: the white man's underdog having an underdog too. (44)

Shockley's narration in this passage is problematic for a multiplicity of reasons: no differentiation between her idiosyncrasies as author, the narrative voice, and the protagonist's thought process exists. What this results in is a series of generalizations about black men and women directly and nationalism indirectly that, left largely unmediated, resonates more as ideological realities than stereotypes. Notwithstanding these shortcomings, Shockley contests the intransigently narrow, myopic, and marginal ways black women are largely conceived within the nationalist imaginary: black women's role as "scapegoats," reproductive entities who produce the nation, and objects upon which black men's resentment against the hegemonic and oppressive white power structure is displaced.

Renay, dismissing Jerome's plea for her to return home, refuses to reunite with him and chooses freely and deliberately to remain with Terry instead. Renay's conscious decision to maintain her interracial same-gender loving union with Terry defamiliarizes black nationalist and American societal fixations on intraracial bonding, racial "purity," and heterosexuality. Of equal if not greater import, it subverts nationalists' and the larger black community's essentialist characterizations of homosexuality or same-sex desire as nonblack or a "white thing": as a site of contamination and disrepair—similar to, yet "*worse*" than, "incest" or "an incurable disease"—and, equally problematic, as a sign of white "decadence."[46] What such sentiments, as inscribed in the novel, do mark is the complicated and vexed relationship between race and sexuality in black lesbian (and gay) experiences. They also contest the black community's sensibilities regarding homosexuality and same-sex desire, as well as destabilize heteronormative history and nationalist polemics that construct black lesbian and gay bodies as having been essentially and "purely" heterosexual until contaminated by encounters with white supremacy.[47] The novel also strikingly animates American scientific sentiments regarding homosexuality as a mental disease, a national "*dis-ease*" that was listed as a mental sickness by the American Psychiatric Association until as late as the mid-1970s; and it was removed from the list around the time of novel's publication in 1974. *Loving Her* thus intervenes, entering into the sociosexual and psychosexual land-scape, by desensitizing and destigmatizing homosexuality and the diversity of sexual expression. Shockley even decriminalizes it, locating criminality and decadence not in the same-sex love act but, rather, in the violent public responses to it.

When Renay, despite her reservations, goes on a double date with her best friend, Fran, and Fran's friend Lazarius, a black nationalist, they encounter a "slim twig of a young black man, wearing a blonde Beatle wig and dressed in tight red pants and [a] matching shirt" with "light powder and eyes shadowed with purple mascara" (153). When he bumps into their table and apologizes "in a high effeminate voice," both Fran and Lazarius respond in highly disparaging heterosexist, homophobic man-ners: Fran, for example, mutters a (sexually) derogatory term, while Lazarius asserts contemptuously that, "Somebody ought to take him out in the alley and beat the shit out of him" (153). Both remarks not only expose deep-seated homophobia and intolerance for sexual difference, but also excoriate those indi-viduals, like Lazarius, who view violence as a "corrective" for so-called black sexual deviancy.

Like Lazarius, Jerome is highly intolerant of individuals, especially black ones, who transgress established (hetero)sexual boundaries. Upon discovering that Renay has left him, not for another black man but for a white lesbian, he confronts her derisively, even referring to her and Terry in derogatory sexual terms. His reaction to Renay's same-gender loving relationship illustrates not only his extremely heterosexist and homophobic attitude, but also his intensely violent condemnation of homo-sexuality. Rather than accept same-gender loving within a black context, he articulates a willingness even to resort to murder as an extreme corrective for black sexual difference. In this case, Jerome, as the author intends, typifies the sexuality-based fears and hostilities of some nationalists and the general American public, as well as castigatory stances toward individuals whose "infractions" threaten established communal standards and cultural norms. Jerome's reaction—as well as his subsequent assertion that he will "whip the pure black shit out of [Renay's] yellow ass"—reflects his insecurities and inadequacies as a man, and problematically suggests that Renay is not "pure" or authentically black (131). For, Renay's having left him in general, and for a woman (and a *white* one at that), not only emasculates him but, far worse in his estimation, undermines his role as a (black) man since, within the nationalist project, women's sexuality is regulated through men who have orchestrated control over female bodies and sexuality.[48] Jerome's desire to beat Renay evidences, then, his need to recover both dominion over Renay and his "lost" manhood.

Renay's response to Jerome's violent reaction evidences the ways black women refuse to capitulate or subscribe to marginalizing nationalist and larger societal proscriptions for women. In challenging heterosexist relationships privileged in nationalist constructions of family—and dictates of women having to "inspire" their men on multiple levels—these women delegitimize the function of the "black man" as they resolutely assert themselves. Renay, aware of Jerome's false sense of security and feelings of masculinity, boldly challenges Jerome's threats:

> Yes. . . . You want to beat me, to trample on me, see me grovel because you despise what you can't change. A man should be able to control his woman—especially a black man who can't control anything else. But do you really want to know why you hate me? Because I've survived your male deterioration. [. . .] Survived. Through the muck and slime you've [. . .] put me through, I've come out of it— our battle of wills. But, you, you're in it and can't get out because you're stuck!
>
> You're too weak to struggle. It's easier to stay in. And you can't stand the idea that I've left the dirt and you, and you can't push me back. (131–32)

Renay exercises not only her agency, but also her transcendent abilities in that she transgresses Jerome's patriarchal authority. Renay, now unencumbered by Jerome's misogynist and confining mandates or her heterosexist marriage with him, articulates her refusal to leave Terry and return to Jerome and "the dirt." In her "talking back," to borrow bell hooks's terminology, Renay denigrates Jerome in language that reverberates with the nationalist discourse that Jerome embodies in order to illustrate the ways in which he, even by certain nationalist standards, does not meet the requirements for manhood.[49] Renay's "back talk" not only demonstrates her unwillingness to be "policed" by Jerome and by nationalist and larger societal circumscriptions for women, but, of far greater import, it signifies her evolution from objectivity to subjectivity—that is, from a largely unautonomous being to an actualized, empowered, liberated self.

"Could It Be Met in this Form?": Shockley and the Ideological Subversion of Convention

In 1969, just five years prior to the publication of *Loving Her*, in the *San Francisco Times*, Marvin Garson—in a move recognizing as well as drawing upon the liberatory politics of the black nationalist call for "Black Power"—makes a similar call: for "Queer Power." Ruminating on the ways in which black people had, through self-determination, appropriation, and self-definition, revitalized the very meaning of "blackness," he uses the (trans)formative power of (racial) self-definition as a model. Once "it was impolite to suggest that a Negro gentleman might have black skin," and "now it's 'Say it loud, I'm black and I'm proud.'" Perhaps, "in a few years [. . .] queers will be saying something like, 'Don't keep trying to rise above it—kiss me, darling, I'm queer and I love it.'"[50]

This redefinition of what's in a name, particularly governing constructions of "lesbian" identity, is precisely what, in part, Shockley's novel anticipates and problematizes. The nexus of black and queer power, a struggle against a desexualized blackness or a construction of sexuality divorced of race, is precisely what *Loving Her* achieves decades before any black and/ or queer theoretical postulations. Exploring vis-à-vis literary

conventions, transgressive embodiment, and racialized expres
sions of sexual "difference," Shockley not only anticipates but
serves as a foundational apparatus and precursor for (post)
modern discourses on black sexuality studies, specifically black
queer—or "quare"—studies. As Shockley and the same-gender
loving movement illuminate the cultural imperative and intersections of race and sexuality (as an act, behavior, and identity),
black queer studies follows in a similar tradition. Simply put,
Shockley serves as a predecessor for black queer theorists in
her focus on the nexus of race and sexuality as black cultural
imperatives. In the spirit of broad inclusivity, and not to perpetuate a sense of communal divisiveness, "black queer" encapsulates "and, in effect, names the specificity of the historical
and cultural differences"—that simultaneous *dialogic* sameness
and difference—"that shape the experiences and expressions of
'queerness.'"[51]

I invoke such discourses and sensibilities in this concluding section, as they provide a lens by which to further assess
Shockley's pioneering work, foregrounding and polemicizing
same-gender loving in ways that challenge the very category of
"non-normative" sexuality: revealing it to be a misnomer. As
same-gender loving is the primary idiom through which transgression is enacted (with its manifestation in an interracial same-
sex relationship), Shockley castigates the ideological conflation
of homosexuality and same-sex desire with nonblackness; "qua-
res," and thus challenges, the putatively inherent whiteness of
homosexuality and same-sex intimacy; and subverts nationalist and larger American constructions of womanhood, family,
and nation. Certainly this differentiates Shockley's novel from
most of its contemporaries, which contributes, to return to my
earlier query, to why the novel has been largely disregarded.[52]
Instead "of dismissing *Loving Her* for its difference," however, "it
may be more illuminating to view this difference as an extreme
narrative choice that sharply highlights [. . .] ideological limits,"
as Dubey avers, that "enables a clearer appreciation of the difficult relation between difference and representative blackness."

Shockley, rather than reify nationalist constructions of "black" identity and the black nation as singular or monolithic, critiques this framework and illustrates, instead, that the black community is an elaborate, dynamic interplay of sociocultural, ideological, sexual and other differences.[53]

Shockley's creation of an interracial same-sex relationship challenges convention, as well as revolts against nationalist and larger societal tendencies that privilege men and their authority at the expense of women. By producing a same-sex union marked with erotic desire, sexual fidelity, and commitment, Shockley threatens the hegemonic domain of heterosexuality by rendering a relationship radically unregulated by men.[54] To this end, she not only destabilizes the very meaning of womanhood and manhood, especially within the context of nation, but also establishes another paradigm for female bodies—along a more diverse and expansive continuum—that extends beyond their narrowly defined roles within the nation and society at large.

3 / Negotiating Cultural Politics

We cannot create community through a collectivism that negates the individual. To erode the personal is to disintegrate the social.

—ROBERT E. BIRT

The relationship between individuality and community, as well as various discourses and epistemologies regarding their nexus and specificities, has received significant attention. Scholars have long theorized about community and its relationship to the individual. In his essay "Of the Quest for Freedom as Community," informed by existential and Marxist ideologies, philosopher Robert Birt asserts that "community is cooperative self-creation, which requires self-creative freedom of its members. [. . .] Individuality is neither denied nor given as atomic individualism. Real community must preserve the Other in his or her Otherness and uniqueness. It must leave room for one to be oneself."[1] Like Birt, public intellectual Cornel West posits that "the norm of individuality reinforces the importance of community"; whereas, a "doctrinaire" individualism "denigrates the idea of community."[2] Not only do both scholars differentiate between individuality and individualism, but they also characterize individuality and community in nonoppositional ways that, without negating "uniqueness" or "otherness," illuminate the symbiosis and/or contingency between these entities.

While their conceptualizations are salient and insightful, what I would add is a consideration of the ways in which gender (and, to an extent, temporality and geography), in addition to race, compound to further complicate the very dynamics of community. As black feminist scholars have long argued, community is mediated by gender, geography and geographical locations, class, and other apparatuses within particular historical moments. "[G]eographic processes important to black women are not just about limitations, captivities, and erasures; they are also about everyday contestation," as Katherine McKittrick posits, "and the possibilities the production of space can engender for subaltern subjects."[3] Furthermore, "transcendent community" is often the ideal rather than the reality or the "norm," as black feminist scholar Joy James avers, since in some "states and societies, black women are subordinated Others. They exist as outsiders within not only American culture but also [. . .] African American cultures."[4] Much like James, Johnnetta Cole and Beverly Guy-Sheftall, in *Gender Talk: The Struggle for Women's Equality in African American Communities*, illumine the extent to which "gender dynamics are embedded in the very structure of Black society," as well as the "complex manifestations and consequences of sexism within African American communities."[5] They explicate the ways race and gender especially collide and have historically been largely ignored in the name of racial and communal solidarity. Such racial/communal dynamics, or the elisions of intraracial gender issues, embrace neither "uniqueness" nor individuality and thereby essentialize community and the role of its members at the expense of "others": namely women.

Such issues surrounding community and individuality, and the deliberate or inadvertent communal suppressions they often engender, especially where women are concerned, are what I find particularly intriguing, as they have larger implications. At the heart of this matter is the very nature of community, with its largely nationalist or nation-like undercurrents, that demands unconditional or ineffable loyalty and solidarity as requisites

for belonging. For community, like "nation," is, as Benedict
Anderson contends, "imagined"; and, "regardless of the actual
inequality and exploitation that may prevail," it is "always conceived as a deep, horizontal comradeship."⁶ What happens when
individuals, particularly black women, transgress such communal "bonds," parameters, or solidarity? And, importantly,
how might a politics of antiracism exist without discounting
intraracial differences, or compromising antisexist and gender
progressive politics, that constitute community?⁷ It is precisely
these communal/cultural questions and predicaments, a largely
though not exclusively postmodern condition, that this chapter
engages.

Previous chapters have illuminated the ways that black female
subjects transgress heteronormativity and regulations of female
sexuality (exclusively) through men, while presenting models
of racialized gendered transgression that rupture the domain
of established convention governing womanhood, nation, and
paradigms for black female bodies. This chapter advances these
very understandings of transgressive behavior, of traversals
or eruptions of the purported "norm" regarding womanhood,
sexuality, and nation—as it intersects with racial longing made
manifest vis-à-vis the sexual—in an exploration that opens
other avenues of consideration of "the transgressive." It does so
through an analysis of Alice Walker's work. Like many African
American women novelists of the post–civil rights era, Walker
explores the precarious relationship between women, resistance,
and familial/communal belonging. In her body of literature are
female characters who negotiate certain cultural dynamics.
When confronted with sociocommunal politics governing race,
gender, sexuality and community or "nation," these characters
usually conform, even if temporarily, or they transgress such
circumscriptions, exerting their individuality. It is precisely
this motif—the dialectics or nexus of transgression and belonging with particular regard to black women, individuality, and
community—that permeates Walker's 1976 novel *Meridian* and
forms the basis of this chapter.

If transgression emblematizes a contestation or destabilization of the supposed "norm," Walker's novel further complicates the relationship between transgressive behavior and established tradition. It illuminates, that is, the ways that even within the context of this disruption and subversion of the "normative," Meridian's racialized gendered transgression—even while "illicit"—is still with the realm of "acceptability."[8] As such, Meridian Hill, the novel's protagonist, is neither shunned, ostracized, nor characterized as anathema in her community. She confronts and ultimately negotiates her transgressive behavior, a particular individuality (that prioritizes a nonconformist self), and communal belonging: struggling against sociocommunal circumscriptions for (black) women, while simultaneously playing a revolutionary activist role within the communities in which she operates. Meridian's ability to function in this mutually (co)operative manner differentiates her from other characters, especially Sula and Renay, analyzed previously, whose transgressive behavior invariably dislocates or relegates them to an "outsiderwithin" status within their respective communal locales.[9] Meridian, unlike Sula and Renay, celebrates her largely uncompromised individuality, transgressing the strictures imposed on womanhood, female sexuality, and motherhood, while concomitantly playing a participatory, activist role within various communities. Meridian not only expands unilateral conceptualizations of womanhood, community, and racialized gender transgression, but also, as this chapter demonstrates, the notion that individuality and community need not exist as mutually exclusive entities in a postmodern society.

A distinguishing element characterizing black politics during the postmodern era is the notion that "race no longer forms the singular axial principle of all political projects affecting African-Americans."[10] Or, the post–civil rights era is marked, as Toni Morrison poignantly avers, as a moment wherein "undiscriminating racial unity has passed."[11] Alice Walker, as a literary activist, explores these very dynamics, the nexus of race and the politics of difference, especially as it pertains to women, not only in fictive characterizations but in activist and theoretical contexts. Influenced by and an active participant in the civil rights movement, as well as the struggle for the liberation of women, Walker coins "womanism"—as theory, praxis, or a way of life—to embody a commitment to the struggles for black women's liberation: one not divorced from the liberation of black people generally. "Womanist," then, denotes "[a] black feminist or feminist of color," one "[c]ommitted to survival and wholeness of entire people, male *and* female. Not a separatist."[12]

It is this type of complex and variegated politics—one in which there are no hierarchies of oppression or proclivities toward (gender) subordination—that informs Walker and is, in turn, inscribed in *Meridian*, wherein the eponymous character navigates the vexed dynamics governing black women's individuality, communal belonging, and racial politics in a postmodern society. In its examination of these dynamics, this chapter explores another dimension of black women's transgressive behavior, one that is mutually inclusive. What I suggest is that racialized gender transgression manifests, in part, vis-à-vis deployments of individuality—that is, strategic prioritizations of (the black female) *self*, as not simply symbolic but rather a conduit of a personal freedom—that are ultimately utilized in the service of a larger communal/collective liberation. The process of establishing an individual self in *Meridian* entails a traversal, and to a greater extent a divestment, of established racial and sociosexual doctrines, logic, and/or conventions; and, this cultivation of such a *self* fosters an actualization of the individual vested in communal/black universal freedom. In Meridian's case, her civil rights struggle is twofold: first, it is a personal one that is embodied—a literal "body politic"—in that she undergoes a corporeal (bodily) struggle against male sexual aggression, compulsory reproduction/motherhood, and matrimonial sexual intimacy. Second, her struggle is one for equality and human rights, as evidenced in her participatory, sociopolitical activist role, which results in self-actualization, in the Atlanta (civil rights) movement.

Climbing As We Lift: Individual
and Communal Liberation

At various junctures Meridian Hill operates within communities that provide little space for individuality to exist, let alone be cultivated. Notwithstanding, she ekes out a uniquely nonconformist livelihood or singularity in each, regardless of the ramifications that might ensue. Meridian's home community, the primary focus of this chapter, is a small rural town in the segregated South that upholds circumscriptions for women embedded in the classical black female script and, as such, is characterized by a particular conservatism surrounding female sexuality. The community's rigidity and gender-specific proscriptions reflect not so much a fixation on morality or moral regulation. Its preoccupation is deeply rooted in a larger concern with female sociosexual behavior and interlocking principles of propriety and respectability. "Because gendered identities define and socialize individuals into unconscious moral senses of appropriate and inappropriate" behavior, "they often become tied to ideals concerning propriety."[13] Such ideals regarding gender and appropriate (sexual) behavior are deeply entrenched in Meridian's community, where they translate into practices of dissemblance or a "politics of silence" surrounding female sexuality, as the novel's narratorial voice asserts:

> [Meridian's] mother, father, aunts, friends, passersby—not to mention her laughing sister—had told her nothing about what to expect from men, from sex. Her mother never used the word, and her lack of information on the subject of sex was accompanied by a seeming lack of concern about her daughter's morals. Having told her absolutely nothing, she had expected her to *do* nothing. [. . .] H]er mother only cautioned her to "be sweet." [Meridian] did not realize this was a euphemism for "Keep your panties up and your dress down," an expression she *had* heard and been puzzled by.[14]

The community, including and emblematized by Meridian's mother, Gertrude Hill, embraces strictures regarding female sexual purity and dissemblance designed strategically, in part, to safeguard black women from sexual violations and vulnerability. Such familial/communal silences regarding black women's sexuality—embodied in misleading and easily misconstrued euphemisms such as "be sweet"—prove ineffectual and, far worse, damaging. Rather than provide Meridian with protection, they contribute paradoxically to her vulnerability to male sexual violence, as her first sexual encounters are acts of molestation she experiences at a local funeral home. Meridian's early experiences with male sexual violation, and her lack of protection against such encounters, inform and influence her subsequent relationship to men and sexuality. Consequently, she establishes a reactive protectionist stance, albeit through sexually intimate relationships with men, as a conduit by which to secure a level of safety from (external) male sexual lust and aggression.

Because she experiences in her early life a rigid avoidance of the topic of female sexuality and has no access to candid, noneuphemistic information on men and female sexuality, Meridian has no familial/communal space in which to engage in dialogues on sex, let alone disclose within these contexts her experiences with male sexual misconduct. Her predicament is neither an isolated circumstance, nor one that should be understood as occurring solely within a literary (con)text. Rather, Meridian's encounters have far greater sociocultural and communal implications, as black feminist scholar Paula Giddings's "The Last Taboo" illumines. Historicizing black sexual politics within a U.S. context, Giddings posits that, given the historically precarious relationship between black people and their perceived sexual pathology within American society, certain "sociosexual conditions," as well as an absence of sex and gender discourses, pervade society and the black community and, in turn, plague black women especially.[15] Not addressing these sociosexual predicaments has "left the community, especially its women, bereft of the help and protection so needed"; and, solutions to these conditions "have not been passed on through families or social institutions."[16]

Much can be extrapolated from Giddings's assertions, which are remarkably applicable to Meridian. Such ideologies and sociosexual conditions apply to the eponymous character, who, in the face of such circumstances, and unprotected by the classical black female script or familial/communal resolutions, deliberately takes it upon herself to mediate her condition. She confronts these larger concerns and silences regarding black sexual politics, as well as the lack of familial intervention, especially on the part of her mother. Mrs. Hill is the embodiment of tradition, as it relates to community and womanhood, which, as socially constructed, entails women's expected sexual innocence and purity. The expectation is that women neither possess sexual knowledge nor exercise sexual desire or agency, all of which are considered outside the realm of femininity and womanhood and are situated within the male/masculine domain. Representative of this traditional position regarding womanhood and sexuality, Mrs. Hill, not unlike Sula's mother, Hannah, never transmits to her daughter fundamental knowledge—whether instructive, cautionary, or empowering—regarding sex or sexuality. While she does not fulfill her expected "mothering" role marked by nurturing and the intergenerational transmission of knowledge from mother to child, she does so in adherence to rigid dictates regarding female sexuality within the community of which she is a product and for which she also serves as a metonym. In this regard, she is a reflection of the community, which embraces tradition, specifically those governing female sexuality and other strictures that have detrimental consequences for women that, ultimately, go unmediated and unresolved.

In the absence of concrete instructions, meaningful discourses on sexuality, and familial/communal protection against sociosexual vulnerability, and unprotected by the script, Meridian strategically mediates her condition in unconventional ways rather than be victimized by male sexual misconduct.

Interestingly enough, her mediation, a direct corollary to having been molested, comes via her deliberate engagements in heterosexual relationships: she seeks and engages in ostensibly committed relationships and the sexual intimacy they entail with men—her "boyfriends" and "lovers"—as protection against external male sexual aggression.

Her relationship with Eddie, a boyfriend who later becomes her husband, is one such scenario. Not attracted to Eddie and utterly disinterested in sex, she engages in the relationship nonetheless. What she desires is not so much Eddie or sex but, rather, the protection that being "his girl" signifies and provides her, as the narrative voice asserts:

> Being with [Eddie] did a number of things for her. Mainly, it saved her from the strain of responding to other boys or even noting the whole category of Men. This was worth a great deal, because she was afraid of men—and was always afraid until she was taken under the wing of whoever wandered across her defenses to become—in a remarkably quick time—her lover. This, then, was [. . .] what sex meant to her; not pleasure, but a sanctuary in which her mind was freed of any consideration for all the other males in the universe who might want anything of her. It was resting from pursuit. (61–62)

Meridian's engagement in committed relationships with men as protection against unwanted external male sexual aggression further underscores the inefficacy and contradictions of strictly gendered expectations for female sexual behavior. Moreover, it reveals the pitfalls and ramifications of absent familial/communal discourses on sexuality and, of equal import, interventions that might protect black women like Meridian from certain sex/gender systems. For, within "sexually aggressive" contexts, young black women who endure such sociosexual conditions have "sexual experiences [. . .] not characterized by learning the meaning or enjoyment of sex, or even making choices about engaging in it, but in protecting themselves from what is viewed [. . .] as the irrepressible sexual drives of the men in their lives."[17] This is precisely the case with Meridian, who "while not enjoying [sex] at all, [. . .] had had [it] as often as her lover [Eddie] wanted it, sometimes every single night" (60–61).

Because she uses it methodically as mediation, Meridian has a vexed relationship to sex that has a certain duplicity that serves a dialogical function. That is, it exemplifies a problematical acquiescence to male sexual desire and irrepressibility or "submission to masculine pleasure"; yet, concomitantly it also signifies, I suggest, a certain agency and resistance on Meridian's part, as she, in her conscious and calculated efforts, utilizes sex, ironically, as a "preventative" measure to regulate the terms of her sexual behavior.[18] As Carole S. Vance argues poignantly in "Pleasure and Danger: Toward a Politics of Sexuality," sexuality is complicated, as an ambiguous and complex relationship exists between female pleasure and danger, empowerment and disempowerment. "Sexuality is simultaneously a domain of restriction, repression, and danger" and also "a domain of exploration, pleasure, and agency"; thus, to characterize sexuality within the realm of "pleasure and gratification" alone "ignores the patriarchal structure" in which women operate. Conversely, to focus on the former—sexual violence, danger, or oppression—"ignores women's experiences with sexual agency and choice," thereby "increas[ing] the sexual terror and despair in which women live."[19]

Vance's assertion encapsulates and speaks to Meridian's sexual behavior, marked by a certain dualism, which should not be read in singular or absolute terms as simply a compliance with male sexual aggression and violation. Rather, her appropriation or manipulation of sex and its functions evidences her agency, as well as her refusal to submit passively to male sexual prerogatives and/or acquiesce to the social and patriarchal systems from which they stem. If sexuality "can be viewed as an entity manipulated" and "as a site of intersectionality, a specific constellation of social practices that demonstrate how oppressions converge," Meridian navigates racial/sexual terrain in her deliberate manipulation of sexuality: her regulating the terms of her sexual behavior, which hinges not upon emotion or desire but that functions methodically as an apparatus.[20] Thus, her duality in terms of sexual behavior and experiences reflects the complex dynamics surrounding female sexuality, especially within black racialized and gendered contexts. As Evelynn Hammonds insightfully asserts regarding black women's sexual experiences and sexualities, "we must think in terms of a different geometry. Rather than assuming black female sexualities are structured along an axis of normal and perverse [. . .], we might find that for black women a different geometry operates."[21] This is not to suggest that black women's sexualities are "anormative," nor is it to render their experiences anomalous or atypical, but rather to allow for a broader and more expansive continuum for black female sexualities and sexual politics—especially given the complexities and historical dynamics governing black women's sexual experiences.

While Meridian's strategic use of sex, unlike dissemblance, proves effectual in safeguarding her from sexual violation, it serves as no substitute for instructive dialogues on sex or its ramifications. She engages in sex methodically, though never fully cognizant of its consequences: and so, having had sex practically "every single night" for "almost two years," as the narrative voice asserts, her "pregnancy came as a total shock" (61). Meridian's unexpected pregnancy is, much like her molestation, one of the damaging and symptomatic outcomes of an absence of familial/communal discourses on sexuality, as well as a result of her unawareness of the reproductive capacities of sexual intercourse. As literary scholar Barbara Christian notes, "no adult, not even Mrs. Hill, gives Meridian information about sex or the prevention of pregnancy—even as the mother knows the drastic changes that motherhood will impose on her daughter."[22] Meridian becomes "prey," ironically, to silences surrounding female sexuality; but, she is also entrapped by problematic politics within heterosexual relationships (like most, if not all, of the female characters of the novel) characterized by limited, confining sociocommunal definitions of racial/sexual identity. In its embrace of a politics of silence, conservatism, and tradition, Meridian's community cultivates, deliberately or inadvertently, an environment regarding sexuality that is threatening and/or detrimental rather than protective to women especially. At the crux of constructions of womanhood, as it is communally defined, is an equally deleterious sensibility that what constitutes femininity and "good"/acceptable womanhood is female sexual ignorance, characterized by a lack of knowledge about, and by extension experience with, sex. As such, female sexuality emblematizes or is conflated exclusively with its reproductive capacity: as a conduit by which to produce life with the expectation that women's relationship to sex is for procreation (childbearing) rather than recreation, or, that is, for pleasure. Such sentiments are concretized in the novel in that Meridian becomes pregnant twice after engaging in sex: the first time is with Eddie, whom she marries as a result, and later she becomes pregnant with Truman, a civil rights worker (a point to which I will return).

This speaks to the larger issues governing black women's sexuality, especially when read within the context of the sociopolitical juncture in which Walker's novel was produced: during the black nationalist era when women were encouraged to "make babies for the revolution"; during the feminist movement when women fought the tyranny of patriarchal and gender oppression; and, even more fittingly in this instance, during the sexual revolution, with its expressed interest in sexual liberation. In this scene reverberates my previous discussion of blacks and the sexual revolution, particularly had it bypassed blacks. Walker demonstrates the deleterious effects of an entrenched communal silence, coupled with a racialized Victorian disposition, that contributes to a lack of sexual knowledge and preventive measures that result in unwanted/compulsory pregnancy—the reproductive consequence of sex. This sensibility and the devastating effects are literalized in the novel by the sexual casualities, the overwhelming number of female characters (Meridian,

Nelda, Wile Child, Fast Mary, among others) who have sex and, consequently, end up pregnant (with stunted lives, literally, since two of these characters die).

This also reflects black women's exigencies of the time, as evidenced in the larger treatment of black female sexuality and black sexual politics in black general-interest periodicals. In 1976, the same year as the publication of *Meridian*, *Essence* magazine featured a monthly question-and-answer column entitled "Your Sexual Health." Joanne H. Tyson, the then codirector of the Institute for Marriage Enrichment and Sexual Studies, responded to the personal, often detailed and explicit questions on topics ranging from birth control pills usage and mishaps, sexual arousal, orgasms, oral sex, and sexually transmitted diseases to pregnancy prevention and the existence of home brews to terminate an unwanted pregnancy to avoid a medical abortion. Alongside such discussions, in the July 1976 issue, an excerpt of Alice Walker's *Meridian* appeared (see Figure 3.1), accompanied by an epigraphic quote: "She had been spasmodic with fear," it read. "Fear because sex was always fraught with ugly consequences for her, and fear because if she did not make out with him she might lose him, and if she did make love with him he might lose interest."[23]

While the epigraph pertains to Meridian's later relationship with Truman, a civil rights worker, it also encapsulates her relationship with Eddie; and, equally consequential, it bears striking semblance to Walker's own personal, sociopolitical, and sexual experiences. As a student at Spelman College, the historically black women's institution in Atlanta, Georgia, where Walker spent two years as a student, she was galvanized and inspired, in part, by another Spelmanite: Ruby Doris Smith Robinson, the legendary civil rights activist and, by Walker's own account, the partial inspiration for the novel's eponymous character.[24] Walker participated in the Atlanta (civil rights) movement before transferring after two years at Spelman, which she considered steeped in Victorian conservatism, to Sarah Lawrence College in New York in December 1963. Her studies commenced in January

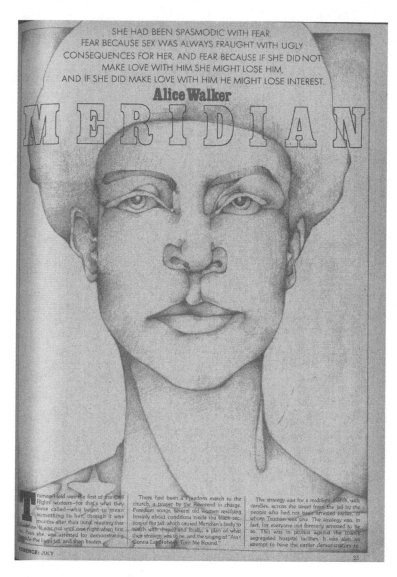

FIGURE 3.1 Excerpt from Alice Walker's *Meridian,* featured in *Essence,* July 1976.

1964, and in the fall of 1965 she learned that she was pregnant: the result of a summer abroad in Kenya and Uganda sponsored by the Experiment in International Living. Walker held the conviction that if she did not have an abortion, she would surely kill herself, asserting that "one or the other of us was not going to survive"; and so, "it was me or it."[25] She succeeded in having an abortion that predated by eight years *Roe v. Wade*, the landmark Supreme Court case that legalized abortion in 1973. Her experience is dramatized in the novel's account of Meridian's abortion after she becomes pregnant by Truman. Walker's experiences, then, inspire Meridian's character(ization).

In terms of her relationship with Eddie, who marries her as he "had always promised he would 'if something went wrong'" (61), Meridian does not fully acquiesce or subscribe to certain marital roles, particularly her sexual role as wife. Instead, she regulates, be it through elusion, the terms of their sex life. Now married and in a union that not only sanctions but legitimates sex, the very meaning of sex and its function changes for Meridian. Whereas it had operated previously as a conduit by which to secure protection from external male advances, now, as Eddie's wife, she no longer contends with such threats—as marriage marks her "unavailable" to men besides her husband. As such, she does not have to contend with male propositions. No longer needing sex as mediation and disinterested in it, Meridian implements certain regulatory practices to curtail and altogether elude sex with Eddie. In addition to "locking" her legs to the point Eddie must "fight to get [them] open," she also relies on seemingly legitimate excuses—grounded in community-based superstitions—to avoid sex: "she put the blame on any handy thing: her big stomach, the queasiness, the coming baby, [and] old wives' tales that forbade intercourse until three months after the baby was born" (65).

In her deliberate and strategic avoidance of marital sex, Meridian circumvents her sexual role as wife and transgresses particular constructions of her, otherwise, restrictive heterosexual relationship—refusing to privilege her husband's sexual desires or allow him to "possess" her body and dictate the terms of her sexual behavior. Moreover, in her conscious use of her pregnancy, a direct repercussion of the reproductive quality of sex, ironically, as a pretext for avoiding sex, she exerts her agency and subjectivity. Through her elusory and regulatory sexual practices, she undermines social prescriptions that contain and require female sexuality within marital domains. And so, just as her methodical use of premarital sex had proven effectual in thwarting external male sexual advances and violations, her strategic circumvention of marital sex is equally efficacious in enabling her to permanently transgress her sexual role as wife. She is altogether "relieved" from sex with Eddie when he, upon the realization that Meridian is disinterested in and does not enjoy (or intend on) having sex with him, engages in an extramarital affair. By the time the baby was born, Eddie had found a "woman who loved sex, and was able to get as much of it as he wanted every night" (65).

Unmoved by Eddie's infidelity or the subsequent collapse of their marriage, Meridian is, instead, perturbed by forced motherhood: Eddie's having left her with the sole responsibility of raising their son. For, as the narratorial voice asserts, he had automatically "assumed [. . .] the baby would remain with her," which, "was, after all, how such arrangements had *always* gone"; he had no intention of "see[ing] much more of either of them" (71–72). What Meridian resents and ultimately challenges, then, is the double standard and gendered nature of parenthood. While Eddie, as a man, shirks fatherhood and his responsibilities without remorse and/or communal repercussions, motherhood is imposed upon and expected of Meridian because she is a woman. "The meaning of 'fatherhood' remains tangential, elusive. To 'father' a child suggests above all to beget, to provide the sperm which fertilizes the ovum," as Adrienne Rich explicates in *Of Woman Born*, versus mothering a child, which necessitates a particular existence, a permanence or enduring presence. "A man may beget a child" and "disappear" to "never see or consider the child or mother again. Under such circumstances, the mother faces a range of painful, socially weighted choices: abortion, suicide, abandonment of the child, infanticide" or raising the child.[26]

Both historically and cross-culturally, women have been defined by motherhood, an identity that has been largely imposed upon them, while no such impositions exist for the "childless man" or the absent/nonfather. What Meridian reacts to and ultimately resists is the vexed and gendered dynamics undergirding parenthood: while Eddie "fathers" a child he eventually abandons without contemplation, stigmatization, or derision, Meridian's responsibility as a woman—in adherence to racial/communal and larger social sanctions—is to fulfill her maternal role of mother as it has been socially constructed. Meridian, however, disrupts these ideals regarding motherhood and all it entails in that she neither possesses nor demonstrates any "maternal" affinities toward her son. Instead of responding to Eddie Jr. with the unconditional love or affection mothers are expected to exude, she rebels, conflating mothering with enslavement:

> It took everything she had to tend to the child, and she had to do it, her body prompted her not by her own desires, but by her son's cries. So this, she mumbled [. . .] is what slavery is like. Rebelling, she began to dream each night, just before her baby sent out his cries, of ways to murder him. [. . . He] did not feel like anything to her but a ball and chain.
> The thought of murdering her own child eventually frightened her. To suppress it she conceived, quite consciously, methods of killing herself. (69–70)

Meridian does not experience the presumably inherent maternal bliss that society associates with motherhood. Rather, she views it and her son as burdens rather than sources of joy or fulfillment meriting idealization. In her evocation of slavery, particularly her equating motherhood with it, Meridian articulates feelings of entrapment and enclosure that society—in its romanticism of the mother role—very rarely, if ever, attaches to motherhood. Meridian perceives motherhood as a hindrance, an institution alienating her from and incarcerating her within herself, that corrupts her potential. As a panacea and contradictory to societal circumscriptions for mothers, she fantasizes about infanticide and suicide as escape mechanisms from what she considers thralldom: unwanted pregnancy and unexpected or compulsory motherhood. Meridian demystifies the largely narrow and myopic conceptualizations of the mother role, as well as ubiquitous mythologies governing the institution of motherhood.

In her allusion to slavery, Meridian also problematizes universal notions regarding motherhood that in her case are further complicated by race and the historical dynamics and nexus between black women and motherhood. Given (enslaved) black women's restricted/denied access to and "ownership" of their children—who, like adult slaves, were commodified and sold as chattel—motherhood within a black racialized context embodies a complex set of meanings beyond the universal. Since motherhood, as a concept and institution, "is of central importance in [. . .] the philosophy of African and Afro-American peoples," it is interconnected with "the historical process within which these peoples have been engaged, a process that is an intertwining of tradition, enslavement, and the struggle for their peoples' freedom."[27] Black motherhood and "the black mother" emblematize, then, something both real and mystical that has historically been revered and idealized. Notwithstanding the historical significance undergirding black motherhood, Meridian, contrary to this "tradition," chooses both freely and deliberately to give her son away rather than kill either him or herself.

Having internalized ideologies concerning black motherhood, Meridian is still both unwilling and unable to serve the role of mother she has been socialized to embrace and fulfill. Unlike her "maternal" ancestors, who had equated the opportunity to keep their children with "freedom," Meridian views slavery and motherhood, specifically raising an unexpected and/or unwanted child, as comparable institutions. In giving away her son, a highly contestatory act, Meridian simultaneously and paradoxically upholds yet diverges from "ideal" black motherhood. That is, she exercises her right as a mother to protect her baby—"believing she had saved [his] life" (91)—by giving him away; yet, conversely, she dissociates herself from the tradition, actual and mythical, by abandoning her child—even if she does so to accept a scholarship to college.[28]

Abandoning Eddie Jr., despite the physical and psychological effects, affords her the opportunity to attend college and play a participatory role in the movement, and thereby liberate her community via sociopolitical activism. As literary scholar Thadious Davis insightfully notes, Meridian "divests herself of immediate blood relations," including her child and parents, "in order to align herself completely with the larger racial and social generations of blacks."[29] Despite her painful private experiences, she "is born anew into a pluralistic cultural self, a 'we' that is and must be self-less and without ordinary prerequisites for personal identity."[30] Moreover, "[i]n order to engage in the intense political struggles of the movement Meridian has to forget the events of her personal past," including her divestment of her child, "that once kept her from the larger historical context of her life."[31] Thus, "the power of public commitment" overshadows, if not overwhelms, "the demands of private ties," as literary scholar Melissa Walker posits.[32] While I concur with both Davis and Walker, I would also suggest that it is precisely because Meridian redefines her *self* in relation to the communal, vis-à-vis participating in sociopolitical activism and uplift, that she "reconciles" her sense of guilt and avoids, unlike other transgressive characters, the communal ramifications that transgressions against motherhood, female sexuality, and strictures for women would otherwise elicit. As such, while she challenges sociocommunal demands and circumscriptions of women where sexuality and motherhood are concerned, her participation in the movement is not seen as deviant. Rather, her activism, a form of racial/communal and sociopolitical work, serves as *expiation* for her racialized/gendered/sexualized transgression. For it is precisely her activism and commitment to liberatory politics that enable her to transgress circumscriptions for women, yet, concomitantly, serve a vital role within varied communities.

In fact, Walker deliberately employs this narrative strategy—characterizing and historicizing Meridian within the context of the movement—to negotiate, as well as problematize, notions regarding black women's individuality, community, and belonging. To this end, her transgressions against motherhood, especially her thoughts of infanticide, are invariably and strategically accompanied by moments of sociopolitical consciousness on her part within the text. Her initial fantasies of murdering Eddie Jr., for instance, are interrupted by a voter registration demonstration led by young activists that she sees on the evening news:

> Now she sat listlessly, staring at the TV. [. . .] There was to be a voter registration drive (she wondered what that was) that would begin [. . .]. Local blacks, volunteers, were needed. [. . .] Black people were never shown in the news—unless of course they had shot their mothers or raped their bosses' grandparent—and a black person or persons giving a news conference was unheard of. But, [. . . it] kept her mind somewhere else while she made her hands play with the baby. (72)

Not only does this interrupt Meridian's thoughts of infanticide, but it introduces and eventually radicalizes her to the civil rights movement, black struggles for equality and sociopolitical subjectivity. Moreover, it helps redefine "blackness"—locating it within the sociopolitical realm of agency with regard to enfranchisement and existential freedom—and rescues black people from the mythology of a pathologized and/or criminalized past. With a newer sense of racial consciousness and political awareness, Meridian, "after the bombing" (80), volunteers at a local movement office and is later radicalized, becoming an active participant in protests, demonstrations, and freedom marches.

Walker problematizes, as well as humanizes, civil rights by illuminating the human element—foregrounding the personal struggles, the faces, black people's dogged determination to attain freedom and equality—in the face of legal rhetoric. This she further achieves in her essay in the civil rights journal *Perspectives*, wherein she ruminates on "civil rights" as more than simply nomenclature, language, and terminology: "It has no music, it has no poetry. It makes one think of bureaucrats rather than of sweaty faces, eyes bright and big for *Freedom!*, marching feet." Moreover, "the term 'Civil Rights' could never adequately express black people's revolutionary goals because it could never adequately describe our longings and our dreams" and "because, as a term, it is totally lacking in color. In short, although I value the civil rights movement itself, I have never liked the term" namely because it "did not evolve out of black culture but rather out of American Law. As such, it is a term of limitation. It speaks only to physical possibilities—necessary and treasured, of course—but not of the spirit."[33]

In her participation in racial/communal uplift and black freedom struggles, Meridian produces and "gives birth" to new opportunities for communities and generations of blacks—disenfranchised and otherwise. She helps to create for them possibilities of racial/sociopolitical equality, as well as greater senses of consciousness and knowledge of their existence in society and the world. This is not to say that the movement is an idealized liberatory experience for Meridian or that she did not confront particular politics that, at times, marginalized her. Yet, it still provides her with a space—unlike the conservative and restrictive community from which she came—in which to achieve selfhood, subjectivity, awareness of her condition, and agency in the face of systematic oppression. For, as Walker asserts, "[t]o know is to exist: to exist is to be involved, to move about, to see the world with [one's] own eyes. This, at least, the Movement has [done]."[34]

In *Meridian*, Alice Walker illuminates the ways in which individuality, especially women's individual freedom, and community are not antithetical or diametrical entities. Through her characterization of Meridian, she demonstrates the convergence, rather than disjuncture, of black women's autonomy in relation to the community at large. Instead of the community serving merely and problematically as a source of entrapment or marginalization for women, it, as Walker illumines, significantly provides a space for women's agency and choice, be it with regard to mothering and/or participating in revolutionary work. In so doing, Walker "takes into account the dynamics of collective identity along with the demands that social codes place upon the group, and she considers the structure of personal identity with its [. . .] social relations, especially family."[35] Moreover, she destabilizes the very meanings and functions of the individual and collective, and their relational aspects to various conventional institutions and social relations: particularly family, motherhood, and community. To this end, she creates transformative and liberatory spaces, not without complications and complexities, for black women as well as generations of blacks.

4 / "That Way Lies Madness": Sexuality, Violent Excess, and Perverse Desire

If post–civil rights black women authors limn the nexus of racialized gender and sexual transgression, employing erotic characterizations and theatricalities of desire, *Eva's Man* does just this. Yet, it goes even farther, exceeding the limit and traversing the boundaries in ways unparalleled in other texts examined in this book. It engages the radical sexual dimension, as well as contests the regulation of female sexuality through men, as does *Sula*. Like *Loving Her*, it refuses to privilege heterosexual intimacy, marked by male dominance, as a singular and solitary option; and, much like *Meridian*, it critiques silence—especially in the form of dissemblance (or the politics surrounding black women's sexuality)—as insidious. Even with these connections, *Eva's Man* is far more aggressive: it agitates; is crude and, at times, simultaneously titillating, pornographic, and offensive; and is both uncensored and unrelenting in its violence, sexual language, imagery, and tone. In fact, Jones's language, her calculated use of the sexually explicit (quasi-pornographic), operates as a direct contestation—a means to overturn—racialized Victorianism. Published during the sexual revolution, the novel reflects the ideological and sociosexual politics of the moment in its effort to liberate sex and libidinal forces from not only repression, but conservatism in terms of morality and what one might engage in during the sex act. Sensibilities undergirding the novel reflect the sociocultural and legal advances in the sexual realm, namely in the arena of the pornographic and public obscenity.

The novel appeared in 1976, only three years after the 1973 Supreme Court case *Miller v. California* that determined the criteria (in a three-tier test) of what constituted obscenity and was, therefore, either protected under or in direct violation of the First Amendment. The Court delineated that something might be adjudged obscene if and only if it presents conspicuously offensive hard-core sexual acts or conducts; is not imbued with (or is essentially void of) serious artistic, literary, scientific, or political value; and, finally, if it appeals to the prurient or arouses the sexual interest of an individual based on the (then) contemporary sociocommunal/community standards. In one of the advances of the sexual revolution, pornography becomes accessible in industrialized form for both public cinematic and private home consumption, changing the sexual landscape in public/private spheres. Some sexual revolutionaries even enacted public displays of nudity and sex acts to rescue sex and sexuality from a domain of repression in demonstrated efforts to reconstitute sex. *Eva's Man* should be read within these sociosexual, cultural, and legal contexts, as Jones participates in these while simultaneously subverting a black Victorianism—a "culture of dissemblance" and politics of silence—that compromises black sexuality.

To this end, *Eva's Man* issues indictments, which, even as they are far more nuanced than overt, are nonetheless extensive. The novel, be it deliberately or inadvertently, offers a harsh castigation (one not always immediately transparent) of all who enable and enforce—whether through silent participation, acquiescence, or violent aggression—problematic racialized sexual entanglements and models. These encompass the infliction of sexualized violence; the suppression of discourses on and progressive practices regarding sexuality; the regulation of female sexuality through men; the embrace of male sexual aggression and domination as intrinsic, rather than detrimental, to hetero-sexual intimacy; and/or the positioning of heterosexuality as normative and hegemonic—which do not go without critique. It becomes an attack not only on the body, a corporeal infliction, but emblematizes a greater symbolic attack on the systematic violence against black women's (and men's) bodies historically.

Published in 1976 during the Black Power and Black Aesthet-ics movements and under the editorship of Toni Morrison at Random House, *Eva's Man* does not subscribe to the conven-tional politics governing black literature or that of the black literary establishment of the post-1960s (nationalist) era. Yet to reduce or subject *Eva's Man* to a narrow reading that sug-gests it excoriates (or dissociates itself from) black politics, such as those of racial uplift and black consciousness advanced by the nationalist agenda, would be simplistic at best and an over-sight at worst. The novel critiques black people, but also, more importantly and harshly, the larger systems that methodically buttress or sanction problematic elements. Institutions that are emblematic of the system at large, including law, the authorities, prisons and law enforcement, are scrutinized in the novel for their accountability in creating social problems.

Thus, even as the novel appears to conspicuously reify stereo-types (such as the black whore and black brute) that have histori-cally pathologized black people and black sexuality, *Eva's Man* also provides insightful commentary, ironically, on stereotypes of black sexual pathology, which it does namely, I would sug-gest, through overexaggeration and titillation. In other words, the novel manipulates and mocks these stereotypes, driving them to extremes in uber-exaggerated form, to illuminate the ludicrous, insanely troubling nature of such skewed construc-tions of blackness and black sexuality. As Madhu Dubey deftly notes in her analysis of the novel in *Black Women Novelists and the Nationalist Aesthetic*:

> *Eva's Man* repeats and recycles a limited number of sexual stereotypes in a stylized manner that forces us to regard

black sexuality as a textual fabrication rather than a natural essence. The problem with *Eva's Man*, then, is not that
it fails to critique the stereotype of the primitive black, but
that this critique is not explicit enough [. . .]. The "perverse ambivalence" of *Eva's Man* derives from its reluctance
to pass unequivocal thematic judgments on the racist and
sexist stereotypes of the past, and its failure to offer a new
set of positive and politically useful images of blacks.[1]

While I concur with Dubey's assertion, I would also suggest
that, in order to engage and critique these larger dynamics, both
ambivalence (vis-à-vis textual incomprehensibility) and madness
serve as means by which this is done. As such, the text never offers
a linear, absolute, or overtly definitive stance or addresses myths
governing black sexual pathology. It is, however, worth noting
that Jones's own use of the narrative defamilarizes convention.
In the same way that Eva transgresses convention, Jones (and the
text) transgresses and elides particular literary "norms," politics,
and "unequivocal judgments," including the dynamics confronting her as a black (female) writer who produced this novel during
the Black Arts/Aesthetics Movement. While there were particular expectations for black writers, as has historically been the
case for African Americans in the literary establishment, Jones
confronted certain choices, if not Black Aesthetic "mandates":
to promote representations of blackness that were racially righteous, that challenged racism and the systematic oppression of
blacks, and that embraced a politics that elevated black identity
rather than issued "assaults" against it. In other words, black writers, including Jones, confronted issues concerning what literary
scholar Biman Basu insightfully recognizes as politics over aesthetics, content or form, and ideology versus ontology.[2]

Eva's Man, and Jones as writer, transgresses categorization in that it does not transparently embrace these dynamics,
which accounts, in part, for its intense scrutiny. In an interview
entitled "About My Work," Jones ruminates on her position as
author, especially as it relates to writing, politics, and artform:

I am interested principally in the psychology of characters [. . .]. For this reason I cannot claim "political compulsions" nor "moral compulsions" if by either of these one
means certain kinds of restrictions on "imaginative territory" or if one means maintaining a "literary decorum." I
am interested in human relationships, but I do not make
moral judgments or political judgments of my characters.
Sometimes I will allow certain characters to make moral
judgments of other characters. I will allow certain characters to be didactic—mostly when I do not share their views.
I am not a didactic writer. Characters and readers have the
freedom of moral judgment. For instance, my disapproval
of Eva's action/choice (in *Eva's Man*) does not enter the
work at all. She simply tells her story. I allow her to tell it,
as much as she will tell.[3]

Jones's reflection reveals the extent to which she does not feel
obliged to acquiesce to the impositions or requisites confronting
black writers. Nor does she feel compelled to uphold a politics of
respectability in terms of representations of blackness. Because
Jones's novel neither overtly embraces certain racial politics nor
transparently resists and/or excoriates racism, it has been scrutinized beyond the point of derision; and, it also has not always
received analyses along the broader spectrum that it merits.

Instead of reading *Eva's Man* as a "depoliticized" text, then,
it might be more beneficial to consider the degree to which it
serves as a "critique of a narrowly defined multiculturalism (and
narrowly defined ideological criticism sometimes associated
with it)" that "in the spirit of broadening its range, may instead
lead to richer readings of black women's fiction."[4] This "multiculturalism," in larger terms, might be read more specifically as
a particular racial politics or politics governing race and racial
representations. Previous scholarship has analyzed this novel in
insightful and provocative ways. I am less interested in reading
Jones's novel in terms of whether it meets or betrays Black Aesthetic politics, privileges feminism, or acquiesces to dominant

pathologies in its depictions of black men and women. Nor am I vested in analyzing madness as either a universal theme or a "sign" rooted in a certain particularity.

Locating *Eva's Man* within a continuum of transgressive black women characters, whose instantiations of (mis)behavior are strategic, I am interested in the ways in which a politics of race is filtered through a nebulous madness, with sex/sexuality ultimately serving as the playing ground of transgression that permeates the novel. In what ways, that is, and as this chapter has already begun to assess, does Jones's novel build upon and utilize transgression, as it intersects with sexuality and pertains to the "norm" and the limit, to broach or circumnavigate particular sociocommunal issues and offer commentary on post–civil rights racial/sexual politics? How does silence in its duplicity function in the text to both maintain and mediate, as well as contest, the problematic politics through deliberate suppression (or nonexpression) in private and public spheres? And, in what ways is madness deployed to the extent that it, in and of itself, operates as transgression that strategically enables a traversal of the established norm and the limit?

In his 1963 essay "A Preface to Transgression," Michel Foucault theorizes about the interface of the limit and transgression, particularly as these relate to sexuality. "We have not in the least liberated sexuality though we have, to be exact, carried it to its limits: the limit of consciousness; the limit of the law, since it seems the sole substance of universal taboos; the limit of language."[5] "It is not through sexuality that we communicate," he further notes, "with the orderly and pleasingly profane world of animals; rather, sexuality is a fissure—not one that surrounds us as the basis of our isolation or individuality" but, instead, one that "marks the limit within us and designates us as a limit."[6] Whether in terms of sexuality or in its various manifestations, transgression has a consequential relationship to the limit. As that act, provocation, or gesture that traverses the limit—crossing and penetrating it—transgression exceeds, if not ultimately violates, the very boundaries the limit regulates. The limit and transgression rely, dialectically, on each other for meaning as well as existence: without the limit, that is, there would be no parameter in need of sanction that transgression might exceed; as such, transgression would cease to exist, at least in its current state, thereby no longer operating with the same essence, meaning, or relevance. What makes the interplay between the limit and transgression even more complex is that "these elements are situated in an uncertain context, in certainties that are immediately upset" by disruption so that "thought is ineffectual as soon as it attempts to seize them."[7]

This section begins with an evocation of transgression and the limit, marked by both certainty and uncertainty as it intersects with "thought," to elaborate on transgressive behavior. Whereas chapter 3 foregrounds an iteration of transgression predicated on the individual, a prioritized self invested in mutual personal and universal racial/communal freedom, transgression might also be understood as contestation or contestatory acts that exceed and violate the limit. "Violates" is the operative word, as it is precisely a violation of—or violence against—boundaries, whether sexual, racial, gender, or psychological, that are not only traversed but obstructed. Such instantiations of transgression are evident in Gayl Jones's 1976 novel *Eva's Man*, which provides rich insight into the linkages between transgression and the limit, as these very dynamics—the "play" between the limit and transgression, and an incessant crossing and recrossing of boundaries—pervade Jones's text. What I suggest is that in *Eva's Man* transgression manifests not only in its physicality but also vis-à-vis linguistics and an iconography marked by a perversity of desire that almost always erupts into violence. These, in turn, are mediated by "the uncertain," as well as "certainties," while shrouded in an ambivalence of madness, the material and psychological embodiment, whether real or performative, of transgression. Put another way, transgression manifests as a dynamic that exceeds comprehension: it cannot be articulated or understood in terms of reason. Jones limns individuals, Eva particularly, ensnared in sexual(ized) violence, transgression, and putative "madness" or mental/psychic instability. Society, including the psychiatrist and cellmates, characterize Eva and the (sexualized) assault of her lover as an irrational act of madness precisely because they cannot convey in words—there is no language, rhetoric, or logic—by which to explicate/understand her extreme excoriation of patriarchal sexual domination. Her violent act should, then, be interpreted as transgressive violence against or the demise of patriarchal racialized/gendered/sexualized limits placed upon her.

Narrated from the vantage point of Eva Medina Canada, the female protagonist incarcerated in the psychiatric ward of a prison (after committing the horrendous, fatal sexualized crime of poisoning and then *orally* castrating her lover Davis), the narrative betrays linearity, logic, and conventional realism in the same way that Eva transgresses boundaries and convention. In her narration, Eva often vacillates between streams of consciousness and linearity (rationality/comprehensibility) and nonlinearity (irrationality/obfuscation), which results in shifts between "the uncertain" and "certainties" in terms of thought, consciousness, and temporality. Past and present, the cerebral and visceral, even sanity and madness collide and, to some extent, emulsify in ways that stymie coherence, order, structure, or the ability to distinguish between varied events.

"Thought," truth, and accuracy/reality are in flux and rendered unreliable, if not downright inexplicable, to the extent that they resist simple or easy interpretability, as the following scene—Eva's recollection of her ex-husband James's reaction when her male classmate randomly appears at their home—makes transparent:

> [James] didn't say anything [. . .], and then he just reached over and grabbed my shoulder, got up and started slapping me.
> "You think you a whore, I'll treat you like a whore." [. . .]
> Naw, he didn't slap me, he didn't slap me, he pulled my dress up and got between my legs.

"Think I can't do nothing. Fuck you like a damn whore."
Naw, I'm not lying. He said, "Act like a whore, I'll fuck
you like a whore." *Naw, I'm not lying.*
I squeezed my legs around his neck.[8] (original emphasis)

This scene makes conspicuous the degree to which interpret
ability and coherence are suspended. Not only does this occur
because of the questionable nature of Eva's recollection, wherein
she asserts one version before digressing into another scenario,
but also because of the degree to which the scene itself, in both
words and actions, resembles Eva's account of other occurrences
that cross time and circumstance. Reverberating in this scene,
then, is another exchange that Eva witnesses several years prior,
at age twelve, between her parents, when a relatively similar
scenario unfolds. Eva's father, John, arrives home from work to
find his wife, Marie, with her lover, Tyrone, who is ten years her
junior. Eva recalls the encounter, particularly how her parents
"dealt" with it, as she listens outside the confines of her parents'
closed bedroom door:

> [I]t was like I could hear her clothes ripping. [. . . N]ow he
> was tearing that blouse off and those underthings. I didn't
> hear nothing from her the whole time. [. . .]
> "Act like a whore, I'm gonna fuck you like a whore. You
> act like a whore, I'm gonna fuck you like a whore."
> He kept saying that over and over. I was so scared. I kept
> feeling that after he tore all her clothes off, and there wasn't
> any more to tear, he'd start tearing her flesh. (37)

The questionable nature of the narrative, based on Eva's recollections, confounds as much, if not more, than it reveals. The
occurrences are imprecise, whether a reflection of the inaccu-
racy of memory, madness, or an otherwise deliberate obstinacy,
as evidenced by the subjective nature of her language. Phrases
such as "it was like" and "I kept feeling that," lack authority,
concreteness, and definitiveness to the extent that the account
is unsubstantiated and, indeed, nebulous. Moreover, they are

characterized by relativity ("it was like") versus a delineation of what it *actually* was, and are described based on the visceral ("I kept *feeling* that") rather than the rational.

This same ambivalence, as well as fluidity of thought and events, permeates the entire novel, erupting invariably into and giving rise to transgression. Sexuality, intimacy, and varying gradations of desire—as this very desire intersects with and spawns violence—are deployed, as is transparent in the above-quoted scenes, and incites transgression, which manifests in actions and words wherein sexuality transposes into an excessive perversity; desire erupts into violence marked by extremities; and silence, while multifaceted, is characterized by an insidiousness that threatens, compromises, and even (especially in Davis's case) exterminates. In the previously quoted scene between Eva and her then husband James, she recounts a violent act—a physical assault, a grabbing of shoulders and slapping—after which she issues a corrective: "Naw, he didn't slap me, he didn't slap me, he pulled my dress up and got between my legs." Even in its unreliability, violence is present and takes shape not only as physical assault, but within a sexual terrain that parallels the sexually aggressive exchange between Eva's parents. Violence is marked by, as well as accompanies, sexual torment, perverse excess, and a maddening silence within the context of punitive sexual recourse. While this interplay among sexuality, (sadomasochistic) violence, silence, and transgression exists—and these entanglements are mediated through "madness"—their overarching function in *Eva's Man* is strategic—to offer larger commentaries on the politics of race, particularly as it interfaces with gender, sexuality, and desire.

As Candice Jenkins asserts regarding sexual intimacy, violence, and desire in *Eva's Man*, "[I]ntimacy among black subjects always brings with it the specter of violent physical and emotional assault. Indeed, representations of desire in Jones's text [. . .] appear to be merely forms of *gendered sexual* interaction" yet might be "better understood as interpretations of *cultural* desire" (emphasis mine).[9] The "perverse and overlapping relation between sex and violence," she further avers, "has a racial component."[10] Much like Jenkins, I recognize these apparatuses as symbolic of a larger racial desire; yet, I would extend this even further by suggesting that this very racial desire, especially as it pertains to transgressive black women characters, is a racialized desire steeped not so much in an assault against black sexuality, literally or metaphorically. Rather, it is geared precisely toward *reconstituting* the politics of race, as it intersects with gender and sexuality, to engender a more complex black identity and postmodern black sexuality.

As I have argued previously, transgressive behavior, as well as racialized gender transgression, and sexuality serve pivotal roles in post–civil rights novels. *Eva's Man* is, of course, no exception. If transgression "is not sexual license," but, rather, "concerns knowledge and power, which are expressed in the conditions of sexuality," then the regulation of sexuality or "prohibition" becomes a source of power that not only restrains the body but also controls "knowledge and social action."[11] In *Eva's Man*, these very sensibilities manifest, taking shape in her sexual interactions with Davis. While she engages in sex with him, and sex that is consensual, it is simultaneously accompanied by restraint and prohibition. Even as she engages freely, she is, all the while, confined to the room in a way that marks her sexual exchange, paradoxically, with consent and constraint, freedom and suppression. If sexuality emblematizes and serves as a means of power that "restrains" when regulated, Eva's killing Davis—especially in a sexualized act that, literally, attacks the phallus and masculinist hegemony—becomes symbolic of agency, the demise of (cumulative) sexual aggression and restraint, and a subversion of patriarchal sexual control. Liberating sexuality, and in this case *black sexuality*, from regulatory practices—whether historically racist and sexually criminal acts or communally inflicted violations, strategic dissemblance, and regulations—rectifies a past, offers possibilities, and shifts the dynamics where power, agency, and autonomy are concerned.

Given this correlation between transgression and sexuality, as well as how they interface with social power and the political, sexuality—in its various enactments and instantiations in *Eva's Man* and other post–civil rights novels analyzed in this study—functions not merely as a trope. As elucidated previously, it also serves as a *signifier* of desire and efforts toward a more complex "blackness" or black identity ungoverned by outmoded racial politics and its attendant conventions regarding gender and sexuality. Black women's transgressive behavior, like transgression itself, functions in *Eva's Man* as a strategy by which to destabilize and disrupt a particular politics governing race: one based on essentialist constructions of "blackness" that circumscribe black womanhood, black female sexuality, and black sexuality at large. As such, the violence that accompanies sexual intimacy is metaphoric: first, it is emblematic of the historical brutalities and sexualized crimes against black bodies—entrenched and exacerbated by a communal silence—that result in an infliction (a re-infliction of sorts) of violence upon itself. Second, it is also indicative of the ways in which race and sexuality imbricate in not only the sexualizing effects of racism but also in the racialization of sex(uality). For, as Sharon Holland notes, the "first sexual revolution" transpired during slavery, wherein black bodies and black sexuality were accessible to whites whose command over blacks took shape in all forms, sexually, corporeally, and otherwise.[12] Sex in slavery entailed, and might indeed be conflated with, atrocities against the body, with the sexual violation of black bodies representative of the wide-ranging dehumanization, historical conquest, and desire to conquer "blackness" that, concomitantly, involves conquering/controlling black sexuality.

"I Got Started Like Everyone Else Does [. . .] I Opened My Legs": Sexual Politics, Violence, and Desire in *Eva's Man*

In *Eva's Man*, Jones illustrates these very notions regarding sexuality as an apparatus that has historically and systematically been used to subjugate, violate, and oppress. Just as sexuality has the ability to restrict and suppress, if it is to be liberated (and *liberating*), it necessitates rescue, and indeed transformation, especially where gender dynamics are concerned. This is, in part, what Jones attempts to illumine in *Eva's Man*. In this regard, the treatment of sexuality, as well as its function, in Jones's text is incomparable to the other novels in this study given the extent to which it is extremely overt and violent—not representative of black sexuality but more a commentary on its potential state. In *Eva's Man*, sexuality, perverse eroticism, and sexualized violence are ubiquitous, as sexual tension pervades and always escalates into violence; and, Eva, unlike most other characters, is always already confronted with it as if it is inevitable. Even as a child, full sexual disclosure is not precluded, as she learns at an early age about the precariousness of sex(uality). As an only child growing up in her two-parent home, one of her earliest recollections is that of her family and its unconventional dynamics. Such memories are not so much of its nuclear structure, but rather an infringement upon it, as evidenced by her mother's lover, Tyrone, and her extramarital affair:

> What I remember about the musician [Tyrone] was that he was ten years younger than my mother. [. . .] When my mother and the musician started going together, my father said nothing. He knew what was going on, but didn't say anything at all. My mother knew he knew, but she would bring the musician home when my father wasn't there. My father would know he'd been there, though, because the musician used to open his packets of cigarettes upside down. [. . .] And so when my father came home, whenever he'd been there, there'd always be an empty packet of cigarettes in the house, opened upside down. After a while it got so every day there was that packet of cigarettes. (25)

While Eva's memory of this is unquestionable, as it is not characterized by a stream of consciousness, the passage is as suggestive and telling as it is rife with symbolism of the sexual. Eva never names Tyrone—consistently referring to him as "the musician," which is, in and of itself, somewhat detached and distancing—in the same fashion that her father, John, while aware of the affair and its intrusion upon his marriage, does not express anything: at least nothing verbally, in a way that evades and makes it appear as if they are "normalized" behaviors/circumstances.

Moreover, the cigarettes, conspicuously symbolic of sexuality, serve as phallic symbols. In the same way Tyrone's presence, sexually and otherwise, inverts and disrupts—even violates, figuratively and literally—the fidelity and sanctity of Eva's parents' marriage (and the family), so, too, are the cigarettes opened backward a metaphoric manifestation of the same inversion of (sexual) access. In other words, Tyrone's uncustomary opening of and access to his cigarettes are emblematic of the same breach and intrusion—adultery and infidelity—that are wreaking havoc in John and Marie's union. Of equal import, whereas there is no "politics of silence" in the form of dissemblance surrounding sexuality, silence is present in another overarching form that is equally deleterious: the silence, that is, that falsely appears as indifference regarding the violation of the sanctity of their marriage. This dynamic appears "normative" since John and Marie go on as if everything were fine: "What was really strange, though, was they still slept together. [. . . T]hey made love as if Tyrone wasn't happening" (29). Yet, on the other hand, in the absence of vocalized contestation, the silence transposes instead into physical enactments of sexualized aggression, such as John's displays of violent desire and perverse excess, in his invective "Act like a whore, I'm gonna fuck you like a whore. You act like a whore, I'm gonna fuck you like a whore" (37). As noted earlier, Jones plays with the pornographic, which reflects the temporal moment in which the book was published during the sexual revolution and "sex wars"/"porn wars" of the 1970s and 1980s. In this context, John and Marie's sexual exchanges lend themselves to a complex, rather than monolithic, reading of the sexual, sexual aggression, and the pornographic—or what constitutes the obscene.

The scene might be read, on the one hand, then, as John's attempts to (over)compensate, through violently aggressive and dominating sexual behavior, for his lack of control over his wife's sexuality and the overall sexual dynamics of their relationship, as well as the state of sanctity (or lack thereof) in their marriage. This sexualized violence and overall sexual exchange, sadomasochism of sorts, between the two is not eroticism but, rather, perversity of desire. In Audre Lorde's theorization of the erotic and pornographic, she argues that "the erotic has often been misnamed by men and used against women. It has been made into the confused, the trivial, the psychotic, the plasticized sensation" and has been falsely confused "with its opposite, the pornographic. But pornography is a direct denial of the power of the erotic, for it represents the suppression of true feeling. Pornography *emphasizes sensation without feeling*."[13]

Lorde's explication of the nexus of eroticism and the pornographic illuminates the textual/sexual dynamics governing John and Marie's sexual exchanges, as well as his language, in which resonates a rhetoric situated within a pornographic lexicon that denies feeling for the sake of sensation, titillation, and sexual fantasy. John's actions, contextualized as such, renders his exchange pornographic, as sensation (without feeling): the ripping of clothes degrades the body in the same fashion that his words—"act like a whore"—diminish and reduce Marie not to a particular humanity or essence but to an empty sexual (and even objectified and pathologized) state. Marie, in turn, is the recipient, quiet and willing to "take it how he gives it," enabling his sensation and sexual domination in his attempts to recover his threatened masculinity. John, through sexuality, virility, and sexual domination, attempts to display masculine strength, or a semblance of it, that is vexed and problematic at best.

On the other hand, one might argue that Lorde's conceptualization of the erotic/pornographic polarizes these entities that are, otherwise, not mutually exclusive. To this end, her assessment of pornography as "sensation without feeling" denies (a politics) of *pleasure* and, furthermore, affect, where sexuality and the pornographic are concerned. Put another way, pornography is not monolithic and embodies a complexity that lends itself (and in turn the scene with John and Marie) to another, more complicated reading that foregrounds sex acts and pleasure outside the domains of "illicit eroticism," to evoke black feminist and sexuality studies scholar Mireille Miller-Young's conceptualization.[14] When analyzing black women's sexuality, it is important, then, to move beyond the "tendency to foreground examinations of black women's sexual exploitation, oppression, and injury at the expense of analyses attentive to black women's sexual heterogeneity, multiplicity," sexual desires, or "the various forms of black women's pleasures," as Jennifer Nash argues.[15] For, even as it is imperative to be "mindful of the ways that dominance can disguise itself as pleasure (and to the ways in which dominance and pleasure are often coconstitutive)," we must be attentive simultaneously "to pleasure in the hopes of creating a rupture in the dominant subordination narrative, a gap that can produce space for imagining the critical linkages between black female sexuality and black female subjectivity."[16] This is, in fact, in part, what Jones does with the novel in that, just as she deploys ambivalence that challenges readability, as well as that suspends judgment with regard to transgression and the incessant crossing of boundaries or the limit, so, too, does she also use ambivalence as a strategy to problematize, if not deconstruct, what constitutes eroticism, obscenity, and the pornographic. For, "theorizing a feminist pornography" necessitates "thinking about a dual process of transgression and restriction" to expose the nexus of race, sex, the pornographic, and how "black female sexuality is sutured to racial histories that inform [. . .] fantasies," even when, at times, the fantasy is "power through aggression and submission."[17] Reading John and Marie's sexual exchange as such underscores, again, Jones's efforts to complicate black sexuality, illuminating not only its complexities but also, vis-à-vis ambivalence, what constitutes pornography, eroticism, and black racialized sexuality.

For Eva, infidelity, perverse excess, and violent sexuality are "instructional" and formative, even as things go unspoken. By her own account, she "kept thinking that [her mother] would start explaining things, but she didn't" (27). What she witnesses in her parents' behavior (and the silence that makes them seem "normative") parallels what characterizes almost all of her own firsthand encounters: sex always manifest as inexplicably violent, excessive, or pornographic. Violated early on with a "dirty popsicle stick" by a little boy her own age, Eva, throughout her childhood and adulthood, is bombarded by inappropriate sexual gestures that run the gamut from sexual "dirty talk" to molestation to rape: "Tyrone puts my hand on his thing. Then he jams himself up inside me" (125). While we learn early on (in the same scene wherein her father comes home and sees Tyrone there) that Tyrone "took my hand and put it on him," it is not until much later, in fact moments before Eva kills then castrates Davis, that we learn that she has, all the while, endured rape by Tyrone. Even in exposing it, this disclosure receives no privileged position but is revealed randomly through interpolation in an amalgamation of thoughts and events that transpired during different junctures rather than sequentially:

> "When you going to feel me again?" [Tyrone]
> No answer.
> "How long has it been, honey?" [Elvira]
> "It's been a long long time." [Eva]
> Mr. Logan is an old owl perched on the stairs.
> Mama says, "Ain't no man I wont but you."
> Daddy says, "Why'd you take him on then?"
> Tyrone put my hand on his thing. Then he jams himself up inside me. (124–25)

Revealed on a relatively climactic note among variegated events, it is abrupt, intrusive, and unexpected—presumably in the same fashion as the rape itself. While each of these is a separate singular experience, they are neither disparate nor extraneous, yet are conflated in the same way they are consolidated in the narrative. At the crux of each is sexuality: predatory like an enactment of molestation as in the case of Tyrone with regard to Eva; solicitous as in the case of Elvira, Eva's same-gender loving cellmate; and adulterous with regard to Eva's parents. She is bombarded by sex—intrusive, predatory, obstructive, and destructive—to the degree that there becomes no real escape. These events become largely conflated and almost indistinguishable, as evidenced in the passage above. As such, time, circumstance, and even the referents—who is saying what, when, and where—elide easy distinction.

The extent to which Eva is inundated by sexually aggressive and inappropriate circumstances, especially to the point that they seem almost monolithic, is also evident in other instances. Beyond her early violation with a "dirty popsicle stick" and later rape by Tyrone, even Eva's cousin Alfonso is relentless in his solicitation of sex that ranges from wanting to "feel her up" to a desire to actually "get her started." Even blood ties or familial relations do not protect her from male sexual aggression. While she runs away, escaping Alfonso, her interactions with Moses Tripp—whom she meets at a bar and stabs in the hand in self-defense from sexual violation—make evident her subsequent refusals to tolerate inappropriate sexual advances. Because she does not delineate to the authorities what circumstances led to her committing the crime, she, at age seventeen, serves time in prison, where, ironically, she meets and later marries her husband, James Hunn: a fifty-two-year-old man whose initial gestures of "tenderness" toward her later evolve into masculine power and domination.

The incident with Moses Tripp foreshadows what happens with Davis Carter, whom she later meets at a bar and "shacks up" with briefly, before killing him with poison and then castrating him. And while she never explicates what exactly led to her horrendous crime—his confining her to his apartment, her discovery that he is married, and/or his sexual dehumanization of her—what does become evident is that Davis embodies the cumulative sexualized aggression and male sexual hegemony that she has experienced throughout her lifetime. "'You know what I think,'" the psychiatrist asserts to Eva during a session, "'I think [Davis] came to represent all the men you'd known in your life'" (81).

In his essay on escape in the fiction of Gayl Jones, literary critic Jerry W. Ward Jr. notes that "the thinking in *Eva's Man* shows paralysis of consciousness, the inability to make certain decisions"; Eva "is the victim of her own passivity, her tendency to accept the *Playboy* fantasy of what a woman is. Her life history contains a series of sordid, dehumanizing sexual encounters."[18] Ward's reading of Eva is based on a characterization of Eva as engendering a passive acquiesce to skewed conceptualizations, based on *Playboy* iconography and constructions, of what constitutes a "woman" that fundamentally implicates her and assumes she is responsible for her own purported degradation—sexual and otherwise. Given the aforementioned instances in which she does *not* acquiesce but rather flees or inflicts violence, I would argue otherwise: that, while Eva is often silent, her nonvocality is a deliberate resistance to vocalized expression that, in and of itself, overturns assumptions regarding her passivity. Such silence should not, then, be confounded and read as indecisiveness, acquiescence, or passivity, especially if passivity signifies silence rooted in Eva's "acceptance of the words and definitions of others."[19] Eva is not so much paralyzed by complacency, nor does she capitulate to narrow masculinist fantasies of women as sexual objects for male sexual gratification or definitions others impose upon her. Such readings castigate, or at the very least implicate, Eva, while exonerating the sexual dehumanization she encounters—and later inflicts upon Davis as retribution for the cumulative sexual violations she has endured—and the larger social structures that perpetuate such conceptualizations of women. Instead, Eva, as well as the men she confronts throughout her life (and even the other couples throughout the novel—John and Marie, Jean and Alfonso, Queen Bee and her string of lovers), is caught in a conundrum of tenuous sexual politics laden with violence, tension, and problematic gender dynamics.

What Eva experiences, along with other couples, are problematic politics governing gender and sexuality that forestall what feminist scholar Barbara Ehrenreich recognizes as "opportunit[ies] for men and women to [. . .] meet as equals without the pretenses involved in gender roles, and to get together against" their "common sources of oppression."[20] In other words, they need models of relationships not fraught with sexual tension but characterized instead by a different set of sexual politics. As Patricia Hill Collins deftly notes, "[s]exual politics can be defined as a set of ideas and social practices shaped by gender, race, and sexuality that frame all men and women's treatment of one another, as well as how individual men and women are perceived and treated by others."[21] These dynamics surrounding sexual politics, particularly men's perception and treatment of women, are concretized in *Eva's Man* and manifest especially in Eva and Davis's interactions.

Upon first meeting Eva, Davis makes certain assumptions that later inform his treatment of her: "'A woman like you.' [. . .] He laughed. 'A mean, tight mama, ain't you? A old woman got me started. [. . .] You a hard woman, too, ain't you? I know you got yourself started. [. . .] Have you been satisfied?'" (8). Davis's perceptions of Eva seem to suggest that he recognizes in her an intrinsic deviation from a particular type of womanhood: one not steeped in convention, especially where sexuality is concerned, but that is, more or less, in tandem with stereotypes of black women as licentious, the embodiment of excessive sexuality, and an insatiable libido, that—resisting masculine regulation—becomes the object of male sexual desire. His designation "a woman like you" situates her outside the "normative"—as uncustomary, atypical, aberrant—with her sexuality neither contained nor defined by anyone outside herself. His vocative, too, has masturbatory implications—"I know you got yourself started"—to which Eva, in an assertion both declarative and corrective, asserts, "'I got started like everyone else does, [. . .] I opened my legs" (8). Eva reveals that her sexuality is marked by not only a "normativity" (like "everyone else"), but, concomitantly, by a sexual agency in that she, in opening her legs, regulates the terms of her sexuality. She resists being categorized or, contrastingly, situated within particular sexual loci that either obfuscate and mark her sexuality as anomalous or that seek to circumscribe it.

Eva later shows the extent to which she is not so much outside conventionality when she analogizes her and Davis's intimate rendezvous to that of a married couple, to which Davis responds otherwise and reveals his own marital status:

> "It's like you were a husband," I said.
> He looked at me hard. He was frowning.
> "I mean you slept with me while I was bleeding, like a husband would, and didn't try to arouse me till I was ready."
> "What's a man for?"
> "Why you want me?" I asked.
> "Only to ride you."
> "You said you used to work with horses."
> "Yeah, that's how I got away from my . . . wife. Brought some horses up this way, and stayed."
> "You didn't tell me you were married."
> "I thought I told you."
> "No, you didn't tell me." (95)

What this passage, which reveals otherwise undisclosed interiorities, exposes is that Eva's and Davis's sexual experiences are polarized. Whereas she analogizes him to a husband—thereby, in essence sanctioning their sexual intimacy—he likens her to a horse, reducing their relations to the animalistic, wherein sex with her translates not into intimacy but copulation. His assertion that he wants her only to "ride her" is reminiscent of his initial impressions of her as the embodiment of unbridled and "anormative" sexuality. To "ride," denotatively speaking, is to sit on, to manage, or to be carried to a finite destination (by an animal or inanimate object). It involves motion and a transitive element that does not entail reciprocity or a mutual exchange, in ways that render it exploitative. Davis's assertion that he wants to "ride" her typifies another dynamic: the sexual, the exploitative nature of sexual regulation, and—to allude to my previous discussion—the nexus of sexuality, power, knowledge, and control/conquest. Eva serves, to this end, as the means by which Davis reaches his "finite destination"—sexual stimulation, gratitude, and climax—in his "rein" (literally and figuratively) over Eva during their sexual engagements. Thus, in his notion of wanting "only" to "ride" Eva reverberate the ways sex, power, and conquest imbricate. Moreover, this scene, surprisingly, is one of the few instances in which, first, Eva is vocally expressive (with her expression marked by comprehension and linearity versus a stream of consciousness and unreliability) and in which *she* initiates dialogue; and, second, sexual intimacy is *not* punctuated by violent excess or other extremities of desire.

The scene is marked, however, by a particular emotional and psychological assault that alters the terms of their sexual engagement. Eva reverts back to and is once again overcome by silence (non-speech or vocality), to which Davis responds by asking her to "[s]ay something." After this she reveals, through narration not verbalization: "He turned me toward him, and went in me" (102). Not only does this reflect the degree to which Eva now experiences sex (not in a matrimonial but rather an intrusive sense), whereby Davis dictates the terms of engagement. But it is also emblematic of the pornographic, based on Lorde's assessment in which Eva merely becomes the conduit by which Davis experiences sensation, simulation, and sexual ecstasy without feeling. In his assessment of the novel, Jerry Ward notes that what Eva learns is sex "got from the street": "From the university of the streets," he writes, "Eva learns that sex is fucking and women are bitches and men are eternally on the watch for a good lay. She has the will to resist sexual abuse, but the will is stunted."²² While provocative in its notion of "sex got from the street," I would argue and indeed add one critical distinction. Eva's will to "resist" sexual abuse is *not* so much stunted as her will to contest and inflict sexual abuse is both *intensified* and *actualized*.

Davis goes even further by locating her outside the "normative" in a degrading fashion that reduces her to stigmatization:

"You ain't natural. [. . .] Shit, if you was natural, you wouldn't even be here, woman. You wouldn't even a let Davis Carter lay a hand on you. Not for free" (121). As when he initially met Eva, Davis imposes certain mischaracterizations upon her that mark her as licentious to the extent she embodies "illicit" sexuality; and his assertion that she is "unnatural" exacerbates things— situating her as the embodiment of promiscuity that exceeds the confines of a sexually conventional and "natural/norm" culture.

Eva's contestation manifests in reciprocity vis-à-vis her infliction of sexualized violence against Davis, who, in his verbal and physical sexual dehumanization, incites transgression. After lacing his drink with poison and killing him, Eva's transgressive behavior extends even further:

> I opened his trousers and played with his penis. My mouth, my teeth, my tongue went inside his trousers. I raised blood [. . .]. I got back on the bed and squeezed his dick in my teeth. I bit down hard. [. . .]
>
> I got the silk handkerchief he used to wipe me after we made love, and wrapped his penis in it. I laid it back inside his trousers, zipped him up. [. . .]
>
> The blood still came through.
>
> "Bastard."
>
> I reached in his pants, got my comb, took the key he'd promised, washed my hands, finished my brandy, wiped his mouth, and left. (129)

Since black male bodies, when sexualized, are reduced to a fixation on the black male penis as "distillation of the essence of Black masculinity," in her contestation, Eva not only kills Davis but, in attacking his penis, the phallus and material embodiment of masculinist sexual hegemony, she also squelches his dominance sexually and otherwise. As sexual power and authority for men are linked to the phallus, it serves as a marker of masculinity.[23] Eva refuses to be a passive or ornamental entity whose sexuality is regulated or confined in the service and sexual gratification of Davis and men. In taking the mutilated penis in bed, engaging with it on her own terms, she executes her own agency, pleasure, and gratification—sexual and empowering, even if grotesque—that diminishes masculinist sexual power and domination. In her transgressive behavior she, like transgression generally, not only marks the limit—crossing and violating it—but also designates the limit. Her contestatory act is, then, an instantiation of transgression. Contestation, as Foucault reminds us, "does not imply a generalized negation, but [. . .] a radical break of transitivity.[. . .C]ontestation is the act that carries them all to their limits"; thus, "to contest is to proceed until one reaches the empty core where being achieves its limit and where the limit defines being."[24]

"A Woman Got to Be Crazy to Do Something Like That. [. . .] Or Want You to Think She's Crazy": Madness and Transgression

The previous section describes contestatory acts as embodiments of transgression that penetrates, defies, and violates the limit. How, then, might we consider these dynamics—transgression and the limit, the boundaries—when they are interspersed with and involve madness? Madness, in this sense, defamiliarizes rationality, reason, and/or linearity and is the very entity that ruptures, if even momentarily, the limit. In *Eva's Man*, "madness," as it intersects with sexualized violence and entrapment, pervades with a certain particularity. As I have illuminated, transgression manifests in enactments of perverse desire and sexuality that erupt into violence that is, in turn, mediated invariably by "the uncertain" and "certainties" embodied in an ambivalence of madness.

As such, madness emblematizes insanity—a fracture or lapse in sanity—as well as operates as a complicated performed action that, calculated, facilitates an evasion of the limit: whether that limit is conventionality with regard to the politics governing sexuality, gender, race, established "normality," or the law. Madness, especially within racialized contexts involving individuals who have been marginalized historically, as is the case with black people, offers possibilities of agency and freedom, if even temporarily, in relation to what was otherwise restricted. Richard Wright's introductory manifesto, "How 'Bigger' Was Born" in *Native Son* helps make this more transparent. In his description of various types of Bigger Thomas(es), the protagonist of his novel, he asserts the following:

> The Jim Crow laws of the South were not for [Bigger]. But as he laughed and cursed and broke them, he knew that some day he'd have to pay for his freedom. His rebellious spirit made him violate all the taboos and consequently he always oscillated between moods of intense elation and depression. [. . . H]e was sent to the asylum for the insane. [. . .]
> The Bigger Thomases were the only Negroes I know of who consistently violated the Jim Crow laws of the South and got away with it, at least for a sweet brief spell.[25]

Wright's description helps elucidate the nexus of madness, race, gender, and the law, wherein a resistance to capitulate or embrace Jim Crow politics (laws that, in and of themselves, were biased and insanely nonsensical) provides momentary subjectivity and liberation for the otherwise disempowered, disenfranchised, and/ or marginalized. Rebelliousness and recalcitrance in the face of restriction (or the limit) land the transgressor in an asylum labeled as "mad," or living out another possible ending that, nonetheless, offers temporary relief and/or freedom from the limit. And so, the "oscillation" of Bigger between "intense elation and depression" is consequential and loaded. It is emblematic of the elation that accompanies the luxury of partaking in the freedoms of indulgence in the putative "norm" (access to which is restricted and not extended to all); yet, it quickly transforms into depression, the material/psychological condition that ensues as a consequence of both denial and the transgressor's reacclimation to disempowerment. This same nature surrounds madness in *Eva's Man*, wherein Eva transgresses several "taboos"—particularly those pertaining to gender, sexuality, and womanhood—while concomitantly gaining access to power in her eventual rejection of gendered sexual hegemony. And, she, too, ultimately lands in an asylum: the psychiatric ward of a prison.

Because of the type of crime Eva commits, her status is dubious and defies comprehension; and, in her resistance to vocalizing precisely why she inflicts sexualized violence of such proportions on Davis, her transgressive behavior is inexplicable, though always associated and linked with a particular "craziness." As Eva's cellmate Elvira asserts, "You know, I ain't seen you laugh, I ain't seen you cry, I ain't seen you do nothing, cept breathe hard last night. You too serene. When a woman done something like you done and serene like that, no wonder *they think* you crazy" (155, emphasis mine). What stand out in Elvira's assertion are the operative words *"they think* you crazy," indicative of thought and a projection of insanity or psychosis onto Eva versus any indication or declarative affirmation (or, for that matter, diagnosis) as to whether she *is* indeed crazy. Because Eva commits a crime, especially one that is unfathomable and a severe breach of convention, she is associated with madness since such behavior, otherwise, has no label—no language, words, or terminology—by which to explain it in a rhetoric that is coterminous with or reflective of the act. It literally *transgresses* language and comprehension. This inability to understand and comprehend is evidenced in the degree to which Eva is interrogated not only by the police, the psychiatrist, and news reporters, but also by her cellmate Elvira. They simply cannot understand—it does not render itself subject to logic or reason—and they are left with the incessant and inevitable question: Why? "Why did you kill him? [. . .] Why did you think you bit it all off?" (167).

Madness, in and of itself, and especially in Eva's case, is an iteration of "the transgressive." Since reason and rationality have been constituted as "normative," reason "is found in the strategies, disciplines, technologies, and tactics which power exercises over the body."[26] Transgression marks, as well as resides in "the divisions that constitute [. . .] rationality: madness and reason, the true and the false, [. . . the individual and society, [. . .] words and things, the confined and the free, repression and liberation, [. . . and] life and death."[27] Given the nexus of reason, which precludes madness and transgression, what disrupts and temporarily suspends these divisions? When calculated and methodical, madness throughout the novel enables Eva to evade these seemingly dichotomous and oppositional divisions, so much so that she does not have to accept or embrace one polarization over the other. All of these, in fact, exist at some point concomitantly. Madness, embodying incoherence, nonlinearity, and a lack of interpretability, also meets with reason. What is true and false meshes, ironically, to the point that they become indistinguishable and resist substantiation. The confined and repressed, paradoxically, are also, if even momentarily, liberated and free; and life, when not extricated and squelched, is characterized by a nihilism or fatalistic quality that resembles a type of (living or social) death. Madness, thus, becomes the guise and a strategic pretense through which transgression is enacted, enabling a suspension of rules in that she engages in a contestatory act—a crossing of the boundaries of acceptable behavior—yet she also does not suffer the most stringent of consequences. Imprisonment, confinement within the psychiatric ward, while a result, still enables Eva to transgress more egregious or harsher forms of criminal punishment.

Madness, whether real or performative, functions as a conduit by which to present these possibilities. What Jones's narrative presents ultimately—in all its extremity, violent excess, and obscurity—is a way of considering racialized sexuality as it relates to the larger politics governing gender ideologies and race. While Jones, to revert to her assertion in an interview, posits that she does not impose judgments or claim that "political compulsion" informs her writing, this does not at all render *Eva's Man* or the characters apolitical. What the novel does do, in fact, is intervene in larger discourses regarding politics of race, gender, and sexuality—about black sexuality and wholeness—and what might disrupt sexualized bondage. And, too, it illuminates other dynamics that somehow fragment and flaw black subjects, as almost all of the characters of the novel themselves are flawed. The novel, thus, "speculates on how the oppressed subject might negotiate these structures of violence," as Biman Basu posits, and "what the dismantling of a phallogocentric structure might entail, so that, if the violence is disturbing," it underscores rather than defines "the violence of the discursive formations which circulate around and circumscribe the subject."[28]

The degree to which this occurs—and to which the text calls to attention the problematic of expressing particular dynamics, especially sexuality within the context of a narrow politics— is concretized in the novel's closing scene. After Eva had long resisted Elvira's sexual advances, her cellmate, in an act of cunnilingus at last, asks Eva to "Tell me when it feels sweet, honey" (177). Eva, leaning back "squeezing Elvira's face between [her] legs," affirms "Now." Whereas sexuality throughout the novel has been marked by violence and a perversity of desire, as well as silence, this same-sex intimate moment, even one Eva herself had resisted, does not incite transgression or violent aggression. On a climactic and conclusive note—"Now"—the text, as does Eva, embraces not limited and rigid expressions of sexuality marked in silence, dissemblance, or heteronormativity. Instead, it vocalizes, in the same manner Eva asserts her voice in the affirmative ("Now"), a transformative way of viewing sexuality and its potentialities. This is not to suggest that the novel presents same-sex intimacy or desire as the only liberatory possibility for racialized subjects. What it does suggest is that transformative politics do not come in restrictive or unitary form. To revert to the novel's title, who, then, is Eva's "*man*," especially since the text concludes with her engaged in the act of cunnilingus with Elvira? While this question and many others throughout the text resist answers or explicability, one thing is transparent: limits, not unlike their counterparts—taboos—may not necessarily be destroyed, but they can indeed be contested and *transgressed*.

5 /   "Between a Rock and a Hard Place": Gloria Naylor's *The Women of Brewster Place*

> *[Black women] writers take us into the minds of their women characters, where, in the silence of their thoughts, the women define their own humanity as something far larger than the sum total of roles and images created by others.*
>
> —GLORIA WADE-GAYLES

Literary theorist Mae Henderson asserts that black women's literature necessitates readings and interpretations of the ways in which "the perspectives of race and gender, and their inter-relationships, structure the discourse of black women writers."[1] What she calls the "simultaneity of discourse" is intended to transcend the relegation of black women's identities to a homo-geneity that does not give credence to their multiplicity of expe-riences. Thus, she proposes a model that addresses "a subject en-gendered in the experiencing of race" while *simultaneously* addressing "a subject 'racialized' in the experiencing of gender."[2] Such an approach lends itself to fuller analyses of the totality of black women's experiences, black womanhood, and paradigms of "otherness."

This last chapter of *Unbought and Unbossed* begins with such an invocation because it is precisely this consideration of race and gender, as they interlock and manifest in conjunction with other dynamics, that informs Gloria Naylor's 1982 novel *The Women of Brewster Place*. A novel in seven stories, Naylor foregrounds and explores the experiences and interiority of seven black women through various personal vignettes within a certain communal/geographical specificity: the dead-end street of Brewster Place. Black women and black women's experiences are not monolithic, hence Naylor's utilization of myriad black female characters: "One character couldn't be *the* Black woman in America," as she notes in an interview, "so I had seven different women, all in different circumstances, encompassing the complexity of our lives, the richness of our diversity, from skin color on down to religious, political and sexual preferences."[3] What she illustrates is a gesture toward a postmodern blackness, in that, while these women share certain affinities as black women, their lives are marked concomitantly by a politics of difference that stymies false assumptions that render black womanhood, sexuality, and experiences absolute, singular, or homogeneous. Naylor illuminates that, in their differences and heterogeneity, each of these women encounters dynamics that expose particular commonalities that govern their lives.

The Women of Brewster Place, much like the other novels examined in *Unbought and Unbossed*, was produced in the post–civil rights era. In its representations, it speaks to the politics of race, particularly with regard to sexuality and black womanhood—addressing larger issues concerning blackness in a postmodern era. If postmodern blackness is characterized by a transcendence of "unitary definitions of racial identity and its centralizing of race," specifically blackness "as the sole axis of all emancipatory politics," Naylor's novel dramatizes this assessment, as the various characters engage these very dynamics and call attention to the politics of race, gender, and sexuality in their transgressive behavior. In its critique of essentialist politics and paradigms, Naylor's novel, like the other texts examined throughout this study, simultaneously privileges *race as engendered* and *gender as racialized*, to advert to Henderson, in ways that illuminate the matrix of experiences, "multiple identities and divergent interests within the category of blackness" that her black women characters embody.

The expression "between a rock and a hard place" used in the chapter title suggests a dilemma, which is remarkably fitting while exploring the vexed dynamics in *The Women of Brewster Place*. Naylor's characters encounter various predicaments that they eventually transcend, all the while negotiating them, particularly in the sexual realm, within the confines and limitations of "a hard place": the brick wall of Brewster Place, which, allegorically, marks certain confines, regulations, or circumscriptions customarily placed on female sexuality and black womanhood. What differentiates Naylor's novel from other texts analyzed in this study, with the exception of *Eva's Man*, is that sexuality is not shrouded in what historian Darlene Clark Hine identifies as a "culture of dissemblance," nor is there typically—as in the case of *Sula*, *Loving Her*, or *Meridian*—a public stigma attached. One exception in *The Women of Brewster Place*, arguably, is the story of lovers Theresa and Lorraine, told in "The Two," which I will examine in greater depth later. Instead, sexuality is acknowledged and embraced, not only in its physicality and complexity, but also within both the public and private sphere. Sexuality is not relegated to a state of pathology, reduced to the stereotypical or homogeneous, or regulated invariably by men. Rather, its various manifestations are explored, rather than suppressed, by women exerting agency.

While myriad representations and experiences of black women pervade Naylor's novel, this chapter explores the ways in which sexuality is interwoven, both overtly and in nuanced ways, into the tapestry of their lives and the larger narrative of individual and, ultimately, communal/collective healing and empowerment. What I suggest is that Naylor utilizes a sexual continuum—from asexuality to hyper(hetero)sexuality, lesbianism and same-gender loving to conventional and compulsory heterosexuality—among other instantiations of sexual expressions and desire as a way of illuminating the degree to which these subjects are, at once, *engendered* by race, *racialized* by gender, and both *engendered and racialized by sexuality*. Ultimately, through their various enactments of sexuality, as well as instantiations of transgression, these women characters offer larger commentaries on race, gender, and sexuality, as well as illuminate their own personal and larger communal exigencies for a new racial politics governing gender, sexuality, and black female sexual citizenship.

In her provocative essay "Framing Sexual Citizenship: Reconsidering the Discourse on African American Families," historian Melinda Chateauvert elucidates the correlation between sexuality and citizenship, particularly in a black racialized context, as well as characterizes sexuality as a locus by which "individuals construct and organize their sexual lives, choose their sexual partners, and discover erotic pleasure."[4] Equality in terms of citizenship necessitates equity in both the social and sexual terrain concomitantly, as well as one's agency with regard to the structure and status of her sexual life, as she insightfully elucidates:

> The concept of sexual citizenship is one approach for framing a racial history of sexuality. Sexual citizenship means the adult right to organize one's sexual life and household as one desires, and to have one's privacy respected and recognized [. . .]. I [. . .] reassess the ways adult men and women organized their households and lives, employing the concept sexual citizenship to consider the ways they challenged the prescriptions for respectability.[5]

Chateauvert's explication of citizenship from a sexual vantage point is revealing, as it calls attention to sexual subjectivity not contingent upon institutions, like marriage, or entities that would otherwise sanction sex; and it also delineates the nexus of race and sexual freedom, as it relates to efforts to exceed respectability, a historic and methodical practice confronting blacks and overshadowing their sexual politics. Whereas sexuality was sanctioned exclusively within the context of marriage—and individuals performing sex outside of those boundaries were penalized (as social policies and some laws indicate)—Chateauvert redefines the function of sexuality, as well as one's right to express it outside of narrow confines.

What she postulates in terms of sexual citizenship, and the freedom to express one's sexual character as the inherent right of all citizens, is provocative; and these very notions of sexual agency and diversity within a black context are, in part, what Gloria Naylor foregrounds in *The Women of Brewster Place*, wherein she addresses black sexual behavior in the era of the sexual revolution, and how sexuality, race, and citizenship imbricate in the lives of black women. Through a literary context in which these dynamics are inscribed and enacted in each of the vignettes of her text, Naylor effectively illuminates the ways in which each of her characters negotiates her sexuality, whether in vexed or tenuous circumstances. Moreover, she demonstrates the degree to which the issue becomes not so much whether the sexual revolution has bypassed black people—to revert to my treatment in the introduction—but, rather, the notion that "the new black reality commands not only greater attention," but also a "new politics of sexuality," to evoke poet-scholar June Jordan, for liberation that is transformative.

"No Young Woman Wants an Empty Bed": Transgressive Black Women and Sexuality in *The Women of Brewster Place*

The Women of Brewster Place opens, not unlike *Sula*, with a genealogy of the community: Brewster Place, with its conception as "the bastard child of several clandestine meetings" between city officials in a smoke-filled room.[6] Its conception was as illegitimate as the individuals, especially its third generation of residents (blacks), were presumed to be. The first character to which readers are exposed is Mattie Michael, with her deep Tennessee southern roots and a respectable livelihood steeped in devout Christianity. Her experience is marked by a fundamentalist-like rigidity concerning sexuality, based on a religious moral code dictating that sex be "saved" until marriage. "Saved" is the operative word, as it evokes the religious sensibility, as well as rhetoric, that characterizes those who abide by the religious dogma, biblical and institutional, and would be "saved": meaning they would enjoy the pleasures of heaven versus their counterparts, "sinners," who would putatively have a less fortune fate.

Mattie's story, her "genesis" and point of unravel, occurs when she, while intending to preserve her sexuality and "save herself" for marriage, gives into carnal pleasures when she accompanies Butch Fuller, a young attractive, agnostic womanizer, to cut sugarcane and pick herbs. The scene/venue is rife with sexual symbolism: the cane, metaphoric phallic symbols, and the herbs are representative of a "naturalness"—the organic bounty and productive/generative aspect of nature—emblematic of the naturalness of sex that, otherwise, in the religious tradition is repressed and associated with sin (unless it is within the sanctioned confines of marriage). While with Butch—and with absolutely no knowledge of sex and deeply grounded in religion, including its dogmatic restrictions governing fornication/sexuality—she feels, for the first time, certain "disquieting stirrings at the base of her stomach": "new feelings" that consume her to the point she "felt she had somehow drifted too far into strange waters and if she didn't turn around soon, she would completely forget in which direction the shore lay—or worse, not even care" (14–15). Having suppressed the sexual, Mattie is unaware of the power of the erotic and her very own sexuality, having been the only child within her deeply devout (respectable) two-parent Christian household, where no discourse on sex existed as it was considered outside religious dialogue or the sanctified church. Caught in a religious and sociosexual conundrum, she succumbs to her carnal pleasures, swept away by Butch's charm, sensuous nature, and virility. After their sexual intimacy in the herb patch, she becomes pregnant (the reproductive capacity of sex), later giving birth to a son she fittingly names Basil. When she refuses to disclose his paternity, it causes an upheaval and beating that accounts for her eventual departure from her parents' home.

Mattie heads to North Carolina, secures a job, and never marries, choosing instead to raise her son alone; and her sexual life is nonexistent by her own choice and inclination. Based on textual inferences, her single sexual encounter with Butch, in which she begets their son, Basil, is her only sexual experience. As a single mother with a child, Mattie's status and subject position are questioned and difficult to negotiate, as is especially evident in her attempts to secure housing. She must confront and navigate her way around interlocking apparatuses: her race, gender, and sexuality concomitantly. Denied housing by white landlords because of her race, she fares no better in the "neatly manicured black neighborhoods," emblematic of a black respectability, in which her gender/sexual status—as an unmarried woman with a child born out of wedlock—marked her as "unacceptable." Moreover, it constitutes an explicit and visible breach of the classical black female script, those culturally prescribed mandates governing "acceptable" black womanhood. As mentioned, it is constituted by black women's expected racial loyalty and solidarity, sexual fidelity to black men, self-abnegation, and the idealization of marriage and motherhood. While she does not violate the script entirely, she does transgress its tenets pertaining to the regulation of black women's sexuality through black men, as well as overstep its mandates governing marriage. Issues of legitimacy, or lack thereof—her being a single mother—take shape in the queries of those she meets, "Where's your husband?" to which her response would invariably incite a disapproving, "'This is a respectable place!'" (30).

As a subject with exterior visible evidence, a child, that she has transgressed the behavioral and sociosexual strictures for women, Mattie is denied far more than housing. "Unmarried persons are punished" and are "denied sexual citizenship" by "society for their 'transgressions'"; and, "as sexual subjects, rather than sexual citizens, African Americans have historically been punished and victimized for asserting their sexual independence and seeking control over their own bodies."[7] Mattie, consequently, is unable to secure housing; and she eventually takes up residence in the private home of Eva Turner, a five-time widowed woman who is raising her granddaughter (Louciela, who is Basil's age) after the child's parents ran off. Unlike those who discriminated against Mattie, "Miss Eva" is nonjudgmental regarding Mattie's breach of the "politics of respectability" and mother-out-of-wedlock status, yet, paradoxically, she later scrutinizes Mattie on the basis of her sexual disposition:

> "'Tain't natural, just 'tain't natural." [. . .]
>
> "What I'm talkin' 'bout is that I ain't hear you mention no man involved in all them exciting goings-on in your life—church and children and work. It ain't natural for a young woman like you to live that way. I can't remember the last time no man come by to take you out." [. . .]
>
> "Ain't you ever had no needs in that direction? No young woman wants an empty bed, year in and year out."
>
> (36–37)

Interestingly, Miss Eva's rhetoric, her assertion that "'tain't natural," resembles—as it alludes to chapter 4's discussion of *Eva's Man*—Davis's assessment that Eva Canada's sex "ain't natural." In Mattie's case, its purported lack of naturalness stems not from her giving sex up but, contrastingly, from her not engaging in sexual intimacy at all. What Miss Eva's commentary regarding Mattie's sexuality does generally is call into question the "normativity" and privileging of sexual preservation, whether abstinence or celibacy, in organized/orthodox religion. What is "unnatural," as Miss Eva underscores, is a polarization or extremity based on the rigidity of religious doctrine and sociocommunal sanctions that renders one's sexuality so close to nonexistent that it is nearly exterminated.

Whereas Miss Eva is not fixated on Mattie's matrimonial status, then, she, diverging from others, interrogates her sexual subject position in ways that, ironically, render Mattie's conscious celibacy, rather than her sexual encounters outside the institution of marriage, as uncustomary. It also importantly marks the often contradictory nature of and impositions on black female sexuality, as well as the ways it is pathologized as unnatural whether it is preserved or deployed. Mattie, particularly her sexuality, indeed transcends homogeneity and is characterized by a complexity that resists singular or absolute terms, definitions, and/or stereotypes. It is marked by unconventionality in the loaded sense of the word. On the one hand, it transgresses convention as being unregulated through marriage and by men, yet it is, on the other hand, not customary in that it embodies celibacy that renders it nonexistent practically to the point of asexuality. As such, her sexuality is, to evoke black feminist scholar Evelynn Hammonds, "simultaneously visible (exposed) and invisible" to the extent she signifies a "black female body [that] has so much sexual potential" while she simultaneously "has none at all."[8]

Replete with both visibility and invisibility, Mattie's sexuality elides categorizations, especially dichotomous constructions as essentially "illicit" and promiscuous/hypersexual or its polar opposite, as wholly nonsexual/asexual. She problematizes these categories, but also personifies a complexity that complicates, if not resists them in ways that not all characters of the novel do. As such, she overturns trite stereotypes of black women, particularly the dominant images in the American literary and cultural imagination that pathologize and obfuscate their sexuality: namely, those of the mammy and the jezebel. While she might seemingly embody the asexual mammy, Mattie's more than latent sexuality (emblematized and made visible by her child) disrupts that paradigm; yet, her conservatism where sexuality is concerned does not align her with the sociosexual qualities, an imputed hypersexuality, of a jezebel. Still, like most of the women who reside in Brewster Place, where Mattie eventually lands, she defines her own sexuality, which encompasses sexual autonomy and freedom. Not only does she control her own body, but also governs the fundamental terms of her sexual expression—if even her desire for a lack thereof.

Etta Mae Johnson, Mattie's good friend with southern roots and a penchant for experiencing the fullness of life, is the quintessence of uninhibited female freedom and sensuality. She is neither restrained by rigidity nor encumbered by sexual codes steeped in dissemblance or provincialism. She embodies a subversive nature and defiant spirit, transgressing circumscriptions governing race, gender, and sexuality while invariably contesting the "norm." As the omniscient narrator delineates, Etta "spent her teenage years in constant trouble. Rock Vale had no place for a black woman who was not only unwilling to play by the rules, but whose spirit challenged the very right of the game to exist" (59). Leaving Rock Vale, she travels abundantly, only to realize that "America" itself "wasn't ready for her yet—not in 1937" (60). Etta, a woman before her time and one unwilling to acquiesce and ascribe to the conventions governing womanhood, leads a life and engages in conduct that are not part of the classical black female script; instead, she is, like the records she carries with her, emblematic of the blues. She possesses a consciousness and has experiences not steeped in victimhood—as in the "my man has done me wrong" blues sense—but, rather, in the female liberatory sense that is marked by enactments of autonomous desire.

As feminist scholar-activist Angela Davis observes, the blues signify a particular "politicalization of sexuality" in that they represent an exceptionally rich locus:

> The overarching sexual themes that define the content of the blues form point the way toward a consideration of the historical politics of black sexuality. Considering the stringent taboos on representations of sexuality that characterized most dominant discourses of the time, the blues constitute a privileged discursive site [. . .], illuminat[ing] the politics of gender and sexuality in working-class black communities.[9]

Moreover, she discusses the relationship of blues to a particular feminist consciousness, which Etta embodies, in that it offers a counternarrative or deviation from the established cultural "norms" and paradigms, especially in terms of sexuality and its provocative depictions of women's independence and "representational freedom." Blues singers often experimented with established sexual "norms" in their performances—discursively, lyrically, and musically—in ways that complicated sexuality.

In her 1928 song "Prove It on Me," Ma Rainey, a leading black woman blues singer, offers a treatment of putatively "non-normative" female sexual longings in overt lyrics in which she openly expresses sexual desire for women. Rainey's performance is emblematic of the performative nature of gender and sexuality, as her song's persona demonstrates. She concomitantly challenges "normativity" and opens space for liberatory sexual politics and nonconformity. The song's persona, its narratorial consciousness, flaunts a particular sexual fluidity and diversity. On the one hand, her sexuality, namely her desire for women, is visible and overt in her declaration of her penchant for female company: when she goes out at night with a group of friends, she asserts it was "women," of course, because she "don't like no men." Moreover, this fluidity manifests in a performative gesture and aesthetic through clothing and the semiotics of attire, as she prefers to dress in "collar and tie" or traditional male accoutrements. Yet, her sexuality and desires remain, contrastingly and paradoxically, private and shrouded: "Don't you say I do it, ain't nobody caught me. You sure got to prove it on me." In its "invisibility" and the fact that "nobody caught" her, as the lyrics suggest, her sexual and intimate preferences, as well as desires, remain within the realm of speculation: the claim goes unsubstantiated without confirmation or proof of the reality of her sexual engagements.

As the discussion of same-gender loving in chapter 2 made transparent, sexual labels do not (always) encompass a person's sexual expression or experiences; and, as the persona of Ma Rainey's song suggests, one's sexuality is complex; as such, anyone who wants to label her or her sexuality will have to "prove it on me." Moreover, like Ann Allen Shockley, Ma Rainey elucidates that sexuality is a constellation of desires and intimate acts along a continuum rather than along a linear or bifurcated trajectory. Rainey thus complicates the working-class blues by imbuing them with a certain black middle-class respectability and formality that resist categorizations as "aberrant." All of this relates to Naylor's character Etta, who is emblematic of a blues lyricism of unbridled sexual pleasure that privileges sexuality, a fullness of life, and "sexual imagery." She experiences what feminist scholar Lynne Segal identifies as a reclamation of "sex for women" that does not merely "liberate women in the process"—whereby sex becomes a conduit *for* liberation—but, rather, whereby women, in this case Etta, engage in "liberated sex."[10] Etta especially demonstrates this in her utilization of sex in what she considers "business opportunities" (61). She ends up on Brewster Place after stealing the car of the affluent married man with whom she had an affair. When he refused to give her either air- or train fare, she takes his car, as she would "be damned if [she] was coming into the city on a raggedy old Greyhound" (58). She is able to not only make it to the city, but is also able to sell the car for a couple of thousand dollars until another "business opportunity" presents itself; and, because her lover was the son-in-law of the sheriff, Etta need not worry about any legal ramifications of her transgressive conduct. Thus, her flouting of sexual codes—breaking of the law and rupturing of the limits constituting transgression—is concretized in her affair with the son-in-law of the sheriff, an allegory for the law, legal authority, and the system itself.

Etta attempts to enact another business opportunity, whereby she would snatch up a visiting pastor, the Reverend Moreland Woods, of Mattie's church, in an effort to secure herself a life of privilege, comfort, and affluence. In a church scene reminiscent of Helga Crane in Nella Larsen's *Quicksand* (1928), Etta enters the church, where "[s]he stood out like a bright red bird among the drab morality that dried up the breasts and formed the rolls around the stomachs of the other church sisters"; she was, as the narratorial voice delineates, a woman "still dripping with the juices of a full-fleshed life" (67). While she attracts the attention of the pastor and leaves the church with him, he recognized the "type of woman" Etta was and "marveled at how excellently she played the game" (71). Their sexual exchange, rather than eventually leading to the marriage that Etta was trying to orchestrate, takes the form of a one-night stand. Her plans are as "dead-end" as Brewster Place. Nevertheless, Etta is not dispirited and remains as transcendent as ever. As the omniscient narrator illumines, both walked away on equal terms:

> [T]he whole business had gone pretty smoothly after they left the hotel. He hadn't even been called upon to use any of the excuses he had prepared for why it would be a while before he'd see her again. A slight frown crossed his forehead as he realized that she had seemed as eager to get away from him as he had been to leave. Well, he shrugged his shoulders and placated his dented ego, that's the nice part about these worldly women. They understand the temporary weakness of the flesh and don't make it out to be something bigger than it is. (73)

Interestingly enough, the passage is narrated from the reverend's perspective. Characterized as "business," as a transaction, the reverend and Etta's sexual exchange is just that; and, more precisely, it reflects the "free love"—sexuality unrestricted or confined exclusively within the realm of heterosexual marriage—of not only blues lyricism but also the sexual revolution era informing the text. Sex between Etta and the reverend, then, is a corporeal enactment characterized by physical gratification devoid of emotion. In it also resonates the notion that, at the crux of women's and sexual liberation was its very "redefinition of sexuality stressing women's autonomy and right to control their own bodies [. . .] in a society at best ambivalent, and more often antagonistic, towards any such notion."[11]

It is precisely this notion with which the reverend must contend; for, upon his realization that Etta is no more intent than he on future encounters and as relieved as himself to part, he attempts to assuage his fractured male ego by characterizing Etta as a "worldly" woman—one outside convention and, even more precisely, the church. The paradox, however, is that his conduct as a preacher is far less conventional than Etta's since he violated the rules of the religious practice he chose and in which he was ordained. The reverend judges his own behavior gently as "temporary weakness of the flesh," displacing his own sexual indiscretion onto Etta, who "got out of the car unassisted and didn't bother to turn and watch the taillights as it pulled off down the deserted avenue adjacent to Brewster Place" (72). "Black male sexuality differs from female sexuality because black men have," as Cornel West posits, "different self-images and strategies of acquiring power in the patriarchal structures of white America and black communities."[12] Whereas Reverend Moreland anticipated governing the terms of their next encounter and having control over whether or not it ever occurs, Etta, in a move that exposes her own sexual autonomy, transgressive behavior, and empowerment, expects nothing more in a mutual discontinuation of sexual engagements. She walks away, disregarding the reverend, just as he ostensibly would have done. And so, even if Etta did not necessarily beat him at his own "game," she did alter the rules of engagement, renegotiating, as she always does, the fundamental right of the game to exist.

This scene and Etta's cumulative experiences with the reverend offer another critique of religion that parallels the problematic dynamics it presents in Mattie's situation regarding sex as unorthodox. Yet, instead of a castigation of religion for a repressiveness that leads to experimentation and negative consequences (pregnancy, in Mattie's scenario), the critique here is of the inhibitions in the preacher, who, despite his religious position, operates off of lust and a masculinist hegemony regarding Etta. He attempts to attain sexual gratification through an objectification and reduction of her to a sexual being—or, in his words, a "worldly" woman. In this regard, he commits "fornication" in the Greek and loaded sense of the word in that he engages in "the objectification of another human being for the purposes of self-gratification."[13]

If Etta Mae Johnson is unconventional, lovers Theresa and Lorraine not only transgress convention, contesting limitations placed on race and gender, but also challenge the narrow confines of female sexuality, especially as it relates to and is encumbered by heterosexism and heteronormativity. Of the various stories and vignettes that comprise the novel, Theresa and Lorraine's narrative is the only one in which the chapter is not titled after the name of its main characters; instead, it is entitled "The Two." This omission of names and lack of specificity is indicative of a larger elision concerning black female same-sex desire, same-gender loving, and lesbianism. It characterizes them, furthermore, as "the two," evoking the notion that they embody a "unit," a togetherness, coupled in ways that both unite and consolidate, as well as conflate.

Theresa and Lorraine's story begins with an "outsider-within" perspective—"At first they seemed like such nice girls"—in the same fashion in which they, as black same-sex lovers, occupy a similar positionality, as both outside and within a sense of belonging and disbelonging, in Brewster Place.[14] What is striking about the opening is the operative word "seemed" is deployed in conjunction with Theresa and Lorraine's status of "nice girls"—the language and rhetoric encapsulates a loaded terminology in which reverberates a "politics of respectability." The assessment of Theresa and Lorraine is, then, that their sexual identities as same-sex lovers, as nonheterosexual women, becomes linked to an intrinsic quality that purportedly precludes "goodness" and thereby marks them as "anormative," aberrant, and far from the "sugar and spice and everything nice" construction of female identity.

Even as they do not receive proper names or distinction in their title, in the narrative they are far from indistinguishable or monolithic, as they are characterized as having various traits, if even, as the narrative demonstrates, based on exterior qualities:

> The women of Brewster had readily accepted the lighter, skinny one. There wasn't much threat in her timid mincing walk and the slightly protruding teeth that she seemed so eager to show everyone in her bell-like good mornings and evenings. Breaths were held a little longer in the direction of the short dark one—too pretty, and too much behind. (129)

Still not yet referenced by name but differentiated based on phenotypic characteristics, skin tone and bodily features, Theresa and Lorraine are reduced to a fixation on their bodies and physical attributes that, problematically, does not extend beyond these aesthetic features; yet, on the other hand, they also embody dimension and characteristics that resist their conflation into absolute or singular categories that would relegate them and lesbians, as well as same-gender loving women generally, to undifferentiated types. They are imbued with a desirability and such qualities as that of being aesthetically pleasing—"pretty"—in ways that disrupt stereotypes and false, illusory conflations of lesbians and same-gender loving women as outside the beauty status quo: as ugly and sexually diverse because of their undesirability which, in turn, links with an inability to attract men. Just as Naylor demonstrates the heterogeneity that exists among black women within a specific communal locale, as evidenced by her dramatization of the lives of seven women, so, too, does she rescue black lesbians and same-gender loving women from a homogeneity that would otherwise render them and their experiences monolithic.

While both of them love women sexually and emotionally, they differ on both experiential and ideological levels. Lorraine's first lover was a woman while she was in high school, and since then she never had a male lover or sexual encounters with men. Because she possesses knowledge of and conviction about her sexual character and intimate desires for women, when her father found a letter from her high school lover, Lorraine refused to lie about its fundamental meanings. As a result of embracing her sexuality and sexual attraction to women, she is kicked out—in an excommunication from her family—and not even allowed to take anything beyond the clothes on her back. Even in her conviction, she has a complex relationship to the designation "lesbian" and what it entails; her very existence, as well as what she embodies, challenges the hegemonic domains of heterosexuality, yet she also does not necessarily embrace, at least not comfortably, a subject position that renders her an outsider in ways that exclude her from community or reduce her to something that, in the words of Miss Eva, "'tain't natural."

> I've accepted it all my life, and it's nothing I'm ashamed of. I lost a father because I refused to be ashamed of it—but it doesn't make me any *different* from anyone else in the world. [. . .]
> There are two things that have been a constant in my life since I was sixteen years old—beige bras and oatmeal. The day before I first fell in love with a woman, I got up, had oatmeal for breakfast, put on a beige bra, and went to school. The day after I fell in love with that woman, I got up, had oatmeal for breakfast, and put on a beige bra. I was no different the day before or after that happened. (165)

Lorraine is wholeheartedly accepting of her sexuality, yet she rejects, as well as excoriates, a relegation to a politics of difference based on her sexual preference and desires. Her essence is intrinsically what it is—constant and stable prior to and subsequent to her acting upon her sexual desires for women—and, as such, no word, especially the designation "lesbian," reflects or defines what constitutes her or her (sexual) existence. Thus, even as she embraces her sexual diversity/identity in the face of her expulsion from her childhood home, she also argues that her very sexuality, in and of itself, is by no means an axis around which a politics of difference operates.

Theresa, unlike her lover Lorraine, has a sexual history characterized by a complexity of diverse sexual experiences with both women and men, complicating efforts to situate or categorize her within a particular type of sexual designation. And, much like Lorraine, she is unapologetic for her sexual history or preferences: "'There's nothing disgusting about [sex with men]," as she tells Lorraine. "You've never been with a man, but I've been with quite a few—some better than others. There were a couple who I still hope to this day will die a slow, painful death, but then there were some who were good to me—in and out of bed" (138). Theresa complicates the rigidity surrounding sexuality, especially what constitutes lesbian identity, much like that of Renay in *Loving Her* who refuses to allow reductive sexual terminology to serve as a reflection of her sexual preferences and sexuality. Theresa, however, embraces the designation "lesbian," even as her experiences exceed myopic categorizations; moreover, recognizing the limitations of labels that do not aptly reflect but rather obfuscate more than they represent her (sexuality), Theresa also refers to herself and Lorraine in a language that is politically incorrect and sexually derogatory. She, on the one hand, uses the very labels to which society at large would, because of their sexualities, reduce them; but, she also uses that particular rhetoric in a way that is somewhat empowering, demonstrating that no words, even those, can define or encompass the complexity of her essence.

Theresa and Lorraine "come to see themselves as lesbians in quite different ways. [. . .] Both women prefer women to men, but they differ dramatically about what that choice means. Theresa insists that being a lesbian means that you are different by nature and thus outside of society, which punishes you so intensely, while Lorraine detests the word *lesbian*, insisting that she is not different from other people."[15] Even while the two women differ ideologically, as well as have their own idiosyncrasies and sexual experiences, their dialogue serves a consequential role in that it is not merely discourse but, rather, is emblematic of the agency these women possess individually in terms of their autonomy, self-definition, and interiority. Delineating the correlation between agency in the narrative sense, which ultimately becomes emblematic of it at large, literary scholar Marilyn Farwell postulates, "Agency in the narrative is a function of women coming together on a narratological level as protagonists of their own story and as narrators of their own inner thoughts. The otherwise confusing set of narrators" puts "in motion a number of separate narratives, a narrative of facts in each woman's life and an inner, psychological narrative explaining her motives and justifying her actions."[16] Its tautological nature notwithstanding, Farwell, like many feminist scholars, illuminates the correlation between narrating one's story and agency. Her assertions, coupled with the experiences of Theresa and Lorraine, illustrate the ways in which the two women, in their very agency, are empowered but also serve as agents or conduits by which female bonding occurs on an individual and larger collective level: they, in what she considers an alterative approach to reading "the two," "are not primarily victims or outsiders; instead, they form the metaphoric center of the female bonding that becomes a powerful narrative agent by the end of the text."[17] The accuracy or validity of her assessment is contingent, however, on what constitutes bonding and also how these dynamics are enacted. Theresa and Lorraine's presence, as well as their status as same-gender loving women, does become the center of attention and discourse within larger communal realms, as evidenced in the Brewster Place Block Association meeting.

While the residents of Brewster Place come together to rally against the negligence they experience as tenants in the building, Sophie, a neighbor who lives across from Theresa and Lorraine—and whose suspicions regarding them are confirmed when she witnesses them in a provocative situation through their unshaded window—attempts to galvanize the community against what she considers "that bad element that done moved in this block amongst decent people" (140). It escalates into a larger conversation, open for public and communal consumption, wherein the other women on Brewster Place disagree with Sophie, whom they essentially think has no business inserting herself into the personal affairs of the two women. Even as Sophie attempts to have the tenants of Brewster Place evict Theresa and Lorraine, whom she argues are "sinning against the Lord," others, especially Mattie and Etta Mae, point to the complexity of the Bible in terms of people, like Sophie, not "be[ing] a busybody in other people's matters," as well as her "let[ting] the Lord take care of it" (140). Ultimately, if anyone is ostracized, it is Sophie rather than Theresa and Lorraine. What this reflects are the redemptive powers of the Bible and biblical discourse that challenge a politics of repression and admonition generally associated with sexuality, especially "illicit" sex outside the confines of marriage, in institutionalized/organized religion. Moreover, even as they question privately the relationship between "the two," Mattie and Etta eventually conclude that, "'I've loved some women deeper than I ever loved any man, [. . . a]nd there been some women who loved me more and did more for me than any man ever did. [. . .] Maybe it's not so different. [. . .] Maybe that's why some women get so riled up about it, 'cause they know deep down it's not so different after all'" (141).

In the public setting and in their private dialogue about Theresa and Lorraine's sexualities, Mattie and Etta, among other tenants, refuse to demarcate and alienate "the two" on the basis of their sexual character, nor do they ascribe power to difference. Instead, they bond together in allegiance rather than allow something, in this case one's sexual preference, to militate against solidarity and divide them. They challenge reductive conceptualizations and notions regarding lesbianism, even delegitimizing rationalizations based on biblical ideologies or readings. What they do, then, is destabilize the politics of difference, engaging instead in the process of female bonding and solidarity. As Audre Lorde contends with regard to black women, sexuality, and bonding:

> As Black women we have the right and responsibility to define ourselves and to seek our allies in common cause [. . .]. But most of all, as Black women we have the right and responsibility to recognize each other without fear and to love where we choose. Both lesbian and heterosexual Black women today share a history of bonding and strength to which our sexual identities and our other differences must not blind us.[18]

Lorde's assertion is remarkably applicable to The Women of Brewster Place, wherein these very dynamics of female bonding, regardless of sexual preferences or parameters, resonate throughout the novel. Lorde's words also substantiate the idea that Theresa and Lorraine are agents of female bonding.

If Theresa and Lorraine function as agents or conduits by which bonding in the female and communal sense transpires, it is not always, if ever, in the most ideal of circumstances, as is the case with Lorraine's horrendously brutal and violent gang rape by C. C. Baker and four members of his outlaw clique. Homophobic beyond the point of viciousness, C. C. and his gang, "born with the appendages of power," vilify lesbianism, same-sex desire, and all that Lorraine embodies. Cornering her in an alley, they gang rape her not only to assert hegemonic masculinity and heterosexuality, but also to "obliterate" her sexual desires for women:

> "I'm gonna show you somethin' I bet you never seen before. [. . .] Bet after we get through with you, you ain't never gonna wanna kiss no more pussy."
> He slammed his kneecap into her spine and her body arched up, causing his nails to cut into the side of her mouth to stifle her cry. He pushed her arched body down onto the cement. Two of the boys pinned her arms, two wrenched open her legs, while C. C. knelt between them and pushed up her dress and tore at the top of her pantyhose. [. . .]
> She couldn't tell when they changed places and the second weight, then the third and fourth, dropped on her—it was all one continuous hacksawing of torment [. . .]
> Her thighs and stomach had become so slimy from her blood and their semen that the last two boys didn't want to touch her, so they turned her over, propped her head and shoulders against the wall, and took her from behind. When they had finished and stopped holding her up, her body fell over like an unstrung puppet. (170–71)

As this brutally violent and grotesque passage reveals, Lorraine is the target of an egregious sexual attack because of her sexuality. The setting in the secluded alley is emblematic of the isolation, emotional and otherwise, that women like Lorraine must endure; and that very isolation lends itself, as Naylor illustrates, to danger and horrendously violent attacks. In the case of C. C. Baker and his gang, they articulate both verbally and physically the degree to which they view lesbianism and same-sex intimacy, or sexuality not regulated by men, as threatening. The violent rape—whereby he attempts to make sure she is "never gonna wanna kiss no more pussy" again—is what he considers a viable method of contestation. In a society wherein heterosexuality is situated as normative, lesbianism and same-gender loving become associated, as emblematized by the gang, with a rejection of the "only visible sign of manhood—their penis."[19] In a broader sense, Lorraine's rape reflects a particular criminalization of the community itself.

While the community, that is, did not violate Lorraine directly, the gestures they did attempt to make were far from comprehensive, effective, or corrective of the hostility toward same-sex desire. To this end, their efforts, much like the wall on Brewster Place, were dead-end and futile. Moreover, that wall—that physical and metaphorical impediment—becomes emblematic, as Naylor illumines, of the ways in which certain politics governing race, particularly where gender and sexuality are concerned, impede communal progress. When the women of Brewster Place bond together to tear down the wall, even if the reader later learns it transpires in a dream, it is representative of hope, transformation, and the liberatory possibilities that, with action and agency, could become a (communal) reality.

Conclusion: "Without Fear of Reprisals": Representation in the Age of Michelle Obama

Unbought and Unbossed is an integrative project—a locus in which black women's literary and cultural production, movement ideologies, and the politics of identity and representation converge, providing an interdisciplinary and broad discursive framework for analyzing these complex issues. What this study has endeavored to examine are deliberate enactments of transgressive behavior that exceed the boundaries governing race, gender, and sexuality, while challenging concomitantly the fundamental categories governing established normativity and politics of identity. The goal of this book has, in part, been twofold: to illuminate these dynamics and how they are engaged and inscribed in post–civil rights black women's literary and cultural production, wherein black women claim a right to subjectivity unencumbered by circumscriptions and other limitations placed on black womanhood. And, second, to provide a historical context for "transgressive" behavior and, in turn, racialized transgression, where black women particularly and black people generally are concerned. Instead of locating black female sexuality within particular confines, whereby it is relegated to the manacles of stereotypes, mythologies, and pathologies, *Unbought and Unbossed* has endeavored to illumine, instead, the ways in which these black women, be they authors, characters, or black women at large, have not fought for the right to be anomalous or aberrant. Rather, they have resisted these designations, exercising the right to not only claim their identities and the politics accompanying those choices, but also to simply exist—participating in behavior that reflects the realm and complexities of humanity, existential experiences, and sexual citizenship.

What I would like to conclude with is a consideration of representations, as they intersect with race, gender, and sexuality, and as they manifest in the contemporary cultural moment. While this project elucidates instantiations of racialized gender transgression of the post–civil rights era, particularly during the interregnum period of the 1970s and 1980s, in what ways might correlations be made—and what are the implications and manifestations of these dynamics—to the contemporary cultural imagination where black womanhood is concerned? In this concluding moment, in these final thoughts, then, I contemplate the significance of the current temporal, sociopolitical moment—one in which we have our first-known African American First Lady of the United States of America: Michelle Obama. Not only does this lend itself to celebration, especially in terms of her very public presence, posture, and positionality, but it also offers a fundamental basis that complicates historical sensibilities and understandings, as well as representations of black womanhood as they operate in the American literary, cultural, and political imagination.

First Lady Michelle Obama, born in 1964 in the midst of the civil rights, black nationalist, feminist, and sexual liberation movements, might be "read"—if we are to engage or pay close attention to the semiotics of race, racialized gendered sexuality, and attire—as the embodiment of a particular duality. She embodies a certain "postraciality," if even illusory, coupled with a postmodern blackness, which I have discussed throughout this work. That is, she embodies a certain complexity of blackness, interestingly one that both deploys and attenuates respectability, that is not unitary, stagnant, or homogeneous, which is especially evident in her attire and fashion sense, which prompts attention and analogies to another First Lady, Jacqueline Kennedy. While her attire is characterized by traditional style (propriety), it is simultaneously marked with a unique distinctiveness that stands out, goes beyond and exceeds—or *transgresses*—the standard and the basic. In fact, it even challenges what constitutes "the norm." This sensibility is typified most transparently in her choice of fashion and style, particularly cut and colors: vibrant and lively (rather than muted, dull, or subdued) yet not over-the-top outrageous or anomalous. Equally significant, Michelle Obama's deliberate exposure of her toned, muscular, and defined arms is emblematic of a certain subjectivity, agency, and orchestrated self-posturing—an "unbought and unbought" gesture—in which reverberates a body in ownership of its own display, which is consequential especially in light of the historical ways in which black women's bodies have been on public display, both literally and figuratively, at the orchestration of others. She transcends and strategically subverts, then, historical ways of situating black female sexuality in that hers is not on literal public display: not, that is, on a slave auction block or exploited in museums with exposed genitalia like the Venus Hottentot—with her sexuality conspicuously invoked or exposed.[1] Yet, here lies the complexity and even tension of blackness in America: her sexuality is "on display" figuratively, metaphorically, and in another less conspicuous form: in the constant, ever-present fixation on her body. That is, not only a fixation on its physicality or its very physique, but also on what *shrouds* it (clothing) and, equally if not more provocative, *what it shrouds*: a latent, ever-present sexuality covertly engaged publicly vis-à-vis the discursive that ranges from pregnancy rumors—a (hyper)sexualizing and encoding of sorts—to the iconographic.

The August 2012 issue of the Spanish magazine *Fuera de Serie* illustrates this point. Its cover image shows Michelle Obama's face photoshopped onto French artist Marie-Guillemine Benoist's classic 1800 *Portrait d'une négresse*, which famously depicts with partial nudity a (former) enslaved black woman in headscarf and white gown with one breast exposed.

FIGURE C.1 Marie-Guillemine Benoist, *Portrait d'une Négresse*, 1800.

The magazine cover concretizes, making tangible and real, a fascination of dominant society with the sexualization and display of black women's bodies in that it, literally, "publicizes" a projection of racialized gendered sexual exposure—a black body rendered subject to the gaze, the fascination, the pleasure and titillation—of others even as it, ironically, also attempts

FIGURE C.2 *First Lady,* by Karine Percheron-Daniels, the basis for a *Fuera de Serie* magazine cover. (Courtesy of artist.)

to celebrate and, indeed, commemorate the moment in which the United States has as its First Lady a woman only generations removed from slavery. In the photoshopped artwork *First Lady,* created by the white mixed-media (French/English) artist Karine Percheron-Daniels, what becomes evident is the precarious association of race—racialized and sexualized vis-à-vis an association with slavery—and the historical as well as contemporaneous public fascination with black women's bodies that extends to a literal and metaphorical voyeurism. Just as the original *Portrait d'une négresse* was Benoist's calculated effort to offer an artistic commentary on larger sociopolitical dynamics, similarly, Percheron-Daniels's superimposed image of Michelle Obama was part of her larger provocative, controversial series of "famous nudes"—including, among others, Abraham Lincoln, President Obama, Princess Diana, and Queen Elizabeth I—created in an effort, she asserts, to provide "an alternative unexpected reality" in which to "view famous individuals in a different way."[2] What becomes ironic about her attempt, especially when considered within a racialized context, is that the "alternative reality" in which she attempts to present these leading figures regardless of their race, gender, or nationality is not much of an "alternative" for black subjects in the sense that black bodies—regardless of gender, positionality, or post (presidential or otherwise)—are always already sexualized in the precise moment of their racialization. Moreover, while *Feura de Serie*, alongside Percheron-Daniels, attempts to commemorate First Lady Obama's rising from a genealogical past of slavery to the rank of First Lady, there is significant irony in such an artistic gesture beyond the exposed breast. While the American flag draped behind Michelle Obama in the portrait suggests that black women and black bodies are integral to the United States, they are, far too often, characterized as having an "external" approximation to America. The U.S. flag behind her, rather than around her or as the garb that shrouds her, resonates precisely as such.[3]

A counterstance, coupled with a politics of recognition, occurs, however, in Michelle Obama's official White House portrait. In her official portrait, First Lady Obama dons a *black* sleeveless dress (baring/bearing arms literally and figuratively), and in the backdrop is a picture of Thomas Jefferson, former U.S. president, writer of the Declaration of Independence, and slaveowner (who fathered children by Sally Hemings, the enslaved half sister of his deceased wife). Michelle Obama's posture, attire, and agency in engaging on her own terms, evidenced in the picture—read within the larger historical context of Jefferson, whom she renders as backdrop as she is foregrounded, centralized and occupying the forefront—represent an interesting counterrepresentation that, whether calculated or inadvertent, achieves a number of results. It not only subverts a precarious historical past that would otherwise render black women's bodies the literal property and object of others' ownership, pleasure, and even disposal (whether physical, sexual, relating to labor, or otherwise). It also reconstitutes the terms of black womanhood, foregrounding it and embodied agency and subjectivity, while rejecting white male hegemonic or patriarchal control, as the Jefferson symbol comes to represent. For, it "executes a self-conscious taunting that reaches across the span of history to repudiate the violence and brutality suffered by so many enslaved women. Michelle [Obama] stands boldly in a White House where she is mistress, not slave. Her body is for her," as political scientist Melissa Harris-Perry cogently posits."[4] And, moreover, it serves, she further asserts, as "an act of resistance" for her, as a black woman, to "demand that her body belong to herself for her pleasure, her adornment, even her vanity, because in the United States, black women's bodies have often been valued only to the extent that they produce wealth and pleasure for others."[5] The photograph is, thus, iconographic and political in that it opposes U.S. historical and contemporaneous proclivities to designate black women's bodies and pleasures within the realm of disbelonging and, thus, at the ownership, voyeurism, and service of others.

She dictates its terms and, concomitantly, "normalizes" black womanhood in a postmodern sense, yet also transgresses totalizing constructions and paradigms in ways that offer possibilities and potentialities, inherently empowering, where black womanhood, racialized gender representation, and sexuality are concerned. Her gesture, and this very spirit, parallels that of this book—a nexus of race, gender, representation, and transgression in relation to black women and their bodies that demonstrates the transhistorical reach and temporal ubiquity of these racial/ sexual/gendered dynamics. This book, like First Lady Michelle Obama's official White House portrait, is a deliberate effort to subvert, reconstitute, and disrupt so that stereotypes or restrictions do not dictate black women's comportment, govern the politics of our intimacies and passion—private or public—or reduce black expression to perversity or aberration but, rather, place it within a continuum constitutive and reflective of the existential human (sexual included) condition.

This is, indeed, a provocative and consequential gesture, with new critical perspectives, approaches, and epistemologies, that interrogates black womanhood within intersectional, integrative, cross-cultural and other frameworks. We need more scholarship that examines, without ambiguity, ambivalence, or "fear of reprisals," the dynamics governing black womanhood and the politics of representation. We need work that transcends ideological and disciplinary boundaries and further engages race, gender, and sexuality. We need discourses that transcend silence, omission, and limitation. We need politics and practices that reflect the totality of our humanity, as well as our individual and collective experiences. We need models and paradigms that broaden our understandings of the functions and conventions governing our identities and representations of them. We need future projects, like this one and our First Lady's official White House photograph, that, simply put, *transgress*.

NOTES

Introduction

1. Chisholm, *Unbought and Unbossed* 19

2. Evelyn Brooks Higginbotham coins the terminology "politics of silence" in reference to the strategic secrecy surrounding black women's sexuality—or what Darlene Clark Hine refers to as a "culture of dissemblance." For discussions, see Higginbotham, *Righteous Discontent*; and Hine, "Rape and the Inner Lives of Black Women in the Middle West."

3. For extensive discussions of the "cult of true womanhood," see Welter, "The Cult of True Womanhood, 1820–1860"; and Carby, *Reconstructing Womanhood*. Carby examines the cultural and political impact of the cult of true womanhood on representations of black women in abolitionist literature, as well as the ways in which these ideologies informed black women's display of propriety and respectability after the cult of true womanhood was no longer "the dominant ideological code."

For scholarship on the gender politics of black nationalism, see Collins, "When Fighting Words Are Not Enough"; Lubiano's "Black Nationalism and Black Common Sense"; and J. H. Scott, "From Foreground to Margin."

4. Dubey, *Signs and Cities* 31.

5. D. Scott, *Extravagant Abjection* 18.

6. See Carby, *Reconstructing Womanhood*; Tate, *Domestic Allegories of Political Desire*; duCille, *The Coupling Convention*; Dubey, *Black Women Novelists and the Nationalist Aesthetic*; Jenkins, *Private Lives, Proper Relations*; and Thompson, *Beyond the Black Lady*.

7. My assertion here benefited from the intellectual insight of literary scholar and critic Cathy Schlund-Vials, who advanced my thinking regarding this interregnum period and multiculturalism.

8. While "mainstream" scholars theorizing about transgression typically ignore issues of race and the racialized dynamics, I do want to acknowledge that a great deal of work is treated by queer of color scholars, as well as theorists in race and sexuality and black queer studies, who do engage racialized blackness and transgression broadly construed.

9. Cohen, "Deviance as Resistance" 24.

10. See, in particular, Cohen, "Deviance as Resistance"; Ferguson, *Aberrations in Black*; Holland, *The Erotic Life of Racism*; Reid-Pharr, *Once You Go Black*; D. Scott, *Extravagant Abjection*; Somerville, *Queering the Color Line*; Stockton, *Beautiful Bottom, Beautiful Shame*; and Abdur-Rahman, *Against the Closet*. Other scholars and texts with which my work intervenes and is in conversation more generally are Reid-Pharr, *Black Gay Man*; Rose, *Longing to Tell*; Collins, *Black Sexual Politics*; McBride, *Why I Hate Abercrombie and Fitch*; and Stallings, *Mutha' Is Half a Word*.

11. Ferguson, *Aberrations in Black* 20–21.

12. Ferguson, *Aberrations in Black* 18, 20–21.

13. Ferguson, *Aberrations in Black* 21, 26, 27, emphasis in quotation mine.

14. Holland, *The Erotic Life of Racism* 11.

15. McBride, *Why I Hate Abercrombie and Fitch* 43.

16. Hine and Thompson, *A Shining Thread of Hope* 303.

17. Babcock, ed., *The Reversible World* 14. For further treatments of transgression, see also Wolfreys, *Transgression*; Jenks, *Transgression*; Stallybrass and White, *The Politics and Poetics of Transgression*; Foucault, "A Preface to Transgression"; and Povinelli's notions of the intersections and dynamics between social constraints and individual freedom in *The Empire of Love*.

18. Wolfreys, *Transgression* 1; see also Jenks, *Transgression*. See also *The City of Women* by Landes, who—through the tropes of race, sexuality, and how "convention" is constituted—offers a lens by which to further scrutinize the "norm," predicating privilege (or the lack thereof) on positionality and context. She complicates and offers a complex modality—through her own embodiment and that of black Bahian women—of racial, gender, and sexual subjectivity. To this end, she, vis-à-vis her work (even as it is not specifically about the United States or black American women) and methodological approach, challenges, as well as problematizes, convention in ways that pertain to my own work; this enables me to reassess and complicate, more specifically, what constitutes the transgressive and its very foundations.

19. Morrison, *Playing in the Dark* 6–7; see also M. M. Wright, *Becoming Black*.

20. Ferguson, *Aberrations* 6.

21. Foucault, "A Preface to Transgression" 446.

22. West, *The Cornel West Reader* 98.

23. Kittredge, ed., *Lewd and Notorious* 1. See also Landes, *The City of Women*, wherein she complicates notions of convention, "normativity," and transgression vis-à-vis Brazilian culture and Bahian women's experiences generally and within the context of Candomblé.

24. Kittredge 1.

25. Carby, *Reconstructing Womanhood* 32.

26. It is important to note that while Timberlake did not suffer certain consequences from the mainstream media and society at large, he did confront a certain amount of criticism and reproach from some artists and circles in the black community.

27. Staples, *Black Masculinity* 2.

28. Kimmel, ed., *Changing Men* 13, 19. See also R. W. Connell, Jeff Hearn, and Michael S. Kimmel, introduction, *Handbook of Studies on Men and Masculinities*, ed. Connell, Hearn, and Kimmel, wherein they assert that since "men and masculinities are shaped by differences of age, by class situation, by ethnicity and racialization," the projection/display of masculinity and the very "gendering of men" exist "in the intersections with other social divisions and social differences" (3).

29. See Wallace, *Black Macho and the Myth of the Superwoman*; and Alexander-Floyd, "We Shall Have Our Manhood."

30. See Evelyn Brooks Higginbotham's salient discussion of "politics of respectability" among black Baptist church women in *Righteous Discontent* (185–229).

31. duCille, *The Coupling Convention* 7. See also Carby, *Reconstructing Womanhood*, for extended discussions on the political and polemical nature of some early black women's novels and their characterizations of black female characters.

32. McDowell, "*The Changing Same*" 38.

33. Christian, *Black Feminist Criticism* 15.

34. Ferguson, *Aberrations in Black*, 45. See also JanMohamed, "Sexuality on/of the Racial Border."

35. I would like to acknowledge literary scholar Nazera Wright, whose intellectual insights influenced my understandings of the nuances of this particular moment and the dynamics surrounding Gwendolyn Brooks's and black women writers' protest literature.

36. A. Walker, "The Civil Rights Movement: What Good Was It?" 122.

37. In *A Shining Thread of Hope*, Darlene Clark Hine and Kathleen Thompson assert that black and white women began questioning "the inequity of their position in society" in part "because of the success of the Civil Rights movement and the addition of the word 'sex' into Title VII of the Civil Rights Act of 1964" (299). For a discussion of the irony behind the inclusion of the word "sex" in Title VII, prohibiting discrimination in employment, see Giddings, *When and Where I Enter* 299–300.

38. Collins, *From Black Power to Hip Hop* 109.

39. Poussaint, "Blacks and the Sexual Revolution" 112.

40. Poussaint 112.

41. Holland, *Erotic Life of Racism* 43.

42. Morrison, What the Black Woman Thinks about Women's Lib" 5.

43. Combahee River Collective, "A Black Feminist Statement" 13.

44. Somerville, *Queering the Color Line* 17.

45. Jordan, "A New Politics of Sexuality" 408

46. In 1960, the Food and Drug Administration (FDA) approved the birth control pill, followed by the 1965 Supreme Court ruling that struck down the Comstack laws that banned contraception. In 1967, the Supreme Court struck down miscegenation laws, regarding interracial marriages, in *Loving v. Virginia*. In 1973, *Roe v. Wade* decriminalized abortion and challenged its illegality. In that same year, the Board of Directors of the American Psychiatric Association removed homosexuality as a mental disorder in the Diagnostic and Statistical Manual of Mental Disorders (DSM); however, in 1974 it appeared with a new diagnosis, "ego-dystonic homosexuality," which was removed in 1986. For further discussions, see Allyn. *Make Love, Not War.*

47. Allyn 7–8.

48. See Huey Newton's "Letter" anthologized in Byrd and Guy-Sheftall, eds., *Traps* 282.

49. Poussaint, "Blacks and the Sexual Revolution" 118, 120.

50. See Holland, *Erotic Life of Racism.*

51. Abdur-Rahman, *Against the Closet* 9.

52. Staples, "Has the Sexual Revolution Bypassed Blacks?" 114.

53. Staples, 114.

54. Cade, "The Pill: Genocide or Liberation?" 205–7.

55. Cade, "The Pill: Genocide or Liberation?" 205–7.

56. DuBois argues: "All womanhood is hampered today because the world on which it is emerging is a world that tries to worship both virgins and mothers and in the end despises motherhood and despoils virgins. The future woman must have a life work and economic independence. She must have knowledge. She must have the right of motherhood at her own discretion" ("The Damnation of Women" 164–65).

57. For extended discussion of "sexual citizenship," see Chateauvert, "Framing Sexual Citizenship."

58. McBride, *Why I Hate Abercrombie and Fitch* 58, 43.

1 / "New World Black and New World Woman"

1. See Gaines, *Uplifting the Race.*

2. For more extensive discussions, see Carby's *Reconstructing Womanhood*, wherein she argues that to comprehend the "cultural effectivity of ideologies of black female sexuality" and black women's narratives, "it is necessary to consider the determining force of ideologies of white female

sexuality," as well as the dominant discourse surrounding it to more deeply understand the ways black women (writers, activists, club women, intellectuals, and race women) broached, transformed, and/or "subverted the dominant ideological codes" (20–21).

3. For extensive discussions of the "cult of true womanhood," see Welter, "The Cult of True Womanhood, 1820–1860."

4. D. G. White, *Ar'n't I a Woman?* 4, 6.

5. Cooper, *A Voice from the South by a Black Woman of the South*, 31.

6. Thompson, *Beyond the Black Lady* 6.

7. Morrison, "Unspeakable Things Unspoken" 390.

8. Johnson, *Appropriating Blackness* 2.

9. Johnson 2.

10. Reid-Pharr, *Conjugal Union* 7.

11. McDowell, *"The Changing Same"* 104.

12. The novel is set against the backdrop of a segregated town, wherein the racial politics resemble precisely what Ruth Landes explicates in "A Northerner Views the South," as well as reflect, in part, her experiences with Jim Crow politics during her time at Fisk University in Nashville, Tennessee (where the novel's protagonist, Sula, also travels).

13. Morrison, foreword, *Sula* xiii.

14. I use "alterity" denotatively to mean a state of being radically different, idiosyncratic, and/or unlike other individuals instead of how it is most commonly applied in postmodern discourse.

15. Morrison, *Sula* 52. Subsequent citations of this novel will appear parenthetically in the chapter text.

16. Ferguson, *Aberrations in Black* 84.

17. Reid-Pharr, *Once You Go Black* 18.

18. See Jennifer C. Nash's "Strange Bedfellows: Black Feminism and Antipornography Feminism," wherein she explicates the nexus and "traffic" between these two feminisms as a way of moving beyond representations and frameworks of black women's bodies and sexualized exploitation, violence, or dehumanization exclusively to a complex interplay with black sexual pleasures, subjectivities, and desires (52–53).

19. Hammonds, "Black (W)holes and the Geometry of Black Female Sexuality" 488.

20. Spillers, "A Hateful Passion, A Lost Love" 315–16.

21. Nash, "Practicing Love" 3.

22. McDowell, 105. See also Docherty, *Reading (Absent) Character*, since his work, as McDowell notes, influences her assertion.

23. For further discussion of gender performativity, as well as fluid gender and sexualities, see Butler, *Gender Trouble* xv.

24. Holland, *Raising the Dead* 5.

25. It is worth noting that, even as Sula and Nel wondered if Shadrack, the shell-shocked male veteran, had witnessed Chicken's death, the ambiguity

(and whether or not he does indeed witness it) is ultimately inconsequential—and nonthreatening—in that he does not witness their homoerotic scene, still left unmitigated by a male presence.

26. For a discussion of the arguments governing women's education, as well as suffrage, and the impact it would have on the race at large, see Gaines.

27. Combahee River Collective, "A Black Feminist Statement" 4.

28. Combahee River Collective 5.

29. Morrison, "What the Black Woman Thinks about Women's Lib" 24.

30. For further discussions of "nonconformity" as transgressive or, more specifically, as "conscious acts of resistance that serve as a basis for a mobilized politics of deviance," see Cohen, "Deviance as Resistance."

31. Lubiano, "Black Nationalism and Black Common Sense" 245.

32. Somerville, Queering the Color Line 17, 16.

33. McClintock, "Family Feuds" 69.

34. McClintock 69.

35. Robert Stepto, "A Conversation with Toni Morrison" 385.

36. Lorde, "Uses of the Erotic" in Sister Outsider 54–55.

37. See Barbara Smith's pioneering "Toward a Black Feminist Criticism" for a parallel assessment—that "Sula uses men for sex which results, not in communion with them, but in her further delving into self" (141).

38. See Candice Jenkins's Private Lives, Proper Relations, wherein she analyzes Sula, sexuality with Ajax, and the erotic in relation to the salvific wish.

39. Holland, The Erotic Life of Racism 12.

40. Reid-Pharr, Once You Go Black 171.

41. Edwards, Charisma and the Fictions of Black Leadership xv.

42. Ferguson, Aberrations in Black 118.

43. For discussions of sexual citizenship, see Chateauvert, "Framing Sexual Citizenship." See also D. T. Evans, Sexual Citizenship; and Richardson, "Constructing Sexual Citizenship" and "Claiming Citizenship?"

44. hooks, "The Politics of Radical Black Subjectivity" 15.

45. hooks, "The Politics of Radical Black Subjectivity" 15.

46. hooks, "The Politics of Radical Black Subjectivity" 15.

47. Washington, "Declaring (Ambiguous) Liberty" 203.

48. Holland, Raising the Dead 5.

49. Dubey, Signs and Cities 5.

50. Johnson and Henderson, "Introduction: Queering Black Studies/'Quaring' Queer Studies" 7.

2 / Toward an Aesthetic of Transgression

1. See Hammonds, "Black (W)holes and the Geometry of Black Female Sexuality"; Rose, Longing to Tell; and Collins, Black Sexual Politics. For discussions of dissemblance and black women's sexuality, see Hine, "Rape and the Inner Lives of Black Women in the Middle West"; and Higginbotham, "The Politics of Respectability."

2. Hammonds argues that lesbian and gay studies, in general, display "consistently exclusionary practices" in that "the canonical terms and categories of the field: 'lesbian,' 'gay,' 'butch,' 'femme,' 'sexuality,' and 'subjectivity' are stripped of context in the works of those theorizing about these very categories, identities, and subject positions. Each of these terms is defined with white as the normative state of existence" ("Black (W)holes and the Geometry of Black Female Sexuality" 483). See also JanMohamed, "Sexuality on/of the Racial Border" 16; and Cohen, "Punks, Bulldaggers, and Welfare Queens," in which Cohen examines the efficacy of "queer" for black lesbian, gay, bisexual, and transgender politics as it relates to issues of gender, sexuality, and social class.

3. The term "same-gender loving" was coined by activist Cleo Manago as a culturally affirming term for black "sexual minorities."

4. I use the term "perceived sexual orientation" to acknowledge that sexual identities and labels are not written on the body in ways that disclose the actualities, specificities, and/or totalities of our sexualities, and to avoid imposing, inscribing, or projecting (otherwise undisclosed) sexual identities and/or labels onto individuals' sexual intimacies and expressions. Within the context of this work, my use of the term "same-gender loving," as it relates to the specific characters' relationship, involves a presence of sexual-relational faithfulness, commitment, and/or love as broadly conceived. My conception of "love" builds, first and in part, upon its denotative meaning as defined in *American Heritage Dictionary*, 3rd ed.: "1. A deep, tender, ineffable feeling of affection and solicitude toward a person [. . .]. 2. A feeling of intense desire and attraction toward a person with whom one is disposed to make a pair; the emotion of sex and romance. 3.a. Sexual passion. b. Sexual intercourse. c. A love affair" (1064). Broadly speaking, same-gender loving applies to physical sexual intimacies anywhere along the emotional-committal continuum, ranging from short- to long-term liaisons to those that fall in between. Second, my notion of "love" reflects what Jennifer Nash identifies as a long history of black feminist "love-politics," wherein love is not coterminous inextricably with romantic love but rather is "celebrated for its advocacy of love as a resistant ethic of self-care" and, in turn, "a politics of claiming, embracing, and restoring the wounded black female self" (see Nash, *Meridians* 3).

The concept "same-gender loving" makes direct use of the term "gender" and does not seem to differentiate—at least in any concrete or transparent way—between sex and gender, which should not be conflated and treated as coterminous. For salient discussions of discourses on gender, particularly in the areas of gender constitution and performativity, consult the works of Judith Butler and Judith Halberstam, who have advanced much of the theory that has broadened our epistemologies regarding gender.

5. Same-gender loving as an analytic responds to Johnnetta Betsch Cole and Beverly Guy-Sheftall's request that "interpretations of same-gender

sexual and emotional bondings among persons of African descent [. . .] take into consideration the cultural specificity of Western categories of sexual identity such as 'heterosexual,' 'homosexual,' 'lesbian,' and 'bisexual,' which have particular meanings in a U.S. context." Failure to recognize that sexual behaviors have different meanings outside Western/American contexts contributes to misinterpretations and skewed perceptions of these sexual acts (Cole and Guy-Sheftall 165).

While this chapter foregrounds and examines black women's sexualities particularly, it is worth noting the "down low" (DL) phenomenon among black men, who self-identify as heterosexual and engage occasionally in clandestine sexual acts with men. In referencing this, it is not my intention to equate same-gender loving with the DL phenomenon but, rather, to draw attention to the limitations of current discourses on sexuality, as well as labels and categories, that do not always reflect the particularities of these subjects' sexualities. For further details, see King, *On the Down Low*.

6. Ferguson, *Aberrations* 3.

7. Johnson and Henderson, *Black Queer Studies* 6–7. Along a similar vein, theoretical and political analyses and field of intellectual inquiry, such as black queer studies, destabilizes "dominant and hegemonic discourses" by unsettling absolute or static conceptualizations of identity in an "interanimation" of race/gender/sexuality, while foregrounding the multiple valences and "subjectivities of the minoritarian subject."

8. Until 1973, homosexuality was identified as a mental illness in the American Psychiatric Association's *Diagnostic and Statistical Manual of Mental Disorders*.

9. Thus, to be clear, this chapter illuminates the ways same-gender loving operates as a postmodern gesture and presage in Shockley's novel to discourses on queer sexuality that would later develop; as such, this chapter does not at all suggest that same-gender loving, as intimacy, framework, or intellectual discourse, functions in contestation, directly or indirectly, with queer identity, theory, intimacies, or studies. While I do not argue that Renay is a lesbian but, rather, that she exceeds such sexual labels and taxonomies, Kara Keeling's work on "black lesbians" does have purchase and does, in ways, describe what Renay does in terms of issuing a "critique of the sexism and heterosexism of dominant articulations of 'blackness,' of the racism and heterosexism of dominant articulations of 'women,' and of the racism of dominant articulations of 'lesbian'" (*Black Queer Studies* 220). And so, while Renay problematizes what constitutes a black lesbian, she nonetheless performs what Keeling identifies as a resistance to hegemony.

10. I use the term "sexual minorities" in direct reference to those individuals who have been marginalized historically and contemporaneously in the United States because their sexual identity, orientation, and/or practices are outside the parameters of so-called "normative" sexual behavior—which, in the United States, translates problematically into heterosexuality.

11. See Hammonds, "Black (W)holes and the Geometry of Black Female Sexuality"; and B. Smith.

12. Quoted in Carbado, McBride, and Weise, eds., *Black Like Us* 113.

13. Clarke, "Failure" 192.

14. Analyzing the ways in which "[gay and lesbian] magazines of the 1960s" galvanized around propagating images of a unified and representative gay and lesbian body, Rodger Streitmatter asserts that "[g]ay people vary widely with respect to factors such as age, socioeconomic level, education, and geographic location. And yet, in order for progress to be made, these diverse individuals ultimately must coalesce to form a single community." Streitmatter's commentary reflects at best the absence of the signifier race in politics surrounding gay and lesbian identities, and evidences gay and lesbian communities' largely inattentive stances toward racialized sexualities (71).

15. B. Smith, *The Truth That Never Hurts* 126.

16. Parker, *Movement in Black* 11.

17. Sexual labels, including the term "queer," especially in relation to African Americans, are "of course controversial"; "many black people across the range of sexual orientation object to its white cultural connotation, if not the word's association with sexual pathology," as Devon Carbado, Dwight McBride, and Donald Weise posit, in *Black Like Us: A Century of Lesbian, Gay, and Bisexual African American Fiction*. As a result, "large numbers of African Americans resist identifying themselves as queer, preferring [. . .] the relatively recent 'same-gender-loving'" (xiv).

18. See note 3 of this chapter.

19. Bristow asserts that "making connections between *sameness* and *difference* (and both terms have their complications), [. . .] signals the overlapping concerns of discrete subcultures." While he relates sameness and difference to "lesbian" and "gay," it is also relevant to same-gender loving which also "designate[s] entirely different desires, physical pleasures, oppressions, and visibilities" (*Sexual Sameness* 2).

20. Foucault, *The History of Sexuality* 43.

21. For an explication of black sexual politics and our need for sexuality and gender discourses in the black community, see Giddings, "The Last Taboo."

22. Also, to reiterate, another source of ambiguity is that same-gender loving privileges the term "gender," seemingly not differentiating—at least in any concrete or transparent way—between sex and gender, which should not be conflated and treated as coterminous. See the works of scholars Judith Butler and Judith Halberstam regarding gender constitution and performativity for more detailed discussions of gender and advanced epistemologies governing it.

23. Holland, *Erotic Life of Racism*, 11.

24. Ross, "White Fantasies of Desire: Baldwin and the Racial Identities of Sexuality" 32.

25. I want to acknowledge the anonymous third reader, whose insights inform not only this intellectual sentiment but the more critical and nuanced approach to same-gender loving advanced in this paragraph and the one thereafter.

26. See Hardt and Negri, *Multitude* 351, qtd. in Nash, "Practicing Love."

27. Ferguson, "Race-ing Homonormativity:" 65.

28. Lane, foreword v.

29. Shockley, *Loving Her* 72. Subsequent citations of this novel will appear parenthetically in the chapter text.

30. See Gayle, "Blueprint for Black Criticism." 44, in which he calls for literary characters imbued with black consciousness and "positive" characteristics to debunk stereotypical images of black people. See also Neal, "The Social Background of the Black Arts Movement."

31. A. Walker, "A Daring Subject Boldly Shared."

32. For reviews of *Loving Her*, see Cordova; and Phillips. Other individuals reference or address aspects of the novel; see Shockley's "The Black Lesbian in American Literature"; Gomez, "A Cultural Legacy Denied and Discovered"; and Schultz, "Out of the Woods and into the World."

33. See Bogus, "Theme and Portraiture in the Fiction of Ann Allen Shockley"; see also Shockley, "The Black Lesbian in American Literature," in which Shockley conjectures that heterosexism and homophobia were additional factors contributing to the neglect of literature with lesbian themes (84). For inimical reviews of *Loving Her*, see Cordova 28; also Phillips scathingly critiques Shockley, who, as "a librarian at Fisk University" whose "short fiction and articles [have] been published in *Black World*[, . . .] should know better" since, in his view, *Loving Her* is "Bullshit that ought not be encouraged" (89–90).

34. The novel's shortcomings are not limited to stylistics, authorial intrusions and interjections, archaic sexual terms, and largely unmediated ideological stereotypes. For further details, see also Lane, foreword, *Loving Her* vii–viii, xiii; and Dubey, *Black Women Novelists and the Nationalist Aesthetic* 151.

35. See Judith Butler, in particular "Performative Acts and Gender Constitution," regarding gender performativity. For discussion of the ramifications of suspicions of "having homosexual relations," and how it was typical for colleges to expel students, see Allyn, *Make Love, Not War* 151.

36. Moynihan, *The Negro Family: The Case for National Action*. For extended literature by black nationalists known for their unabashed appropriation and propagation of black matriarchy rhetoric, see Hare, "Will the Real Black Man Please Stand Up?"; Cleaver, *Soul on Ice*; and Staples, "The Myth of the Black Macho."

37. Stokely Carmichael asserts that "[t]he position of women in SNCC is prone." Though Carmichael was joking, his remark reflects some of the prevailing gender politics and ideologies regarding women undergirding the movement (*Ready for Revolution* 431–32).

38. It is worth noting here that while Shockley critiques nationalist politics, she focuses more on individuals like Jerome who, under the guise of nationalism, evade their own shortcomings and/or failures and overcompensate for them by exerting masculinist and patriarchal control.

39. Dubey, *Signs and Cities* 33. For extended discussions of racial identity and racial politics with a centralizing of race and "universalizing agenda," see also hooks, "Postmodern Blackness" and "The Chitlin Circuit: On Black Community" in *Yearning*.

40. Dubey, *Signs and Cities* 34.

41. Lane, foreword, *Loving Her* xii.

42. Abdur-Rahman, *Against the Closet* 84, 85.

43. Rpt in Allyn, *Make Love, Not War* 85.

44. Mayer, ed., *Gender Ironies of Nationalism* 7.

45. Mayer, ed., *Gender Ironies of Nationalism*, 2.

46. See also Thomas, "Ain't Nothin' Like the Real Thing" 126; and R. M. Williams, "Living at the Crossroads" 146, for scholarship that discusses nationalist articulations of homosexuality as both a sign of white decadence and ramification of white supremacy. See also Michel Foucault's *History of Sexuality* for discussions of the association of homosexuality with pathology and dis/ease.

47. Thomas, "Ain't Nothin' Like the Real Thing" 123.

48. Mayer, ed., *Gender Ironies of Nationalism* 7.

49. bell hooks, "Talking Back" 9.

50. Marvin Garson, qtd.in Allyn, *Make Love, Not War* 155.

51. Johnson and Henderson, *Queer Black Studies* 7.

52. For example, Morrison, *The Bluest Eye* (1970) and *Sula* (1973); Meriwether, *Daddy Was a Number Runner* (1970); A. Walker, *Third Life of Grange Copeland* (1970); and Jones, *Corregidora* (1975) and *Eva's Man* (1976). Codified same-sex desire is not foreign to black women's literature or the African American literary tradition. Much of the literature of the New Negro Renaissance, otherwise known as the Harlem Renaissance, by black women writers, notably Nella Larsen, Angelina Grimké, Alice Dunbar Nelson, presents race longing and desire as intertwined with (a masked) sexual longing. Other authors and contemporaries of Ann Allen Shockley, such as Toni Morrison, Alice Walker, Gayl Jones, and Gloria Naylor do have more sexually explicit expressions of homoeroticism and same-sex desire among women. Shockley is, however, in a trailblazing category of her own when it comes to foregrounding a treatment and sustained exploration of same-gender loving and black women's sexualities as operating along a continuum or constellation of desire.

53. Dubey, *Black Women Novelists and the Nationalist Aesthetic* 153.

54. See Mayer, ed., *Gender Ironies of Nationalism* 14. See also Kemp, "When Difference Is Not the Dilemma" 87, where she asserts that lesbianism and same-sex desire, especially within the context of the black community,

is conflated with "unbridled female sexuality" unregulated through men and, as such, is seen as threatening.

3 / Negotiating Cultural Politics

1. Robert E. Birt, "Of the Quest for Freedom as Community," *The Quest for Community and Identity*, ed. Birt 92.

2. West, *Prophesy Deliverance* 17.

3. McKittrick, *Demonic Grounds*.

4. James, *Shadowboxing* 40.

5. Cole and Guy-Sheftall, *Gender Talk* xxii.

6. Anderson, *Imagined Communities* 7.

7. See Dubey, *Signs and Cities*, 31, wherein she poses a similar inquiry that she identifies as one of the fundamental challenges of the postmodern era in African American studies.

8. See Jenks, *Transgression*, whose discussion of the nexus of transgression and the illicit as within the category of acceptable behavior informs my assertion here.

9. Patricia Hill Collins coins the terminology "outsider-within" to discuss "a peculiar marginality" and "social locations or border spaces marking the boundaries between groups of unequal power"—for instance, black female domestics in white people's homes, and black women in the academy—wherein the "marginalized" are privy to, though not able to fully or readily partake of, the privileges afforded the "dominant" group. I appropriate Collins's theory of "outsider-within" to mean those individuals, specifically black women characters, who have membership within certain (racial/ethnic) communities; yet their transgressions against established communal "norms" relegate them to isolation or marginalization within their communal locales (see Collins, *Black Feminist Thought* 11, 300).

10. Dubey, *Signs and Cities* 30.

11. Morrison, "Introduction: Friday on the Potomac" xxx.

12. A. Walker, *In Search of Our Mothers' Gardens* xi.

13. Bannerji, Mojab, and Whitehead, eds., *Of Property and Propriety* 4.

14. A. Walker, *Meridian* 60. Subsequent citations of this novel will appear parenthetically in the chapter text.

15. Giddings, "The Last Taboo" 423.

16. Giddings, "The Last Taboo" 425.

17. Giddings, "The Last Taboo" 425.

18. Dubey, *Black Women Novelists and the Nationalist Aesthetic* 128.

19. Carole Vance, "Pleasure and Danger: Toward a Politics of Sexuality," in Vance, ed. *Pleasure and Danger* 1.

20. Collins, *Black Sexual Politics* 11. In light of stereotypes and associations with illicit and pathologized sexuality, as well as in the absence of meaningful discourses on sexuality, black women like Meridian—and other

minor characters, such as Fast Mary and Wile Chile—become sexually vul
nerable, pregnant, and suffer fatal consequences.

21. Hammonds, "Black (W)holes and the Geometry of Black Female
Sexuality" 492–93.

22. Christian. *Black Feminist Criticism* 240.

23. *Essence*, July 1976, 35. It is worth noting that in this same issue appears
an interview by Jessica Harris in which Walker talks about her then recently
published novel *Meridian*. Among other topics, she discusses the motivation
behind it (see A. Walker, "An Interview with Alice Walker" 33).

24. I wish to acknowledge the intellectual insight of Beverly Guy-Sheftall,
who made me aware of Ruby Doris Smith Robinson's influence on Walker's
development of her protagonist Meridian. See also A. Walker, "An Interview with Alice Walker" 33, in which Walker notes that "Ruby Doris [Smith]
Robinson, one of the founders and backbone members of SNCC, provided
the germ for the book."

25. Byrd, ed., *The World Has Changed* 8.

26. Rich, *Of Woman Born* 13.

27. Christian, *Black Feminist Criticism* 213.

28. This notion of "ideal" black womanhood—black women protecting
their children so that they might live—is also complicated by historical
accounts of slave women who took their children's lives as emancipatory
acts to save them from the institution of slavery.

29. T. M. Davis. "Alice Walker's Celebration of Self in Southern Generations" 49.

30. T. M. Davis 49.

31. M. Walker, *Down from the Mountaintop* 176.

32. M. Walker 175.

33. A. Walker, "The 'Silver Writes' Movement" 22–23.

34. A. Walker, "The Civil Rights Movement: What Good Was It?" 126. For
others, such as the historian Berneice Johnson Reagan, who recount experiences like Walker's of having gained a sense of self-awareness, existential
consciousness, and purpose from the civil rights movement, see Crawford,
Rouse, and Woods, eds. *Women in the Civil Rights Movement*.

35. T. Davis, "Alice Walker's Celebration of Self in Southern Generations" 48.

4 / "That Way Lies Madness"

1. Dubey, *Black Women Novelists and the Nationalist Aesthetic* 95.

2. Basu, "Public and Private Discourses and the Black Female Subject"
193.

3. Jones, "About My Work" 233.

4. Basu, "Public and Private Discourses and the Black Female Subject"
194.

5. Foucault, "A Preface to Transgression" 442.

6. Foucault, "A Preface to Transgression" 442–43.
7. Foucault, "A Preface to Transgression" 445.
8. Jones, *Eva's Man* 162–63. Subsequent citations of this novel will appear parenthetically in the chapter text.
9. Jenkins, *Private Lives, Proper Relations* 153–54.
10. Jenkins, *Private Lives, Proper Relations* 153.
11. Lemert and Gillan, eds., *Michel Foucault* 26.
12. Holland, *Raising the Dead*, 120.
13. Lorde, *Sister Outsider* 54.
14. For an explication of "illicit eroticism," see Miller-Young.
15. Nash, "Strange Bedfellows" 52–53.
16. Nash, "Strange Bedfellows" 53.
17. Miller-Young, "Interventions."
18. Ward, "Escape from Trublem" 254.
19. Dixon, "Singing a Deep Song" 246.
20. Ehrenreich, "The Decline of Patriarchy" 290.
21. Collins, *Black Sexual Politics* 6.
22. Ward, "Escape from Trublem" 255.
23. See Collins, *Black Sexual Politics* 206.
24. Foucault, "A Preface to Transgression" 447.
25. R. Wright, *Native Son* xi.
26. Lemert and Gillan, eds., *Michel Foucault* 69.
27. Lemert and Gillan, eds. 69.
28. Basu, "Public and Private Discourses and the Black Female Subject" 207.

5 / "Between a Rock and a Hard Place"

1. Mae Gwedolyn Henderson, "Speaking in Tongues," in *Changing Our Own Words*, ed. Wall 17.
2. Henderson, "Speaking in Tongues" 17.
3. Naylor asserts this in her 1989 interview in *Ebony*, qtd. in Whitt, *Understanding Gloria Naylor* 2.
4. Chateauvert, "Framing Sexual Citizenship" 198–99.
5. Chateauvert 199.
6. Naylor, *The Women of Brewster Place* 1. Subsequent citations of this novel will appear parenthetically in the chapter text.
7. Chateauvert, "Framing Sexual Citizenship" 204.
8. Hammonds, "Black (W)holes and the Geometry of Black Female Sexuality" 487.
9. A. Y. Davis, *Blues Legacies and Black Feminism* xvii.
10. Segal, *Straight Sex* 30.
11. Segal 33
12. West, "Black Sexuality" 305.

13. Jeremiah Wright, as qtd. in *Silence: In Search of Black Female Sexuality in America*.

14. For an explication of the terminology "outsider-within," see Collins, *Black Feminist Theory*.

15. Christian, *Black Feminist Criticism* 195.

16. Farwell, *Heterosexual Plots and Lesbian Narratives* 154.

17. Farwell 160.

18. Lorde, *Sister Outsider* 52.

19. Christian, *Black Feminist Criticism* 196.

Conclusion

1. See Harris-Perry's chapter "Michelle" in her work *Sister Citizen*, wherein she illuminates the way in which the public fixation on and scrutiny of Michelle Obama's body resembles the historical treatments of black women, including Saartjie Baartman, famously known as the Hottentot Venus.

2. *Portrait d'une négresse* represents Benoist's artistic effort to recognize her nation's abolition of slavery on the one hand, while offering larger commentary on racism and sexism in France, thus serving as a marker of emancipation and a feminist moment.

3. While this is the case with *First Lady*, it is worth noting that Karine Percheron-Daniels later created *Our First Lady Liberty*, her recent artwork featuring First Lady Michelle Obama as the Statue of Liberty with the U.S. flag as the garb that shrouds her body.

4. Harris-Perry, *Sister Citizen* 280.

5. Harris-Perry, *Sister Citizen* 280.

Bibliography

Abdur-Rahman, Aliyyah I. *Against the Closet: Black Political Longing and the Erotics of Race.* Durham: Duke University Press, 2012.

Abelove, Henry, Michèle Aina Barale, and David M. Halperin, eds. *The Lesbian and Gay Studies Reader.* New York: Routledge, 1993.

Ahad, Bahia. *Freud Upside Down: African American Literature and Psychoanalytic Culture.* Urbana: University of Illinois Press, 2010.

Alderson, David, and Linda Anderson, eds. *Territories of Desire in Queer Culture: Refiguring Contemporary Boundaries.* Manchester: Manchester University Press, 2000.

Alexander-Floyd, Nikol G. "'We Shall Have Our Manhood': Black Macho, Black Nationalism, and the Million Man March." *Meridians* 3.2 (2003): 171–203.

Allyn, David. *Make Love, Not War: The Sexual Revolution: An Unfettered History.* New York: Routledge, 2001.

Anderson, Benedict. *Imagined Communities: Reflections on the Origin and Spread of Nationalism.* London: Verso, 1983.

Aptheker, Bettina. *Women's Legacy: Essays on Race, Sex, and Class in American History.* Amherst: University of Massachusetts Press, 1982.

Austin, Algernon. *Achieving Blackness: Race, Black Nationalism, and Afrocentrism in the Twentieth Century.* New York: New York University Press, 2006.

Babcock, Barbara A., ed. *The Reversible World: Symbolic Inversion in Art and Society.* Ithaca: Cornell University Press, 1978.

Bannerji, Himani, Shahrzad Mojab, and Judith Whitehead, eds. *Of Property and Propriety: The Role of Gender and Class in Imperialism and Nationalism*. Toronto: University of Toronto Press, 2001.

Basu, Biman. "Public and Private Discourses and the Black Female Subject." *Callaloo* 19.1 (1996): 193–208.

Battle, Juan, and Sandra L. Barnes, eds. *Black Sexualities: Probing Powers, Passions, Practices, and Policies*. New Brunswick, NJ: Rutgers University Press, 2010.

Bell, Roseann P., Bettye J. Parker, and Beverly Guy-Sheftall, eds. *Sturdy Black Bridges: Visions of Black Women in Literature*. New York: Anchor, 1979.

Bell-Scott, Patricia. *Flat-Footed Truths: Telling Black Women's Lives*. New York: Henry Holt, 1998.

Bendel-Simso, Mary Michele. "The Politics of Reproduction: Demystifying Female Gender in Southern Literature." Diss. State University of New York at Binghamton, 1992.

Bennett, Michael, and Vanessa D. Dickerson, eds. *Recovering the Black Female Body: Self-Representations by African American Women*. New Brunswick, NJ: Rutgers University Press, 2000.

Birt, Robert E., ed. *The Quest for Community and Identity: Critical Essays in Africana Social Philosophy*. Lanham, MD: Rowman and Littlefield, 2002.

Bliss, Rebecca D. "Dangerous Women: The Quest for Alternative Narratives as Feminist Revolution in Contemporary American Women's Fiction." Diss. Purdue University, 1998.

Boggs, Nicholas. "Queer Black Studies: An Annotated Bibliography, 1994–1999." *Callaloo* 23.1 (Winter 2000): 479–94.

Bogus, Sdiane. "Theme and Portraiture in the Fiction of Ann Allen Shockley." Diss. Miami University, 1988.

Booker, M. Keith. *Techniques of Subversion in Modern Literature: Transgression, Abjection, and the Carnivalesque*. Gainesville: University of Florida Press, 1991.

Boykin, Keith. *One More River to Cross: Black and Gay in America*. New York: Anchor, 1996.

Bracey, John H., Jr., August Meier, and Elliott Rudwick, eds. *Black Nationalism in America*. Indianapolis: Bobbs-Merrill, 1970.

Braxton, Joanne, and Andrée Nicola McLaughlin, eds. *Wild Women in the Whirlwind: Afra-American Culture and the Contemporary Literary Renaissance*. New Brunswick, NJ: Rutgers University Press, 1990.

Bristow, Joseph, ed. *Sexual Sameness: Textual Differences in Lesbian and Gay Writing*. London: Routledge, 1992.

Brooks, Daphne A. *Bodies in Dissent: Spectacular Performances of Race and Freedom, 1850–1910*. Durham: Duke University Press, 2006.

Brooks, Gwendolyn. *Blacks*. Chicago: Third World, 2001.

———. *Maud Martha*. 1953. Chicago: Third World, 1993.

Bryant, Jacqueline. "'Clothed in My Right Mind': The Foremother Figure in Early Black Women's Literature." Diss. Kent State University, 1998.

Bryce, Jane, and Karl Dako. "Textual Deviancy and Cultural Syncretism: Romantic Fiction as a Subversive Stain in Africana Women's Writing." *Arms Akimbo: Africana Women in Contemporary Literature*. Ed. Janice Lee Liddell and Yakini Belinda Kemp. Gainesville: University Press of Florida. 219–29.

Butler, Judith. *Bodies That Matter: On the Discursive Limits of Sex*. New York: Routledge, 1993.

———. *Gender Trouble: Feminism and the Subversion of Identity*. New York: Routledge, 1999.

———. "Performative Acts and Gender Constitution: An Essay in Phenomenology and Feminist Theory." *Performing Feminisms: Feminist Critical Theory and Theatre*. Ed. Sue Ellen Case. Baltimore: Johns Hopkins University Press, 1990. 270–82.

Byrd, Rudolph P., ed. *The World Has Changed: Conversations with Alice Walker*. New York: New Press, 2010.

Byrd, Rudolph P., and Beverly Guy-Sheftall, eds. *Traps: African American Men on Gender and Sexuality*. Bloomington: Indiana University Press, 2001.

Cade, Toni, ed. *The Black Woman: An Anthology*. New York: New American Library, 1970.

———. "The Pill: Genocide or Liberation?" *The Black Woman: An Anthology*. Ed. Toni Cade Bambara. 1970. New York: Washington Square, 2005. 205–7.

Carbado, Devon W., Dwight A. McBride, and Donald Weise, eds. *Black Like Us: A Century of Lesbian, Gay, and Bisexual African American Fiction*. San Francisco: Cleis, 2002.

Carby, Hazel. "It Jus Be's Dat Way Sometime: The Sexual Politics of Women's Blues." *Radical America* 20.4 (1986): 9–22.

———. *Reconstructing Womanhood: The Emergence of the Afro-American Woman Novelist*. New York: Oxford University Press, 1987.

Carmichael, Stokely. *Ready for Revolution: The Life and Struggles of Stokely Carmichael (Kwame Toure)*. With Ekwueme Michael Thelwell. New York: Scribner, 2003.

Chateauvert, Melinda. "Framing Sexual Citizenship: Reconsidering the Discourse on African American Families." *Journal of African American History* 93.2 (Spring 2008): 198–222.

Chisholm, Shirley. *Unbought and Unbossed*. 1970. Washington, DC: Take Root Media, 2010.

Christian, Barbara. *Black Feminist Criticism: Perspectives on Black Women Writers*. 1985. New York: Teachers College, 1997.

———. *Black Women Novelists: The Development of a Tradition, 1892–1976*. Westport: Greenwood, 1980.

———. "The Race for Theory." *African American Literary Theory: A Reader*. Ed. Winston Napier. New York: New York University Press, 2000. 280–89.

Clarke, Cheryl. "The Failure to Transform: Homophobia in the Black Community." *Home Girls: A Black Feminist Anthology*. Ed. Barbara Smith. 1983. New Brunswick, NJ: Rutgers University Press, 2000. 190–201.

———."Lesbianism: An Act of Resistance." *This Bridge Called My Back: Writings by Radical Women of Color*. Ed. Cherríe Moraga and Gloria Anzaldúa. 1981. New York: Kitchen Table, 1983. 128–37.

Cleaver, Eldridge. *Soul on Ice*. New York: Dell, 1968.

Cohen, Cathy. "Deviance as Resistance: A New Research Agenda for the Study of Black Politics." *Du Bois Review: Social Science Research on Race* 1.1 (2004): 27–45.

———. "Punks, Bulldaggers, and Welfare Queens: The Radical Potential of Queer Politics?" *GLQ: A Journal of Lesbian and Gay Studies* 3.4 (May 1997):437–66.

Cole, Johnnetta Betsch, and Beverly Guy-Sheftall. *Gender Talk: The Struggle for Women's Equality in African American Communities*. New York: Ballantine, 2003.

Collins, Patricia Hill. *Black Feminist Thought: Knowledge, Consciousness, and the Politics of Empowerment*. 1990. New York: Routledge, 2000.

———. *Black Sexual Politics: African Americans, Gender, and the New Racism*. New York: Routledge, 2004.

———. *From Black Power to Hip Hop: Racism, Nationalism, and Feminism*. Philadelphia: Temple University Press, 2009.

———. "When Fighting Words Are Not Enough: The Gendered Content of Afro-centricism." *Fighting Words: Black Women and the Search for Justice*. Minneapolis: University of Minnesota Press, 1998. 155–83.

Combahee River Collective. "A Black Feminist Statement." *Still Brave: The Evolution of Black Women's Studies*. Ed. Stanlie M. James, Frances Smith Foster, and Beverly Guy-Sheftall. New York: Feminist Press, 2009.

Connell, R. W., Jeff Hearn, and Michael S. Kimmel, ed. *Handbook of Studies on Men and Masculinities*. Thousand Oak, CA: Sage, 1987.

Cooper, Anna Julia. *A Voice from the South by a Black Woman of the South*. 1892. New York: Negro Universities Press, 1969.

Cordova, Jeanne. Rev. of *Loving Her*, by Ann Allen Shockley. *Lesbian Tide* (October 1974): 28.

Crawford, Vicki L., Jacqueline Anne Rouse, and Barbara Woods, eds. *Women in the Civil Rights Movement: Trailblazers and Torchbearers, 1941–1965*. Bloomington: Indiana University Press, 1993.

Dandridge, Rita B. "Gathering Pieces: A Selected Bibliography of Ann Allen Shockley." *Black American Literature Forum* 2.1–2 (Spring-Summer 1987): 133–46.

Davis, Angela Y. *Blues Legacies and Black Feminism*. 1998. New York: Vintage, 1999.

———. *Women, Race, and Class*. 1981. New York: Vintage, 1983.

Davis, Thadious M. "Alice Walker's Celebration of Self in Southern Generations." *Southern Quarterly* 21.4 (Summer 1983): 49.

de Lauretis, Teresa, ed. *Feminist Studies, Critical Studies*. Bloomington: Indiana University Press, 1986.

——— *The Practice of Love: Lesbian Sexuality and Perverse Desire*. Bloomington: Indiana University Press, 1994.

———. "Queer Theory: Lesbian and Gay Sexualities, an Introduction." *Differences: A Journal of Feminist Cultural Studies* 3.2 (1991): iii–xviii.

———. "Sexual Indifference and Lesbian Representation." *Performing Feminisms: Feminist Critical Theory and Theatre*. Ed. Sue-Ellen Case. Baltimore: Johns Hopkins University Press, 1990. 17–39

Dixon, Melvin. "Singing a Deep Song: Language as Evidence in the Novels of Gayl Jones." *Black Women Writers, 1950–1980*. Ed. Mari Evans. New York: Anchor, 1984.

Docherty, Thomas. *Reading (Absent) Character: Toward a Theory of Characterization in Fiction*. Oxford: Clarendon, 1983.

Du Bois, W. E. B. "The Damnation of Women." *Darkwater: Voices from Within the Veil.* 1920. New York: Schocken, 1969. 163–87.

Dubey, Madhu. *Black Women Novelists and the Nationalist Aesthetic.* Bloomington: Indiana University Press, 1994.

———. *Signs and Cities: Black Literary Postmodernism.* Chicago: University of Chicago Press, 2003.

duCille, Ann. *The Coupling Convention: Sex, Text, and Tradition in Black Women's Fiction.* New York: Oxford University Press, 1993.

———. "The Occult of True Black Womanhood: Critical Demeanor and Black Feminist Studies." *Signs* 19.3 (Spring 1994): 591–629.

———. "Phallus(ies) of Interpretation: Toward Engendering the Black Critical 'I.'" *African American Literary Theory: A Reader.* Ed. Winston Napier. New York: New York University Press, 2000. 443–59.

Edwards, Erica R. *Charisma and the Fictions of Black Leadership.* Minneapolis: University of Minnesota Press, 2012.

Ehrenreich, Barbara. "The Decline of Patriarchy." *Constructing Masculinity.* Ed. Maurice Berger, Brian Wallis, and Simon Watson. New York: Routledge, 1995. 284–90.

Evans, David T. *Sexual Citizenship: The Material Construction of Sexualities.* New York: Routledge, 1993.

Evans, Mari. *Black Women Writers, 1950–1980 .* New York: Anchor, 1984.

Faderman, Lillian. *Surpassing the Love of Men: Romantic Friendship and Love between Women from the Renaissance to the Present.* 1981. New York: Quality Paperback, 1994.

Farwell, Marilyn R. *Heterosexual Plots and Lesbian Narratives.* New York: New York University Press, 1996.

Ferguson, Roderick A. *Aberrations in Black: Toward a Queer of Color Critique.* Minneapolis: University of Minnesota Press, 2004.

———. "Race-ing Homonormativity: Citizenship, Sociology, and Gay Identity." *Black Queer Studies.* Ed. E. Patrick Johnson and Mae G. Henderson. Durham: Duke University Press, 2006. 52–67.

Flowers, Sandra Hollin. *African American Nationalist Literature of the 1960s: Pens of Fire.* New York: Garland, 1996.

Foucault, Michel. *The History of Sexuality: An Introduction.* Trans. Robert Hurley. Harmondsworth: Penguin, 1981.

———. "A Preface to Transgression." *The Essential Foucault: Selections from the Essential Works of Foucault.* Ed. Paul Rabinow and Nikolas Rose. 1994. New York: New Press, 2003.

Gaines, Kevin K. *Uplifting the Race: Black Leadership, Politics, and Culture in the Twentieth Century.* Chapel Hill: University of North Carolina Press, 1996.

Gates, Henry Louis, Jr., ed. *Reading Black, Reading Feminist: A Critical Anthology.* New York: Meridian, 1990.

Gates, Henry Louis, Jr., Nellie McKay, et al., eds. *The Norton Anthology of African American Literature.* New York: Norton, 1997.

Gayle, Addison, Jr., ed. *The Black Aesthetic.* Garden City: Doubleday, 1971.

———. "Blueprint for Black Criticism." *First World* 1.1 (January/February 1977): 41–45.

Ghasemi, Parvin. "Revision of Motherhood, Maternity, and Matriarchy in Toni Morrison's Novels." Diss. Pennsylvania State University, 1994.

Giddings, Paula. "The Last Taboo." *Words of Fire: An Anthology of African-American Feminist Thought.* Ed. Beverly Guy-Sheftall. New York: New, 1995. 414–28.

———. *When and Where I Enter: The Impact of Black Women on Race and Sex in America.* New York: Quill, 1984.

Gilman, Sander. "Black Bodies, White Bodies: Toward an Iconography of Female Sexuality in Late Nineteenth Century Art, Medicine, and Literature." *"Race," Writing, and Difference.* Ed. Henry Louis Gates Jr. Chicago: University of Chicago Press, 1986. 223–40.

Gomez, Jewelle. "A Cultural Legacy Denied and Discovered: Black Lesbians in Fiction by Women." *Home Girls: A Black Feminist Anthology.* Ed. Barbara Smith. 1983. New Brunswick, NJ: Rutgers University Press, 2000. 110–23.

Griffin, Farah Jasmine. "Textual Healing: Claiming Black Women's Bodies, the Erotic and Resistance in Contemporary Novels of Slavery." *Callaloo* 19.2 (1996): 519–36.

Guy-Sheftall, Beverly, ed. *Words of Fire: An Anthology of African-American Feminist Thought.* New York: New Press, 1995.

Hammonds, Evelynn. "Black (W)holes and the Geometry of Black Female Sexuality." *African American Literary Theory: A Reader.* Ed. Winston Napier. New York: New York University Press, 2000.

Hardt, Michael, and Antonio Negri. *Multitude: War and Democracy in the Age of Empire.* New York: Penguin, 2004.

Hare, Nathan. "Will the Real Black Man Please Stand Up?" *Black Scholar* 2:10 (June 1971): 32–35.

Harley, Sharon, and Rosalyn Terborg-Penn, eds. *The Afro-American Woman: Struggles and Images*. New York: Kennikat, 1978.

Harper, Frances. *Iola Leroy*. 1892. New York: Oxford University Press, 1988.

Harper, Phillip Brian. *Framing the Margins: The Social Logic of Postmodern Culture*. New York: Oxford University Press, 1994.

Harris, Laura Alexandra. "Queer Black Feminism: The Pleasure Principle." *Feminist Review* 54 (Autumn 1996): 3–30

Harris, Trudier. *From Mammies to Militants: Domestics in Black American Literature*. Philadelphia: Temple University Press, 1982.

———. "Greeting the New Century with a Different Kind of Magic: An Introduction to Emerging Women Writers." *Callaloo* 19.2 (1996): 232–38.

———. *Saints, Sinners, Saviors: Strong Black Women in African American Literature*. New York: Palgrave, 2001.

———. "This Disease Called Strength: Some Observations on the Compensating Construction of Black Female Character." *Literature and Medicine* 14 (1995): 109–26.

Harris-Perry, Melissa V. *Sister Citizen: Shame, Stereotypes, and Black Women in America*. New Haven: Yale University Press, 2011.

Hays, Sharon. *The Cultural Contradictions of Motherhood*. New Haven: Yale University Press, 1996.

Helly, Dorothy O., and Susan M. Reverby, eds. *Gendered Domains: Rethinking Public and Private in Women's History*. Ithaca: Cornell University Press, 1992.

Henderson, Mae. "What It Means to Teach the Other When the Other Is the Self." *Callaloo* 17.2 (1994): 432–38.

Henderson, Mae Gwendolyn. "Speaking in Tongues: Dialogics, Dialectics, and the Black Woman Writer's Literary Tradition." *Changing Our Own Words: Essays on Criticism, Theory, and Writing by Black Women*. Ed. Cheryl A. Wall. New Brunswick, NJ: Rutgers University Press, 1989. 16–37.

Hendrickson, Roberta M. "Remembering the Dream: Alice Walker, *Meridian* and the Civil Rights Movement." *Melus* 24.3 (Autumn 1999): 111–28.

Hernton, Calvin C. *The Sexual Mountain and Black Women Writers: Adventures in Sex, Literature, and Real Life*. 1987. New York: Anchor, 1990.

Higginbotham, Evelyn Brooks. "African-American Women's History and the Metalanguage of Race." *Signs: Journal of Women and Culture in Society* 17.2 (Winter 1992): 251–74.

———. *Righteous Discontent: The Women's Movement in the Black Baptist Church, 1880–1920.* Cambridge: Harvard University Press, 1993.

Highwater, Jamake. *The Mythology of Transgression: Homosexuality as Metaphor.* New York: Oxford University Press, 1997.

Hine, Darlene Clark. "Rape and the Inner Lives of Black Women in the Middle West: Preliminary Thoughts on the Culture of Dissem blance." *Words of Fire: An Anthology of African-American Feminist Thought.* Ed. Beverly Guy-Sheftall. New York: New, 1995. 380–87.

Hine, Darlene Clark, and Kathleen Thompson. *A Shining Thread of Hope.* New York: Broadway, 1998.

Holland, Sharon Patricia. *The Erotic Life of Racism.* Durham: Duke University Press, 2012.

———. *Raising the Dead: Readings of Death and (Black) Subjectivity.* Durham: Duke University Press, 2000.

Holloway, Karla F. C. *Codes of Conduct: Race, Ethics, and the Color of Our Character.* New Brunswick, NJ: Rutgers University Press, 1995.

hooks, bell. *Black Looks: Race and Representation.* Boston: South End, 1992.

———."Continued Devaluation of Black Womanhood." *Ain't I a Woman: Black Women and Feminism.* Boston: South End, 1981. 51–86.

———. *Feminist Theory: From Margin to Center.* 1984. Boston: South End, 2000.

———. "The Politics of Radical Black Subjectivity." *Yearning: Race, Gender, and Cultural Politics.* Boston: South End, 1990. 15–22.

———. "Talking Back." *Talking Back: Thinking Feminist, Thinking Black.* Boston: South End, 1989.

———. *Yearning: Race, Gender, and Cultural Politics.* Boston: South End, 1990.

Huffer, Lynne. *Mad for Foucault: Rethinking the Foundations of Queer Theory.* New York: Columbia University Press, 2010.

Hull, Gloria T., Patricia Bell Scott, and Barbara Smith, eds. *All the Women Are White, All the Blacks Are Men, but Some of Us Are Brave.* New York: Feminist Press, 1982.

Jagose, Annamarie. *Queer Theory: An Introduction.* New York: New York University Press, 1996.

James, Joy. *Shadowboxing: Representations of Black Feminist Politics.* 1999. New York: Palgrave, 2002.

James, Joy, and T. Denean Sharpley-Whiting, eds. *The Black Feminist Reader.* Malden, MA: Blackwell, 2000.

James, Stanlie M., and Abena P.A. Busia, eds. *Theorizing Black Feminisms: The Visionary Pragmatism of Black Women.* London: Routledge, 1993.

James, Stanlie M., Frances Smith Foster, and Beverly Guy-Sheftall, eds. *Still Brave: The Evolution of Black Women's Studies.* New York: Feminist Press, 2009.

JanMohamed, Abdul R. "Sexuality on/of the Racial Border: Foucault, Wright, and the Articulation of 'Racialized Sexuality.'" *Discourses of Sexuality: From Aristotle to AIDS.* Ed. Domna C. Stanton. Ann Arbor: University of Michigan Press, 1995. 94–116.

Jenkins, Candice Marie. "Cultural Infidels: Intimate Betrayal and the Bonds of Race." Diss. Duke University, 2001.

———. *Private Lives, Proper Relations: Regulating Black Intimacy.* Minnesota: University of Minnesota Press, 2007.

Jenks, Chris. *Transgression.* London: Routledge, 2003.

Johnson, E. Patrick. *Appropriating Blackness: Performance and the Politics of Authenticity.* Durham: Duke University Press, 2003.

Jones, Gayl. "About My Work." *Black Women Writers, 1950–1980.* Ed. Mari Evans. New York: Anchor, 1984.

Jordan, June. *Eva's Man.* 1976. Boston: Beacon, 1987.

———. "A New Politics of Sexuality." *Words of Fire: An Anthology of African-American Feminist Thought.* Ed. Beverly Guy-Sheftall. New York: New Press, 1995. 407–11.

Keeling, Kara. "'Joining the Lesbians': Cinematic Regimes of Black Lesbian Visibility." *Black Queer Studies.* Ed. E. Patrick Johnson and Mae G. Henderson. Durham: Duke University Press, 2005. 213–27.

Kemp, Yakini B. "When Difference Is Not the Dilemma: The Black Woman Couple in African American Women's Fiction." *Arms Akimbo: Africana Women in Contemporary Literature.* Ed. Janice Lee Liddell and Kemp. Gainesville: University Press of Florida, 1999. 75–91.

Kendrick, Gerald D. Review of *The Women of Brewster Place,* by Gloria Naylor. *Journal of Black Studies* 14.3 (March 1984): 389–90.

Kimmel, Michael S., ed. *Changing Men: New Directions in Research on Men and Masculinity.* Newbury Park, CA: Sage, 1987.

King, J. L. *On the Down Low: A Journey into the Lives of 'Straight' Black Men Who Sleep with Men.* New York: Random House, 2004.

Kirsch, Max H. *Queer Theory and Social Change*. London: Routledge, 2000.

Kittredge, Katharine, ed. *Lewd and Notorious: Female Transgression in the Eighteen Century*. Ann Arbor: University of Michigan Press, 2003.

Ladner, Joyce. *Tomorrow's Tomorrow: The Black Woman*. Garden City: Doubleday, 1971.

Landes, Ruth. *The City of Women*. 1947. Albuquerque: University of New Mexico Press, 1994.

———. "A Northerner Views the South." *Social Forces* 23:3/5–79.

Lane, Alycee J. Foreword. *Loving Her*. By Ann Allen Shockley. 1974. Boston: Northeastern University Press, 1997. v–xvi.

Larsen, Nella. *Quicksand*. Ed. Deborah E. McDowell. 1928. New Brunswick, NJ: Rutgers University Press, 1986.

Lee, Shayne. *Erotic Revolutionaries: Black Women, Sexuality, and Popular Culture*. Lanham, MD: Hamilton, 2010.

Lefever, Harry G. *Undaunted by the Fight: Spelman College and the Civil Rights Movement, 1957–1967*. Macon, GA: Mercer University Press, 2005.

Lemert, Charles C., and Garth Gillan, eds. *Michel Foucault: Social Theory and Transgression*. New York: Columbia University Press, 1982.

Lorde, Audre. *Sister Outsider*. Freedom, CA: Crossing, 1984.

Lubiano, Wahneema. "Black Nationalism and Black Common Sense: Policing Ourselves and Others." *The House That Race Built*. 1997. New York: Vintage, 1998. 232–52.

Matus, Jill L. "Dream, Deferral, and Closure in *The Women of Brewster Place*." *Black American Literature Forum* 24.1 (Spring 1990): 49–64.

Mayer, Tamar, ed. *Gender Ironies of Nationalism: Sexing the Nation*. London: Routledge, 2000.

McBride, Dwight A. *Why I Hate Abercrombie and Fitch: Essays on Race and Sexuality*. New York: New York University Press, 2005.

McClintock, Anne. "Family Feuds: Gender Nationalism and the Family." *Feminist Review* 45 (Autumn 1993): 69–79.

McDowell, Deborah E. *"The Changing Same": Black Women's Literature, Criticism, and Theory*. Bloomington: Indiana University Press, 1995.

———. "New Directions for Black Feminist Criticism." *African American Literary Theory: A Reader*. Ed. Winston Napier. New York: New York University Press, 2000. 167–78.

———."'The Self and the Other': Reading Toni Morrison's *Sula* and the Black Female Text." *Modern Critical Views: Toni Morrison*. Ed. Harold Bloom. Philadelphia: Chelsea House, 1990. 149–63.

McKinley, Catherine E., and L. Joyce DeLaney, eds. *Afrekete: An Anthology of Black Lesbian Writing*. New York: Anchor, 1995.

McKittrick, Katherine. *Demonic Grounds: Black Women and the Cartographies of Struggle*. Minneapolis: University of Minnesota Press, 2006.

Meriwether, Louise. *Daddy Was a Number Runner*. 1970. New York: Feminist Press, 2002.

Miller-Young, Mireille. "Interventions: The Deviant and Defiant Art of Black Women Porn Directors." *The Feminist Porn Book: The Politics of Producing Pleasure*. New York: Feminist Press, 2013. 125–44. E-Book.

Mitchell, Angelyn, ed. *Within the Circle: An Anthology of African American Literary Criticism from the Harlem Renaissance to the Present*. Durham: Duke University Press, 1994.

Morrison, Toni. *The Bluest Eye*. 1970. New York: Pocket, 1972.

———. "Introduction: Friday on the Potomac." *Race-ing Justice, Engender-ing Power*. Ed. Morrison. New York: Pantheon, 1992.

———. *Playing in the Dark: Whiteness and the Literary Imagination*. 1992. New York: Vintage, 1993.

———. *Song of Solomon*. 1977. New York: Plume, 1987.

———. *Sula*. 1973. New York: Plume, 1982.

———. "Unspeakable Things Unspoken: The Afro-American Presence in American Literature." *Within a Circle: An Anthology of African American Literary Criticism from the Harlem Renaissance to the Present*. Ed. Angelyn Mitchell. Durham: Duke University Press, 1994. 368–98.

———. "What the Black Woman Thinks About Women's Lib." *What Moves at the Margin: Selected Nonfiction*. Ed. Carolyn C. Denard. Jackson: University Press of Mississippi, 2008. 18–30. .

Morton, Patricia. *Disfigured Images: The Historical Assault on Afro-American Women*. New York: Greenwood, 1991.

Moynihan, Daniel Patrick. *The Negro Family: The Case for National Action, 1965*. *The Moynihan Report and the Politics of Controversy*. Ed. Lee Rainwater and William L. Yancey. Cambridge: MIT, 1967.

Mullings, Leith. *On Our Own Terms: Race, Class, and Gender in the Lives of African American Women*. New York: Routledge, 1997.

Muñoz, José Esteban. *Disidentifications: Queers of Color and the Performance of Politics*. Minneapolis: University of Minnesota Press, 1999.

Nagel, Joane. *Race, Ethnicity, and Sexuality: Intimate Intersections, Forbidden Frontiers.* New York: Oxford University Press, 2003.

Nash, Jennifer C. "Practicing Love: Black Feminism, Love-Politics, and Post-Intersectionality." *Meridians* 11.2 (2013): 1–24.

———."Strange Bedfellows: Black Feminism and Antipornography Feminism." *Social Text* 26.4 (Winter 2008): 51–76.

Naylor, Gloria. *The Women of Brewster Place.* New York: Penguin, 1982.

Neal, Larry. "The Social Background of the Black Arts Movement." *Black Scholar* (January/February 1987): 11–22.

O'Brien, Colleen Claudia. "Contested Visions of a New Republic: Race, Sex, and the Body Politic in American Women's Writing." Diss. University of Michigan, 2001.

Papastergiadis, Nikos. "The Home in Modernity." *Ex-cavating Modernism.* Ed. Alex Coles and Richard Bentley. London: BACKless, 1996. 96–110.

Parker, Andrew, et al., eds. *Nationalisms and Sexualities.* New York: Routledge, 1992.

Parker, Pat. 1978. *Movement in Black.* Ann Arbor, MI: Firebrand, 1990.

Parvin, Ghasemi. "Revision of Motherhood, Maternity, and Matriarchy in Toni Morrison's Novels." Diss. Pennsylvania State University, 1994.

Pellegrini, Ann. *Performance Anxieties: Staging Psychoanalysis, Staging Race.* New York: Routledge, 1997.

Penelope, Julia, and Susan Wolfe, eds. *Lesbian Culture: An Anthology: The Lives, Work, Ideas, Art and Visions of Lesbians Past and Present.* Freedom: Crossing, 1993.

Phillips, Frank Lamont. Rev. of *Loving Her,* by Ann Allen Shockley. *Black World* (September 1975): 89–90.

Pifer, Lynn. "Coming to Voice in Alice Walker's *Meridian*: Speaking Out for the Revolution." *African American Review* 26.1 (Spring 1992): 77–78.

Poussaint, Alvin. "Blacks and the Sexual Revolution." *Ebony,* October 1971, 112–20.

Pryse, Marjorie, and Hortense J. Spillers, eds. *Conjuring: Black Women, Fiction, and Literary Tradition.* Bloomington: Indiana University Press, 1985.

Puhr, Kathleen M. "Healers in Gloria Naylor's Fiction." *Twentieth Century Literature* 40.4 (Winter 1994): 518–27.

Rabinow, Paul, and Nikolar Rose, eds. *The Essential Foucault.* New York: New Press, 1994.

Reid-Pharr, Robert. *Conjugal Union: The Body, the House, and the Black American.* New York: Oxford University Press, 1999.

———. *Once You Go Black: Choice, Desire, and the Black American Intellectual.* New York: New York University Press, 2007.

Rich, Adrienne. *Of Woman Born: Motherhood as Experience and Institution.* New York: Norton, 1986.

———. *On Lies, Secrets, and Silence: Selected Prose, 1976–1978.* 1979. New York: Norton, 1995.

Richardson, Diane. "Claiming Citizenship? Sexuality, Citizenship and Lesbian/Feminist Theory." *Sexualities* 3.2 (2000): 255–72.

———. "Constructing Sexual Citizenship: Theorizing Sexual Rights." *Critical Social Policy* 20 (2000): 105–35.

Ristock, Janice L. *No More Secrets: Violence in Lesbian Relationships.* New York: Routledge, 2002.

Robinson, Dean E. *Black Nationalism in American Politics and Thought.* Cambridge: Cambridge University Press, 2001.

Rodgers-Rose, La Frances, ed. *The Black Woman.* Beverly Hills: Sage, 1980.

Romano, Renee C. "Talking Black and Sleeping White." *Race Mixing: Black-White Marriage in Postwar America.* Cambridge: Harvard University Press, 2003.

Rose, Tricia. *Longing to Tell: Black Women Talk about Sexuality and Intimacy.* New York: Straus and Giroux, 2003.

Ross, Marlon B. *Manning the Race: Reforming Black Men in the Jim Crow Era.* New York: New York University Press, 2004.

———. "Some Glances at the Black Fag: Race, Same-Sex Desire, and Cultural Belonging." *African American Literary Theory: A Reader.* Ed. Winston Napier. New York: New York University Press, 2000. 498–522.

Ruff, Shawn Stewart, ed. *Go the Way Your Blood Beats: An Anthology of Lesbian and Gay Fiction by African-American Writers.* New York: Henry Holt, 1996.

Ruitenbeek, Hendrik M., ed. *Psychoanalysis and Female Sexuality.* New Haven: College and University Press Services, 1966.

Samuels, Wilfred D., and Clenora Hudson-Weems, eds. *Toni Morrison.* Boston: Twayne, 1990.

Sargisson, Lucy. *Utopian Bodies and the Politics of Transgression.* London: Routledge, 2000.

Schultz, Elizabeth. "Out of the Woods and into the World: A Study of Interracial Friendships between Women in American Novels." *Conjuring: Black Women, Fiction, and Literary Tradition.* Ed.

Marjorie Pryse and Hortense J. Spillers. Bloomington: Indiana University Press, 1985. 67–85.

Scott, Darieck. *Extravagant Abjection: Blackness, Power, and Sexuality in the African American Literary Imagination.* New York: New York University Press, 2010.

———. "Jungle Fever? Black Gay Identity Politics, White Dick, and the Utopian Bedroom." *GLQ: A Journal of Lesbian and Gay Studies* 1 (1994): 299–321.

Scott, Joyce Hope. "From Foreground to Margin: Female Configurations and Masculine Self-Representations in Black Nationalist Fiction." *Nationalisms and Sexualities.* Ed. Andrew Parker, et al. New York: Routledge, 1992. 296–312.

Segal, Lynne. *Straight Sex: Rethinking the Politics of Pleasure.* Berkeley: University of California Press, 1994.

Shockley, Ann Allen. "The Black Lesbian in American Literature: An Overview." *Home Girls: A Black Feminist Anthology.* Ed. Barbara Smith. 1983. New Brunswick, NJ: Rutgers University Press, 2000. 83–93.

———. *Loving Her.* 1974. Boston: Northeastern University Press, 1997.

Shockley, Ann Allen, and Veronica E. Tucker. "Black Women Discuss Today's Problems: Men, Families, Society." *Southern Voices* 1.3 (August-September 1974): 16–19.

Smethurst, James Edward. *The Black Arts Movement: Literary Nationalism in the 1960s and 1970s.* Chapel Hill: University of North Carolina Press, 2005.

Smith, Barbara, ed. *Home Girls: A Black Feminist Anthology.* 1983. New Brunswick, NJ: Rutgers University Press, 2000.

———. "Toward a Black Feminist Criticism." *African American Literary Theory: A Reader.* Ed. Winston Napier. New York: New York University Press, 2000. 132–46.

———. "The Truth That Never Hurts: Black Lesbians in Fiction in the 1980s." *Wild Women in the Whirlwind: Afra-American Culture and the Contemporary Literary Renaissance.* Ed. Joanne Braxton and Andrée Nicola McLaughlin. New Brunswick, NJ: Rutgers University Press, 1990. 213–45.

———. *The Truth That Never Hurts: Writings on Race, Gender, and Freedom.* New Brunswick, NJ: Rutgers University Press, 1998.

Smith, Valerie. "Black Feminist Theory and the Representation of the 'Other.'" *African American Literary Theory: A Reader.* Ed. Winston Napier. New York: New York University Press, 2000. 369–84.

———. *Not Just Race, Not Just Gender: Black Feminist Readings*. New York: Routledge, 1998.

Somerville, Siobhan B. *Queering the Color Line: Race and the Invention of Homosexuality in American Culture*. Durham: Duke University Press, 2000.

Spelman, Elizabeth V. *Inessential Woman: Problems of Exclusion in Feminist Thought*. Boston: Beacon, 1988.

Spillers, Hortense J. "A Hateful Passion, a Lost Love." *Feminist Studies* 9.2 (Summer 1983): 293–323.

Stallings, L.H. *Mutha' Is Half a Word: Intersections of Folklore, Vernacular, Myth, and Queerness in Black Female Culture*. Columbus: Ohio State University Press, 2007.

Stallybrass, Peter, and Allon White. *The Politics and Poetics of Transgression*. Ithaca: Cornell University Press, 1986.

Stanton, Domna C., ed. *Discourses of Sexuality: From Aristotle to AIDS*. Ann Arbor: University of Michigan Press, 1992.

Staples, Robert. *Black Masculinity: The Black Male's Role in American Society*. San Francisco: Black Scholar, 1982.

———. *Exploring Black Sexuality*. Lanham, MD: Rowman and Littlefield, 2006.

———. "Has the Sexual Revolution Bypassed Blacks?" *Ebony*, April 1974, 111–14.

———. "The Myth of the Black Macho: A Response to Angry Black Feminists." *Black Scholar* 10.6, 7 (March-April 1979): 24–33.

———. "The Myth of Black Sexual Superiority: A Re-Examination." *Black Scholar* 9.7 (April 1978): 16–22.

Stepto, Robert. "'Intimate Things in Place': A Conversation with Toni Morrison." *Conversations with Toni Morrison*. Ed. Danielle Taylor-Guthrie. Jackson: University Press of Mississippi, 1994. 380–81.

Stockton, Kathryn Bond. *Beautiful Bottom, Beautiful Shame: Where "Black" Meets "Queer."* Durham: Duke University Press, 2006.

Streitmatter, Rodger. *Unspeakable: The Rise of the Gay and Lesbian Press in America*. Boston: Faber and Faber, 1995.

Tate, Claudia, ed. *Black Women Writers at Work*. New York: Continuum, 1983.

———. *Domestic Allegories of Political Desire: The Black Heroine's Text at the Turn of the Century*. New York: Oxford University Press, 1992.

Terborg-Penn, Rosalyn, and Andrea Benton Rushing, eds. *Women in Africa and the African Diaspora: A Reader*. 1987. Washington: Howard University Press, 1996.

Thomas, Kendall. "'Ain't Nothin' Like the Real Thing': Black Masculinity, Gay Sexuality, and the Jargon of Authenticity." *The House That Race Built*. Ed. Wahneema Lubiano. 1997. New York: Vintage, 1998. 116–35.

Thompson, Lisa B. *Beyond the Black Lady: Sexuality and the New African American Middle Class*. Urbana: University of Illinois Press, 2009.

Vance, Carole S, ed. *Pleasure and Danger: Exploring Female Sexuality*. 1984. London: Pandora, 1992.

Varga-Coley, Barbara Jean. "The Novels of Black American Women." Diss. State University of New York at Stony Brook, 1981.

Wade-Gayles, Gloria. *No Crystal Stair: Visions of Race and Gender in Black Women's Fiction*. 1984. Cleveland: Pilgrim, 1997.

Wagner Martin, Linda, and Cathy N. Davidson. *The Oxford Book of Women's Writing in the United States*. Oxford: Oxford University Press, 1995.

Walker, Alice. "Alice Walker's Appeal." Interview by Paula Giddings. *Essence*, July 1992, 58–60, 62, 102.

———. "The Civil Rights Movement: What Good Was It?" *In Search of Our Mothers' Gardens: Womanist Prose*. San Diego: Harcourt Brace Jovanovich, 1983.

———. "A Daring Subject Boldly Shared." Review of *Loving Her*, by Ann Allen Shockley. *Ms.*, April 1975, 120–24.

———. *In Search of Our Mothers' Gardens: Womanist Prose*. San Diego: Harcourt Brace Jovanovich, 1983.

———. "An Interview with Alice Walker." Interview by Jessica Harris. *Essence*, July 1976, 33.

———. *Meridian*. 1976. New York: Pocket, 1986.

———. *Revolutionary Petunias and Other Poems* . New York: Harcourt Brace Jovanovich, 1973.

———. "The Silver Writes Movement." *Perspectives: The Civil Rights Quarterly* (Summer 1982): 22–23.

———. *The Third Life of Grange Copeland*. New York: Harcourt, Brace, Jovanovich, 1970.

Walker, Melissa. *Down from the Mountaintop: Black Women's Novels in the Wake of the Civil Rights Movement, 1966–1989*. New Haven: Yale University Press, 1991.

Wall, Cheryl A, ed. *Changing Our Own Words: Essays on Criticism, Theory, and Writing by Black Women*. New Brunswick, NJ: Rutgers University Press, 1989.

———. "On Dolls, Presidents, and Little Black Girls." *Still Brave: The Evolution of Black Women's Studies.* Ed. Stanlie M. James, Frances Smith Foster, and Beverly Guy-Sheftall. New York: Feminist Press, 2009. 435–39.

———. *Worrying the Line: Black Women Writers, Lineage, and Literary Tradition.* Chapel Hill: University of North Carolina Press, 2005.

Wallace, Michele. *Black Macho and the Myth of the Superwoman.* 1978. London: Verso, 1990.

Wallace-Sanders, Kimberly. *Mammy: A Century of Race, Gender, and Southern Memory.* Ann Arbor: University of Michigan Press, 2008.

———. *Skin Deep, Spirit Strong: The Black Female Body in American Culture.* Ann Arbor: University of Michigan Press, 2002.

Ward, Jerry W. "Escape from Trublem: The Fiction of Gayl Jones." *Black Women Writers, 1950–1980.* Ed. Mari Evans. New York: Anchor, 1984.

Washington, Mary Helen, ed. *Black-Eyed Susans: Classic Stories by and About Black Women.* New York: Anchor, 1975.

———. "'The Darkened Eye Restored': Notes toward a Literary History of Black Women." *Within the Circle: An Anthology of African American Literary Criticism from the Harlem Renaissance to the Present.* Ed. Angelyn Mitchell. Durham: Duke University Press, 1994. 442–53.

———. "Declaring (Ambiguous) Liberty: Paule Marshall's Middle-Class Women." *Sister Circle: Black Women and Work.* Ed. Sharon Harley and the Black Women and Work Collective. New Brunswick, NJ: Rutgers University Press, 2000. 199–217.

———, ed. *Invented Lives: Narratives of Black Women, 1860–1960.* New York: Anchor, 1987.

———, ed. *Midnight Birds: Stories of Contemporary Black Women.* New York: Anchor, 1980.

Welter, Barbara. "The Cult of True Womanhood, 1820–1860." *Dimity Convictions: The American Woman in the Nineteenth Century.* Athens: Ohio University Press, 1976. 21–41.

West, Cornel. "Black Sexuality: The Taboo Subject." *Traps: African American Men on Gender and Sexuality.* Ed. Rudolph P. Byrd and Beverly Guy-Sheftall. Bloomington: Indiana University Press, 2001.

———. *The Cornel West Reader.* New York: Basic Civitas, 1999.

———. *Prophesy Deliverance!: An Afro-American Revolutionary Christianity.* Philadelphia: Westminster, 1982.

White, Deborah Gray. *Ar'n't I a Woman?* 1985. New York: Norton, 1999.

———. "The Cost of Club Work, the Price of Black Feminism." *Visible Women: Essays on American Activism.* Urbana: University of Illinois Press, 1993. 247–69.

White, E. Frances. *Dark Continent of Our Bodies: Black Feminism and the Politics of Respectability.* Philadelphia: Temple University Press, 2001.

Wilcox, Janelle. "Constructed Silences: Voice and Subjectivity in the Resistance Texts of Gayl Jones, Alice Walker, and Toni Cade Bambara." Diss. Washington State University, 1995.

Williams, Rhonda M. "Living at the Crossroads: Explorations in Race, Nationality, Sexuality, and Gender." *The House That Race Built.* Ed. Wahneema Lubiano. New York: Vintage, 1998. 136–56.

Williams, Sherley Anne. "Some Implications of Womanist Theory." *African American Literary Theory: A Reader.* Ed. Winston Napier. New York: New York University Press, 2000. 218–23.

Wolfreys, Julian. *Transgression.* New York: Palgrave Macmillan, 2008.

Wright, Beryl. "Back Talk: Recoding the Body." *Callaloo* 19.2 (Spring 1996): 397–413.

Wright, Michelle M. *Becoming Black: Creating Identity in the African Diaspora.* Durham: Duke University Press, 2004.

Wright, Richard. *Native Son.* 1940. New York: Harper-Perennial, 1989.

Wyatt, Gail Elizabeth. *Stolen Women: Reclaiming Our Sexuality, Taking Back Our Lives.* New York: John Wiley, 1997.

INDEX

About the Author

Trimiko Melancon is an Assistant Professor of English, African American Studies, and Women's Studies at Loyola University New Orleans.